Northfield Ink
Community Stories Along Division Street

Maggie Lee

Northfield Ink
Community Stories Along Division Street

Maggie Lee

LOOOMIS HOUSE PRESS
NORTHFIELD, MINNESOTA

Published by Loomis House Press, Northfield, MN.
ISBN: 0-9707020-9-4

Cover and interior design by Mark F. Heiman.
Cover art "Snow on Division" by David F. Allen, Northfield.

Printed in the United States of America.

Contents

Hiram Scriver	6	Ervin G. Farrankop	107
Ross C. Phillips	8	George Campbell	110
A. K. Ware	11	Willard 'Red' Nelson	113
Charles D. Orr	13	Henry B. Kump	116
Lincoln Fey	15	Solomon P. Stewart	118
Samuel L. Manhart	18	Ralph Fjelstad	121
Dr. W. A. Hunt	20	Frank DeMann	124
Dr. K. J. McKenzie	23	George Christian	126
Effie Stranahan		Harvey H. Mader	128
& Gustaf Santino	25	Norman Olsen	130
John & Elizabeth Nutting	28	Fred B. Arneson	132
Frank E. Drake	32	Charlie Nichols	134
H. A. Whittier	34	William E. Revier	136
Laura Baker	37	Leal A. Headley	138
Edwin R. Rice	40	Marie Piesinger	141
Carl Heibel	43	W. W. Pye	144
Alfred J. Lashbrook	46	George J. Zanmiller	147
Louis Tschann	49	Casper Peterson	149
Frank Curren	52	Christian M. Grastvedt	151
Henry A. Boe	55	Sid Freeman	153
Horace Baldwin	58	Ralph A. Jacobsen	156
Guy Wells	60	A. E. Armstrong	158
Walter E. Johnson	63	William R. Gill	160
Oakey S. Jackson	66	Burnett Voss	163
Alex MacKay, Sr.	68	Everett L. Dilley	166
Carl Weicht	70	Clarence Albers	168
George Bickel	73	Lee Dahl	171
Harry O. Dilley	75	John E. Fremouw	173
C. L. Brown	77	Frank Gallagher	175
Ralph B. Goodhue	80	George Machacek	177
Orval Perman	83	Robert Swanson	179
Nels Parson	86	Dacie Moses	181
Sanford L. Haugen	89	Sidney Rand	184
Alvin Houston	92	Thomas J. Bunday	188
Dr. Bernard Street	95	Ted Scott	191
Stanley 'Tiny' Johnson	98	Les Drentlaw	194
John Larson	101	Carl Swanson	196
Victor E. Carlson	103	Robert Shumway	198
Endre B. Anderson	105	Dallas Haas	201

Individuals are listed chronologically by the date of the historical article referenced in each *Northfield News* column. For an alphabetical list, see the index at the end of this book.

I've been writing "Do You Remember?" columns in the present form for 19 years — a total of about 990 columns.

Most small city newspapers publish in some form a column of significant occurrences from 100, 75, 50, 25, 10 years ago. But when I was 65 and stepping down from editing the *Northfield News*, the publisher and I dreamed up the combination now used. Some person or event mentioned in the week's "Do You Remember?" column is chosen for a detailed story to appear alongside.

The new idea immediately attracted the favorable attention of University of Minnesota communications professors whom I much respected and the combination has proved to be a favorite feature in Northfield. Old timers like the column because it brings back memories. Newcomers enjoy learning about Northfield's past.

When it was decided that some of the columns should be published in book form during Northfield's sesquicentennial observance, I was assigned the task of choosing about 75 that should be included — roughly one out of every 10½ columns that I've written.

I tried to choose columns about people most significant in Northfield's development, but also the most interesting stories. This was not, as you can guess, easy.

And then I ran into an unexpected problem. Because of the way the subject is chosen, there are people who have been very significant in Northfield's development about whom a column has not been written.

Some names have just not appeared in the particular combination of papers. About some from a century ago there is not enough material available to write a good story. And then there are weeks when there are several possible names and I've made a choice based on how much material I could find — or maybe just a personal preference — and not on how comparatively important the person was.

Personal preference may still be entering into the choices for inclusion in this book. Please forgive me if your favorite significant person is missing!

Maggie Lee

Stories are the lifeblood of a community. They remind us of who we are and how we got here. They are spiritual sustenance, nourishment that shapes our collective identity, lifts up our values and reveals our character. They help us understand what sets us apart from the rest of the world, or at least from that community down the road.

Maggie Lee knows a good story when she sees one. For more than six decades, a remarkable tenure by any standard, she has shared them with readers of the *Northfield News*. She came to the *Northfield News* in 1944 to assume bookkeeping duties, but she was miscast. There was a journalist — a storyteller — inside waiting to emerge. That calling could not be ignored.

Maggie soon became a reporter, a news editor, then an associate editor, the editor and finally managing editor of the *Northfield News*. She covered city council, school board, agriculture and business development. She wrote editorials, columns, obituaries; reviewed local concerts and plays; and roamed Division Street year-after-year promoting local businesses and the people who ran them. She has been the community's historian, its promoter, its confidante, its ombudsman, its conscience. And, all the while, Maggie did it with a unique blend of compassion, sensitivity, Main Street diplomacy and professional resolve.

But Maggie was thick-skinned and tough. She did not shrink from controversy. She knew the hard truth is good in both the short run and the long run. It was always the community that was most important to Maggie. She rose to defend important environmental resources. She opposed short-sighted development and those who were willing to chase dollars at the expense of community cohesion. She cheered for the underdog and celebrated the innovators who built better mouse traps. She advocated for investment in projects and initiatives that preserved our heritage and nurtured that sense of community that makes Northfield, well . . . . Northfield.

There are a couple of key elements to Maggie's remarkable success. First is her willingness to devote her entire professional life to her community. Few among us are willing to demonstrate that kind of loyalty. Second is her stance as a life-long learner. Maggie has never lost her curiosity or thirst for learning something new.

Just ask her about the waves of technology she has endured over the years. And last, Maggie covered the news with a "democratic" eye. It's a trait she shares with noted Minnesota author Garrison Keillor. His genius is in his celebration of the ordinary. He draws our attention to the mini dramas that propel all of us through life, the self-doubt, the modest triumphs, and our reluctant submission to age and circumstance.

Maggie understands that, too. All of us have a story to tell. And while some are perhaps more dramatic, more compelling than others, all of them are valuable and most are pretty good. By sharing these "ordinary" stories about the people who lived and worked in Northfield, Maggie provides us a window to the ideas and the values, the community themes that have been handed off from one generation to another for more than 150 years. By telling these stories, Maggie has helped us remember what is important to be doing while we call Northfield home. They call upon us to honor those who have come before us by being good stewards of this community until we hand that responsibility off to those who will follow.

Thank you Maggie Lee. You are a gift to the community. You are one who understands the value of stories and devoted a life time to telling them.

Scott Richardson
Former *Northfield News* Editor
February 17, 2005

Northfield Ink
Community Stories Along Division Street

1890: Scriver quits mercantile business
Scriver one of most active citizens

After being actively engaged in mercantile business since 1856, Hiram Scriver has decided to retire from business, said the May 17, 1890, *Northfield News*. He barely escaped dying in the saddle; he died June 1, 1890. He was only 60 years old.

Scriver was one of Northfield's first business people and he was the city's first mayor. He was extremely active in bringing the college to be sponsored by the Congregational Church (Carleton) to Northfield.

The *News* said of him when he died, "The death of Honorable Hiram Scriver removes from our midst one of Northfield's most respected and highly valued citizens. Coming to Northfield when the future of the town was unknown and investing his money with other pioneers, he has always been a man whose interest in the welfare of Northfield has been uppermost.

"His death, which occurred last Sunday evening, was not unexpected as he has been a sufferer from paralysis during the past 20 years, but always lived in hope that his condition would improve and bore his sufferings with patience and Christian fortitude."

Scriver was born in Hemmingford in the Canadian province of Quebec on April 22, 1830. He attended high school in Potsdam, N.Y., and worked with mercantile businesses from the time he left school.

Traveling across country in June of 1856, he arrived in Northfield by stage coach. He later wrote, "As the prairies spread, out before us in their living green, dotted with the wild rose and other flowers, was it any wonder that the heart of the traveler from

the barren hills of the East or the wilds of Canada should leap for joy within him, and that he should feel that this is indeed a goodly land? And as we came over the hill east of the village and the noble forest with the then magnificent grove of elms near the mill broke upon our view as the stage drove into the embryo City of Northfield, need you be surprised that I ordered my trunk taken off, and felt that at last I had reached my journey's end, and in the old settler's parlance, 'struck my stake.'" We have not found any reference as to where he would have gone on the stage coach had he not "ordered the trunk taken off" at Northfield. It is recorded that he had previously decided that this region was the place he would spend his life.

We do know that he rented sleeping space in Jenkin's Tavern, a small hotel near the corner of Fifth and Division, adjacent to the site of Grundy's Corner Bar. On June 12, he bought the business of N. B. and T. R. Coulson who had in March installed a small stock of merchandise in a rude building on what later became Bridge Square. He bought them out and established himself in business with a capital of $10,000.

John W. North, founder of the city, persuaded him to accept for his store, property lots further south to make room for a square in the heart of the city. Scriver agreed and moved the wooden building to the current site of the Scriver Building. It was about a decade later that he built the stone building that is named for him. The wooden frame building was then moved north along Division to the site of the recent addition to the public library. Used as a residence hall for Carleton men students, it became known as Pancake Hall.

During part of the time Scriver was in business here, he was not married and occupied sleeping space in the wooden frame building. It seems that cows wondered around town at night in those days, just as some dogs and cats do today. They were prone to enter the shallow basement of the business building, then move about, bumping into the floor joists. Remembering his disturbed sleep, Scriver was determined to put up a substantial structure when he put up a business block.

His store occupied the corner space when the building was completed in the early '60s. And of course the building became famous for housing the First National Bank at the time of the James-Younger bank raid.

In 1860 Scriver married Clara E. Olin. She was killed in a run-away horse accident. The couple's only child had died at the age of 2. Scriver was married in 1886 to Delia M. Vanderbelt. About her, his obituary said, "whose devotion during the last years of his life did much toward alleviating his sufferings."

A *News* clipping in the Scriver file that is not dated states that Hiram was "early identified with the Lyceum Society in Northfield, that organization of pioneer days where culture and public spirit were fostered. As secretary of that organization, he became virtually the 'father of the Northfield library.' At a later period he was a generous benefactor of the library, and Mrs. Scriver at her death left in his honor a substantial memorial fund, the income of which is used for the purchase of books."

He belonged to a small group of Northfielders who were, according to the aforementioned clipping, "responsible not only for the location of Carleton College in this city, but who led the way for the creation of a college by the Congregationalists of the state. He was named on the first board of trustees (of the college) in 1866 and served until his death.

"There appears on the minutes of the board of trustees of Carleton this tribute to Scriver, adopted shortly after his death: 'A trustee from the organization of the college and recording secretary until 1882, whose sacrifices, labors and benefactions have been numerous and generously bestowed from the first days of its existence, and whose faith in its future, whose counsels in its behalf, whose care and prudence in the management of its affairs, made him one of the most valuable and trustworthy counsellors.'"

Scriver's obituary stated that although he was "not a politician in the general acceptance of the term, he has repeatedly been elected to positions of trust by his fellow citizens. He was the first mayor of Northfield (he was elected in March of 1875 after the city charter had been obtained) and has represented this part of Rice County in the state legislature."

His funeral was held in the Congregational Church of which he had been a member for 27 years. The service was conducted by the pastor, The Rev. J.E. McConnell, assisted by J.W. Strong, president of Carleton College. Interment was in Northfield Cemetery at the south edge of town.

Delia Scriver, who lived her last years in Geneseo, N.Y., died in the late '20s.

3 May, 1990

1897: Chief Ross Phillips develops new fire alarm system

Phillips serves as fire chief for 42 years

"R.C. Phillips, chief of the fire department, appeared with a request for an electric bell at his house to be used in a new telephone fire alarm system he is arranging," was part of a story about a Northfield City Council meeting that appeared in the Saturday, Nov. 6, 1897, *Northfield News.* The paragraph continued, "The request was granted by the council."

Phillips (grandfather of present-day Northfielder Margaret Starks) joined the fire department in 1876 and was elected chief in 1884. He headed the department until 1926 and during that long period was present at every single fire. He also missed very few meetings of the department.

He had to be inventive because the department had very little equipment through the years. In an interview in his later years, Phillips said, "Those were the days when a fire was about

as colorful and romantic as the visitation of a pestilence. No horses with glittering, burnished trappings, no red-wheeled fire wagon, no flying hoofs striking sparks from the paving, not even a hydrant to connect a hose to, and maybe we weren't out of luck if the fire happened to get started a long way from one of the town cisterns. It was just grim work, back-breaking toil, arm power and leg power, hope against hope, and almost certain failure."

Phillips was not a native of Northfield. He was born in Ashtabula, Ohio, on Sept. 11, 1853. He came to Minnesota with his parents very soon after the state had been ad-

mitted to the union. He, his mother and his siblings came to Northfield in 1862 when his father was away in the Civil War.

He learned to be a tinsmith and was engaged in that trade and in hardware business during much of his life. For several years he was employed by the Northfield Furnace Co. which produced furnaces highly regarded over several states. For a time he was in business for himself. For the last two years of his life, he was the city weighmaster.

As a child, Phillips observed the fighting of fires by bucket brigade. By the time he joined the department, it had a hand-drawn hook and ladder cart. A pump and hand engine was added in 1880. In 1894, three 500-barrel cisterns were built around the city — one at Carleton College, another in the present location of the Middle School, and the third at Longfellow School — to provide water for the department.

Horse-drawn vehicles were first used in the spring of 1897. The department experienced some excitement in connection with that development. Apparently the department did not have its own team of horses and the first team to come along after a fire alarm had sounded was pressed into service. Because the owner of the team so utilized was given $4, there was a race to arrive first.

The first motor truck was obtained in 1916.

In the early days of the department, it worked out of the Lyceum Building on

Fourth St., now the property of Agu Lukk. In 1880 the city erected the building in which Three Acres Antiques has been located. The fire apparatus was kept on the main floor and some members of the department slept on the second floor, sharing the upstairs with the city council room.

Fighting fires did not provide the only excitement in young Phillips' life. The same year that he joined the fire department, the James-Younger gang came to Northfield to raid the First National Bank. The bank, of course was located where it has been reproduced in the Scriver Building and Phillips was working in the shop of A. R. Manning's hardware on Bridge Square, the back doors of the two places opening across from each other onto an eight-foot alley.

Interviewed in 1897 regarding the raid, Phillips recalled, "The first thing I heard was some loud talking in the bank and then I heard a shot.

"When I heard the shot, I started for the front of the store where Manning was working on his books. I asked him what that shot was and he said, 'I think it's that show that's going to be here tonight.' I started to go up around the corner when I met John Tosney and John Archer who shouted, 'They're robbing the bank.'

"At the same time, five men whom I saw on the bridge started to ride rapidly across the square, firing right and left and shouting, 'Get in, you sons of b——s.'

"I ran back into the store, took the guns and revolvers we had and threw them out on the show case, handing at the same time a single shot Winchester to Manning. In doing so, however, I made a mistake and gave him the wrong size shells, so that after he went out and attempted to load his rifle, he had to come back to get new shells. I took two revolvers and went to the corner with him.

"The robbers were going up and down the street, firing and yelling. As soon as we got to the corner, Manning pulled up his gun and fired at the man in front of the opera house across the street (now Jacobsen's) who

at once threw up his hands and before he had gone 15 feet, fell off his horse dead. This was the man who was called Stiles.

"I then slipped up on the steps by the side of the (Scriver) building and putting my left hand over the rail and concealing my body as well as I could, began firing at the robbers. At that time I saw that there was a man under the stairs trying to get a pop at Manning and Manning in front was trying to get a shot at him. While I was standing on the third step, this robber — supposed to be Bob Younger — fired a shot at Manning which went through the step I was standing on. After that Manning told me to get down as they were shooting through the stairs.

"I went down and stood beside Manning and about then George Bates shouted across the street to us that they were leaving town. We came around the corner and looking saw two men getting onto one horse and the rest riding away.

"Elias Stacy and I then rushed out into the street and each took a shot at them as they were passing Holland's corner (now De-Grood's), which did not, however, take effect.

"While I was on the steps, I saw Dr. Wheeler fire out of the third story window in the corner of the Central House across the street, the shot that killed Miller. I could not see Miller, however, as he was close to the door of the bank and the stairs were between me and him. I was one of the first of those who went to him after the other robbers had gone. He was trying to get up, on his hands and knees, but he died within 15 or 20 minutes after he was shot."

Four years later, in August of 1880, at All Saints Episcopal Church, Phillips married Ellen E. Whitford who had come to Minnesota from Kansas as a baby in a covered wagon. She had lived at Hampton and Waterford before Northfield. Her obituary said that during the 50 years her husband was a member of the fire department, she "was keenly interested in its work and especially in its members who came to regard her with the same affection they felt toward their veteran chief."

When Phillips retired, the city council presented him with $100 (worth far more than $100 today) "in recognition of his honest, faithful and efficient service."

His obituary stated that he came from a family of fire fighters. His brother, H. L. Phillips, was assistant chief at Jamestown, N.Y. A nephew, Len Phillips, was captain of Hose Co. No. 3 in Jamestown. Another brother, J. W. Phillips, was chairman of the Minneapolis city council's fire department committee and the latter's son Jay was a Minneapolis fireman.

The obituary said that Phillips had been in frail health for some time, but suffered only a brief illness before dying on Dec. 24, 1926, shortly after midnight, as the result of heart disease.

The death occurred only a few months after Phillips' retirement from the fire department. Asked in the spring of 1926 whether, if he could go back 50 years, he would go for fire department service. "Damn right I'd join," was his prompt and spirited response, according to the *News*. "I suppose when I retire I'll still be going along with the fire boys. I don't see how I can keep away from it unless I break all my ribs or something."

He had been a member of the Odd Fellows Lodge for 57 years. He also belonged to Social Lodge No. 48, AF&AM, and Corinthian Chapter No. 33, RAM, Masonic orders. He was a member of All Saints Church.

His wife survived him (she died in 1933) as did one daughter, Nellie W. Phillips. The couple had brought up another daughter, Maude Phillips Evenson, who preceded her father in death.

The funeral services were held at the Phillips home and across the street at All Saints Church. Among those who attended from out of town were fire chiefs from Rush City, Owatonna, Faribault, Albert Lea, Waseca and Minneapolis. Northfield fire fighters were present in uniform to serve as an escort.

7 November, 1997

1899: A. K. Ware, builder of Grand, buys house in Northfield

In a decade, Ware very active in local politics and business

The Northfield News reported that A. K. Ware, a businessman planning to move to Northfield from the East, had purchased a most unusual house, the residence of Mrs. Sophronia Dean located at Third and Maple. He and his family would be moving into the house on about May 1, 1899.

Through the years a number of prominent Northfielders resided in this house and finally, the property of Carleton College, it was used to house women students. Fire destroyed the unusual structure in the early 1940s.

Ware was born in Waterloo, Iowa, on Aug. 23, 1863, and attended the schools of Evanston, Ill. He started his business career in Lake Benton, Minn.

In 1887 he married Harriet Fletcher of Winona and they made their home in Minneapolis. Soon, however, they moved to points east including Elmwood, Ill., and Fredericksburg, Va.

In March of 1899, the *News* picked up an item from the *Elmwood Gazette* stating that Ware, who had left for Virginia the year before, had just sold his Fredericksburg farm, "Snowden," and would move to Northfield. The story explained, "Northfield is the location of one of the best Congregational colleges in this country (Carleton was established by the Congregational Church) and Ware makes this move for the purpose of educating his children."

The Elmwood paper quoted the *Fredericksburg Free Lance,* "It will be a source of regret to our people generally that we are to lose Ware and his family from the community. During the short time he has resided here, Ware has become very popular with our citizens, and he and his interesting family will be greatly missed."

The *Fredericksburg* item continued, "Ware is largely engaged in the breeding of high class, standard bred trotting horses and while much pleased with our section and people,

there is but little demand here for such fancy bred, expensive horses and his main object in disposing of his property here is to settle in a section where the demand for fine horses in greater."

Although Ware lived in Northfield just over 10 years, he became a very influential citizen. He erected the Ware Auditorium which later became the Grand Theater and is now an entertainment center. He owned and operated a racetrack, had the controlling interest in the Northfield Light, Heat and Power Co., was elected to the city council, served as mayor of Northfield from 1902 to 1905, then served in the Minnesota state legislature.

Ware brought about 30 horses with him and established a stock farm named Alcantara. The farm was named for his famous stallion who had the reputation of being third in his rank of trotting sires in the world.

Within a few months of his arrival Ware was erecting a building. The *News* stated that citizens had been "crying for an opera house" but that no one had ever taken action. "Now it comes that A. K. Ware, who has cast his lot among us and who has taken a great interest in Northfield and its welfare, is willing to go ahead and give our city a first class opera house."

He secured the lots at the corner of Washington and Fourth in April of 1899. Citizens encouraged him to erect a larger building than he had planned.

The opera house, named the Ware Auditorium, was designed by Henry Carter, architect. It was known for its unusually good acoustics. It featured dressing rooms, equipment for operating the stage, an orchestra pit.

The auditorium had its formal opening on Dec. 26, 1899, with Walter Whiteside starring in "The Red Cockade."

Many plays traveled by train from city to city in those days. Local events were also held in the auditorium such as home talent plays and concerts. High school commencements and Memorial Day exercises were conducted there. Ware himself established an oratorical contest between Carleton and St. Olaf Colleges that took place in the building, a tradition that was continued until around 1930.

While he was mayor, he made the statement, "So confident and trustful are our citizens that a large portion never lock their doors to either house, barn or garage. Also there are no great feuds or quarrels in our city. People are sociable, generous, kind to the unfortunate and sick."

He added, "Hardly a paradise as yet, but nevertheless a place where a good honest man is respected whether he has money or education or breeding and where a home is sweet, be it ever so humble. Surely a resident of Northfield has much to be thankful for and little to growl about."

However Ware ran into plenty of bickering while he was mayor, being a Republican working with a Democratic council. The *News* accused the council of illegal transfers of funds.

When Ware won a seat in the legislature, he worked on bills for improved roads, reformed railroad rate system, iron ore tonnage tax, railroad rate tonnage tax, county potion.

When he was re-elected to the legislature, the *News* said it was because "he stood for something and by something."

Mr. and Mrs. Ware had nine children — Roger, Marjory, Cecil, Theodore, Mildred Alfreda, Ralph, Alexander and Fletcher. Roger died by drowning while the family lived here.

When his term in the legislature expired, Ware purchased a fruit ranch planted to apples and pears near Medford, Ore. He offered the auditorium for sale and Northfield business and professional people formed the Ware Auditorium Co., contributing to the fund.

Ware said that he had brought $65,000 to Northfield and was leaving with only $35,000. "No one can say that Mr. Ware made money out of the Northfield people and took it all to Oregon."

Mrs. Ware died in 1912 and her remains were brought to Northfield for burial at Oaklawn Cemetery. Ware married twice more, in 1913 and 1915, but the *News* offers no clue as to whether the marriages were dissolved or whether the wives died. Ware was not married when he died on June 26, 1931, at Rochester. He had been living in Minneapolis for four years and had lived in southern California previously. He is buried in Oaklawn.

26 March, 1999

1901: C. D. Orr moves here, will operate grain elevator
Orr, nearly 80, dies while visiting family in Florida

"C. D. Orr of Osage, Iowa, who will conduct the new elevator, moved his family to this city this week and located in the Bullock residence at Eighth and College," said a news item in the April 6 , 1901, *Northfield News.*

The April 27 *News* reported that Orr would be ready to purchase grain on May 1.

The story stated, "The new elevator of C. D. Orr on the Great Western tracks at Second St. will be ready for business on May 1 and Orr has arranged everything for the convenience of the farmer.

"The building is 24 by 24 feet on the ground and cribbed 34 feet high. There are nine grain bins, the six outside being eight feet square. The capacity of the building is 15,000 bushels.

"Orr has everything arranged to handle grain very rapidly and has placed two sets of scales in his elevator. One is a dump scale and all the farmer has to do is drive upon the bridge and with a simple devise the back end of the wagon is dropped and the load can be unloaded without lifting a sack. He has also arranged a hopper scale for those who prefer it.

"Across the driveway from the elevator the two-story office is located, the first story being used for the engine room and the second for office purposes.

"All in all, Orr has a very complete elevator and will handle grain in a manner which he hopes will please the farmers of this section."

The next mention of Orr in the *News* files has to do with a fire at his home. Mr. and Mrs. Orr had gone "over town" on a mid-June evening in 1903, leaving their young daughter and their baby daughter at home. Preparing to put the baby to bed, the older girl filled a small oil lamp. She filled it too full and lighted it, causing an explosion that set fire to a window shade and the adjacent woodwork.

The daughter pumped water in the adjacent sink to dash the flames, but was not successful in extinguishing them. So she ran to the door and screamed for help. Guy Page, a passerby, ran in, soaked a small rug from the kitchen floor, using it to smother the flames.

The May 3, 1913, *News* reported that Orr had started the erection of a coal shed and a flour, bran and feed house contiguous to the side of his elevator that fronted West Second. The 16 by 30-foot addition was built of cement blocks and was one story high.

Actually Orr was no stranger to Northfield when he moved here in 1901. He had been born on a farm in Northfield Township, six miles southeast of the city of Northfield, on Feb. 5, 1866. He was the son of David H. and Armaninda (Tiffany) Orr.

His father had come to Rice County in 1857, farming until 1883. That year he bought an interest in a mill at Cascade near Randolph. C.D. (Charles), the oldest son, was bookkeeper at the mill for a few years in his youth.

On July 1, 1890, Charles married Lillian Simpson in a double ceremony with her sister, Marion Simpson, and Thomas Wallace.

The *News* reported, "A very pleasant double wedding took place at the residence of

Mr. and Mrs. B. Simpson at Cannon Falls. . . . The rooms throughout the house were decorated with flowers. The soft, sweet music by the Cannon Falls band rang out on the cool night air with a sublimity that enraptured all present. There were 85 guests."

For several years Orr was ad agent for Northwestern Elevator and the family lived at Pipestone, Cottonwood and Minneapolis while he managed elevators in those cities. Later he was one of a firm, Orr & Lewis, with three elevators in Iowa. He made his home in Osage. After coming to Northfield, he was an active member of the Methodist Church, serving for many years as a deacon, as a trustee and as a steward. He was a member of Masonic orders, Social Lodge No. 48, AF&AM, and Sheba Chapter No. 73, OES.

In August of 1913, Orr was the subject of a story in *The American Elevator and Grain Trade* which was published in Chicago.

Accompanied by a large picture of the elevator, the story stated: "The elevator of C. D. Orr, Northfield, Minn., is one of the most successful plants of its size in southern Minnesota. Orr has been located in the same place for about 13 years and has been constantly making improvements to his elevator so as to keep pace with the growth of his business.

"The elevator proper is of cribbed construction containing nine bins. Its equipment includes a wagon dump, grain cleaner, automatic scales. There has recently been added a concrete annex which will be used principally for the storage of coal. Electric drive is employed throughout, power being secured from a nearby central station.

"Much of the success enjoyed by Orr is attributed by him to the fact that he practices the Golden Rule 365 days every year. He has aimed to make customers his friends and his straightforward methods of conducting business have produced excellent and lasting results."

When he was 63, Orr took a year's vacation, part of which he and his wife spent in travel. But on June 27, 1930, the *News* reported that he was "back in business at Orr's Elevator which he has operated for nearly 30 years."

While he was gone, he leased out the elevator but, the *News* reported, he "found it hard to even consider retiring from the business which he has spent so many years building."

We have been unable to locate in either the *News'* biographical files or the newspaper index at the public library the date of the fire that destroyed the Orr Elevator, apparently in the mid 1930s. He did not rebuild the elevator, but continued to deal in coal.

There is a clipping in the Orr file about C. D. Orr's birthday anniversary in February of 1939. With Orr's picture, a paragraph states: "One of Northfield's veteran businessmen, Orr celebrated his 73rd birthday anniversary Monday. He was a birthday guest of the Lions Club at noon and on Wednesday his anniversary was recognized by the men of the Methodist Church at their meeting. Orr has been in the coal and grain business in Northfield for 38 years."

In 1945, the Orrs celebrated their 55th wedding anniversary with a family dinner at their home and an evening gathering of friends.

Only a half year later, while he and his wife were vacationing — along with their son-in-law and daughter, Col. and Mrs. James T. Watson of Washington, D.C. — in Bartow, Fla., Orr died in his sleep on Jan. 26, 1946.

The funeral was conducted in the Northfield Methodist Church. Burial was in Northfield Cemetery.

His widow then lived with the Watsons, much of the time in Washington, but also in Puerto Rico and Fort Sheridan, Ill. She died on Jan. 18, 1951.

Your writer remembers Orr, particularly since he was a prominent businessman. But she has also fondly tucked away in her "file" of humorous memories a tale that began when Mrs. Orr was off on vacation — probably visiting the Watsons. Orr noticed some onions in the basement and fixed himself an onion sandwich. It didn't live up to his expectations, but he didn't find out why until Mrs. Orr returned. He had eaten a couple of her prize gladioli bulbs.

7 April, 2001

1901: Lincoln Fey, Northfield youth, builds horseless carriage
Fey avoided allergies by developing, riding in automobiles

"Since early boyhood I was more or less troubled by asthma, caused mostly by mill dust with which I had come in contact in the mills where my father was a miller," Lincoln Fey remembered when he was 60 years old.

"I loved to hunt and fish, but found it extremely difficult to ride behind horses. It always seemed queer to me that the railroad trains had to have steel rails on which to travel. Why couldn't a vehicle be constructed to travel on the road? Threshing engines traveled the road, but at a very slow rate of speed. Why not a light type of vehicle?" Fey asked.

The car mentioned in the *News* of Aug. 17, 1901, was the second built by Fey. Newspaper feature stories credit him with 'building a horseless carriage when he was only 17 years old, but he was 24 when this story appeared.

It stated, "The new automobile which has been in action on the streets of Northfield the past week is the outcome of the inventive genius and persistent energies of Lincoln Fey, son of Mr. and Mrs. Henry Fey of this city.

"For several years Fey has been working on his machine but until the present was unable to perfect his plans. The entire work, in detail, is that of Lincoln Fey. . . . Through much careful thought, hard work and mechanical skill, Lincoln has realized his ambitions and has his automobile successfully constructed and in perfect running order.

"A number of trials have been given the machine and its speed tests about 25 mph with no extra effort in climbing hills. It develops nearly 3 horsepower and consumes a gallon of gasoline in a distance of 75 miles. The wheels have rubber tires 2½ inches wide and the action is easy and free.

"Altogether the automobile is a work of genius and does great credit to the young mechanic of whom Northfield is justly proud."

Fey, who was best known by his nickname, Link, was born Oct. 26, 1878, at Waterford where his father was for several years the miller at the Grange Mill as well as the nearby Cascade Mill. Henry Fey had come to America at age 19 from Germany where his father had been a miller. He worked in mills in the Eastern states and in Minneapolis before coming to Waterford in 1877. He married Emily Tramm in 1878 and the couple had two sons. The younger son, Frank, often helped Link with his mechanical adventures.

The family moved from Waterford to Lime Springs, Iowa, where Henry Fey was miller for five years.

They returned to Northfield in the mid 1890s, buying the house at 310 E. Sixth. Henry Fey became the miller for the Ames Mill.

Link spent much of his time observing the workers at the Fox & Ferris Foundry in Northfield. One of the machinists was developing a single cylinder, slide valve steam engine for boat use.

Fey recalled in his old age, "I learned all about the working parts and how they functioned. This led to my decision to build a steam-driven vehicle to use on the road and after a time, I completed some crude pencil drawings of a steam engine."

Patterns were made with the aid of the head molder, Lambert E. Spears, whom Fey called one of the best mechanics in the Northwest. "Through his teaching and advice, the importance of accuracy and design was impressed on my mind." He also received advice from Fred Bates, Greenvale Township native who had moved into Northfield in the mid 1890s and had opened a bicycle shop in the present location of Hodge Podge Que antique shop. Bates was working on a horseless carriage that would make use of a gasoline engine after earlier experimenting with a steam engine.

Link's steam boiler and engine had proved to be too heavy for the bicycle-type frame he had built. About then he was able to observe a one ton four-cycle gasoline engine in use at the Stanton elevator. With a great deal of thought, he decided to go with a gasoline engine on a tricycle, using tandem bicycle wheels in front with one driving wheel in back.

His father, a lover of horses, thought that Link's hobby was keeping him from his schoolwork. He also thought it was dangerous because of the gasoline. But Link's mother and brother encouraged him. He was 17 and entering eighth grade.

With Frank running behind, Link tried out his new machine on snowy roads in early 1897. A local wagon maker had made a wooden seat and footboard and a blacksmith had forged the front axle. As the levers had not been perfected, Link had to run into a snowbank to stop the vehicle.

As Link sought to improve his tricycle-car, the millwright at New Prague offered to buy it for $65, a goodly sum in those days. Link quickly accepted the offer.

Next he commenced building a four-wheel horseless carriage. The body was built by Martin Tholstrup, local carpenter.

In old age, Fey recalled. "Along in the winter of 1898, the machine was completed and ready for a test run. On account of frightening horses and receiving unjust comment from illiterate bystanders, the machine was not taken out until midnight. The carriage was pushed over to the drinking fountain in the Square and the water tank filled. The engine was started and away we went with a lantern tied to the front of the rig as a headlight. The machine continued on its run without a hitch until 3 in the morning, a continuous run of three hours covering most of the streets in town."

Link continued, "My brother and I were two very happy lads and well pleased with the performance of the rig which functioned perfectly except for a little undue vibration. Three hours of continuous operation may have been a record at the time for hydrocarbon, motor-driven vehicles. We got quite a kick out of the fact that the people next day were having considerable trouble getting information as to 'what that thing was going around town last night.'"

Link continued to work on this car, the one described in the 1901 news story. He sold this car for $170 to Bates who rebuilt it somewhat, added a jump seat for his two sons and used it as a family car for seven years.

Link graduated from high school when he was 21. After spending several months in Denver, seeking a cure for his asthma and working as a mechanic, he returned to Northfield and started work on his third car. This time he wanted a four-passenger car with a three-speed and reverse transmission. He was trying to develop a float-feed carburetor which would assure a constant mixture of gasoline.

His brother helped him financially by working in the Ames Mill and playing in an orchestra.

Again seeking help for his asthma, Link spent the winter of 1904–5 in Los Angeles where he studied car design. On his return he was eager to build a four-cylinder, air-cooled car. He was still working on the third car when he began the fourth.

In 1905 he joined Henry Meacham to make air-cooled farm engines. They removed the engine from the third car for use as power for their machine tools. But finally, hampered by lack of capital, they sold everything to a Minneapolis firm.

The bright red third car was sold in 1907 to a man connected to the American Bridge Co. He returned the motor to Link in 1949. Witnessed by Bates and three other old car aficionados, Link set the old motor up in his garage and coaxed it back to life.

Link worked at times in Minneapolis for the A. F. Chase Automobile Co., distributor of the Mitchell auto, and a Corliss Co. He then rented an office in the Central Block, hoping to establish an industry, the manufacture of cycle cars. This did not work out and later he became the local Hudson and Essex dealer, working from his home garage.

In 1944 he was granted a patent covering two types of anchor raising and lowering devices what were put into production by Dr. W. D. Amundson, local optometrist. For many years, Link served as a freelance mechanical trouble shooter around Northfield.

Link, who did not marry, spent the last month of his life at the Odd Fellows Home. He died Sept. 18, 1956, at Northfield Hospital.

He had been a member of Northfield Lodge No. 50, IOOF, since 1916. His funeral was conducted from the Northfield Methodist Church.

His brother, who had been sales manager for U.S. Steel Corp. in Portland, Ore., for many years, preceded Link in death in 1946.

18 August, 2001

1901: Sam Manhart recalls experiences in 1888 blizzard

Manhart becomes prominent Northfield businessman

"Sam Manhart's Close Call — Story of fast riding in a blizzard on the old H & D," was a headline in the Nov. 16, 1901, *News*.

The story started, "Everybody south of Minneapolis and north of Austin who has ever been near a railway depot has heard of Sam Manhart and knows that his energy and nerve coupled with a first-class locomotive has made rolling stock on the Milwaukee Road pay dividends. . . . For some 10 years Sam had been running on what is known as 'The Special' on the I & M division and he was not troubled to any great extent with time cards as he was dodging in and out of switches and stealing stations here and there to make time. During this period, which very unfortunately terminated last Fourth of July by having his right hand blown off with a fire cracker, Sam has had enough close calls to turn silvery his once jet black hair. He has cut freight trains in two and smashed up a few loaded push cars, disfiguring his engine, but has always come out without a scratch."

The writer, who is not identified, said that while a group of men was sitting around telling about their hair breadth escapes, Manhart came up with the following story:

"We were in Milbank, S.D., on Jan. 26, 1888. I was firing at the time and was placed on the rear engine of a double header pulling passenger train No. 3 to the Twin Cities. The government thermometer registered 42 below zero and a fresh northwestern blizzard was blowing 38 mph and snow was in the air in clouds.

"Bird Island was the first division and we changed engines and again pulled out to make the cities. By this time the wind had increased to 58 mph and the worst blizzard I ever saw was raging. We left Bird Island with orders to meet No. 2 at Hector nine miles distant.

"We went out and soon the engineer turned to me, and as he looked at his watch said, 'Unless our wheels are slipping, we should be in Hector.' He asked me what I could see and I said not a thing.

"We supposed the crew on the front engine knew where they were at. We put on the air and shut down and inquired into the situation. We found we were 4½ miles past our station and on the same track with another double header coming our way that we should have side tracked for at Hector.

"We were in a horrible fix and the storm was raging faster and more furious every moment. I took my lantern and went up the track and finally heard her whistle. I gave the danger signal in all the languages of the lantern, but got no response.

"She came on, her windows covered with ice and snow so that the engineer could see nothing. Quick as a flash a thought struck me. I pulled off my overshoe and as the first engine came to me, I threw the shoe through the window and as the second came up, I fired my lantern through the cab window. In this way I communicated to them that there was trouble ahead. They brought their train to a halt just as she bumped our pilot.

"This was the closest call I ever had to being in a genuine smashup and our train, going with the wind, made faster time than I have ever made since — 13½ miles in 11 minutes. Had No. 2 been on time at Hector, we would have had the worst smashup in front of the depot ever known on the H & D as she had the right of way and would have been holding the main line."

Samuel L. Manhart was born Nov. 30, 1861, in Ottawa, Ont., Canada. When he was six years old he came with his parents to Dakota County in Minnesota.

They settled first in Lewiston, which was a boom town located on the Cannon River north of Northfield (and long since gone). Later they lived in Northfield for a short time and then they engaged in farming in Greenvale Township.

Manhart was 15 years old at the time of

the James-Younger raid on the First National Bank of Northfield and he recalled in his later years that he had ridden into town just a few minutes after the street battle had taken place.

He was scarcely 20 when he entered railroading, rising rapidly from fireman to freight engineer, and later to passenger locomotive engineer on the I & M division of the Milwaukee Railroad between Minneapolis and Owatonna and Minneapolis and Austin.

He had been engaged in railroading for 20 years when he lost his right hand when he was handling a giant firecracker in a celebration at Owatonna.

He spent the next year working in a drugstore, then came to Northfield in 1902. He established the Manhart Coal Co. here, continuing to head the business until his death. For a while his brother, W. F. Manhart, was associated with him. That partnership continued until 1928 and the brother died in 1930. In 1928 George B. Larkin became associated with Manhart.

Manhart served for many years as a director of the Northfield National Bank, eventually as the bank's vice president. He served as president of the Commercial Club (forerunner of the Chamber of Commerce), the Oaklawn Cemetery Assn., and was active in other civic bodies.

The *News* stated in Manhart's obituary that he "took a zestful interest in politics, both local and national.

In 1885 Manhart married Mary Fishback who died in 1908. Their only child, Arthur, died when he was 14. On Nov. 3, 1910, Manhart married Nellie Revier.

Manhart died March 15, 1937, in Hot Springs, Ark. He had gone to Hot Springs on March 6 for treatment for what he believed to be a minor ailment.

The *News* reported that he had not been in his usual health for several months and after he reached Hot Springs, a critical illness developed unexpectedly. Mrs. Manhart, who had been called to Hot Springs on Saturday, was with him when he died on Monday at St. Joseph's Hospital in Hot Springs.

The funeral was held in St. Dominic's Church, the service conducted by a longtime close friend of Manhart, the Rev. C. J. Normoyle of Two Harbors. Interment was in Oaklawn Cemetery, adjacent to the graves of his first wife and his son.

The pallbearers and honorary pallbearers represented associates of Manhart in his career as a railroad man, businessman, banker and civic leader.

The *News* commented in the obituary that "Manhart's death came as a great shock to friends in Northfield where, despite his 75 years, he had continued his usual business activities and his zestful interest in local affairs to within but a short time of his death.

"Forceful, energetic and aggressive. Manhart made an outstanding success of his business following a period when he rose rapidly in the railroad field. He was a man's man who counted his friends by the score, but who was always ready to take a decided stand for what he believed to be right.

"Manhart was especially well known among railroad men and those engaged in similar businesses to his. Because of his witty nature, his wide reading, and his interest in the affairs of the town, his office on West Third St. (a space in the same building and behind what is now Northfield Travel) was long a popular gathering place for his friends. He was trusted by many, and had helped many less fortunate that he was."

17 November, 2001

1914: Hunt retires from service as mayor
Hunt becomes city's 'leading citizen'

"After guiding most efficiently the administration of the city's affairs for four years during a critical period in its history, Dr. W. A. Hunt retires to join the class of ex-mayors," said the *Northfield News* of March 20, 1914.

The story also stated, "The doctor is being urged by his friends to become a candidate for higher honors and may file for the legislature."

The newswriter commented, "During his tenure of office, the city's business has been, of necessity, economically administered and several important permanent public improvements (have been) effected.

"When a man of the type of Dr. Hunt," the story

continued, "gives four years of service to a city at a considerable sacrifice of time and money and no other compensation than the criticisms and complaints of the disgruntled few, he is at least entitled to a hearty 'well done' as an expression of the public's appreciation."

Dr. Hunt had been elected mayor of Northfield the first time in the spring of 1910, the *News* reporting that the election would be remembered "as one of the most exciting and strenuous in the history of the city." Hunt had been running against R. D. Barrett from the non-partisan convention; he himself had been a candidate by petition. On the eve of the election, Barrett made a statement that split his followers on the main issue of the campaign, whether Northfield should be "wet" or "dry."

"At a gathering held last Saturday night in John Way's blacksmith shop, the Wets decided upon Everett Spear as their new standard

bearer and admonished 'to throw all personal feeling aside' and work in earnest. . . . Pressure was brought to bear on all quarters and the Dries rallied to the support of Dr. Hunt who received a majority of 22 over his opponents and a plurality of 76 over Spear.

The story also reflected some excitement at the first ward polling place. "There was found on opening the polls Tuesday morning a stranger, a rather meek-looking individual who had been stationed there by 'the good government committee' to watch for fraudulent voters. As far as can be learned, he spoke to no person and in no way disturbed the peace of the voting place. Soon it was learned that he was a regular detective, a real live detective in Northfield and stationed at the first ward polls. This was too much for some of the voters who passed the word around that the man was placed there to intimidate the voters of the district. 'Regular Southern intimidation' it was called. As far as the number of votes polled, the results showed that not many were kept from the polls, but steps were taken by some to have the 'detective' ejected. The judges of the election board were appealed to, but they found no objection to his presence in the room. The city attorney was asked for an opinion. He found nothing which would bar the man from the room. The attorney general was telephoned and he agreed with the city attorney. The county attorney was finally asked for a warrant for the arrest of this detective, but he found no ground for the issuance of such a bill and refused the request."

That section of the story concluded with the statement that detectives had been placed at both the first and third ward polling places "to keep track of student voters." The story said that the election judges themselves were very careful to question each student casting a vote and predicted that soon there would be a test case in district court to test the right of Carleton and St. Olaf students to vote in Northfield.

The story concluded that as far as the *News* could learn, there were no actual fisticuffs during the day, but there were many "curb orators at large on Tuesday."

Dr. Hunt's reelection in 1912 was extremely quiet — he was unopposed.

Dr. Hunt was a Republican and according to his obituary (in 1921), he was "well known in state Republican circles. In 1912 he was an alternate to the Chicago national convention. He was deeply interested in the state and national government and worked consistently in the interests of his party."

The obituary said of his years as mayor, "his tactful and far-sighted administration proved of great value to the city in a critical period. . . . Despite the loss of $4,800 annually (much money in those days) in the city revenue during his term in office, the city tax was decreased.

"So many friends did he gain by his economical and efficient management of public affairs that he was induced to run for representative in the legislature from Rice County. Running under the handicap of a 'dry' label in a 'wet' county, he was defeated by a small margin. Characteristically he gave every support to his opponent during the time the latter served as representative."

For more than 15 years Dr. Hunt served on the Northfield Board of Education, being president of the board much of that time. There he also concentrated on getting the schools on a sound financial basis, according to the *News*.

Dr. Hunt was on his way to a school board meeting — crossing from his house (no longer standing) that was directly across Union St. from what is now the middle school and was then Northfield High School — when he slipped on ice on the school lawn and suffered a head injury. That injury was not understood and he died about two weeks later on Jan. 27, 1921, when only 63 years old.

He had been the first Northfield-born person to serve Northfield as mayor, born here on Jan. 2, 1858. He attended local schools and graduated from Carleton in 1878. He studied medicine at the University of Michigan, graduating with honors in 1882, and immediately returned to Northfield to practice.

The late Bill Schilling wrote briefly about Dr. Hunt in his "Up and Down Main Street," revealing that his medical office was over Finkelson's Drug Store (now part of the Community National Bank site on the Bridge Square side). "Dr. Hunt was a very fine citizen," Schilling wrote, "a good practitioner, and was always for everything that was for the best interest of the city. . . . It can well be said that he was an ideal citizen, highly respected by all."

The obituary commented on Hunt's medical practice — "he gave to it such a high ideal, from which he never faltered. Little cared he for the time of night, the condition of the weather or his own physical comfort — when the call came he was ready. Never in the memory of those who have known him most intimately has Dr. Hunt failed to respond to the call for the relief of suffering.

"That he might better serve his patients and have a clearer knowledge and understanding of his profession, Dr. Hunt had frequently taken post-graduate courses in New York and Chicago. . . . His patients loved him and had a sublime confidence in him."

The fall before he died he had been elected vice president of the Minnesota Medical Society. He had frequently served in office in the Rice County Medical Society.

He was also a 32nd degree Mason, a member of Osman Temple Shrine, and an active Odd Fellow.

He and his wife Florence (she died in March of 1920) were the parents of three sons, William, Harold and Arthur.

Nearly 800 attended the funeral service in the Congregational Church (now First United Church of Christ) where he had been an active member.

The obituary concluded, "Dr. Hunt was at the time of his death, Northfield's leading citizen. There are no words that can express the feeling of the people of this community nor the sense of keen personal loss which many of them feel in Dr. Hunt's death."

It seems likely that the obituary was put together by the late Carl Weicht, long news editor and editor of the *News* who was an intimate friend of Dr. Hunt's sons.

16 March, 1989

1914: McKenzie serves professional group
Veterinarian leads active civic life

"Northfield contributes largely from its business, professional, educational and agricultural workers to the official roster of state organizations of various kinds," said a page one story in the *Northfield News* of Jan. 23, 1914.

The story stated that "Dr. K. J. McKenzie was elected a director of the Minnesota Veterinary Medical Association at the annual meeting in Minneapolis last week."

"Doc" McKenzie had been a charter member of the group and later was to serve as its president. He also served as president and secretary of the Minnesota State Veterinary Examining Board. When he died in February of 1946, more than 20 veterinarians from other cities, including the state's most prominent, attended his funeral service.

president, Andrew Jackson.

McKenzie served on the Northfield City Council for 12 years before becoming mayor.

McKenzie and his wife helped Northfield in another little way that seems amusing this much later; we can only hope it won't happen again. Northfield was served by two telephone companies for quite a number of years and of course a veterinarian would need to have the two lines, both in the office and at home. People would frequently call the McKenzies and ask them to give a message to someone who had the other kind of telephone!

Picton, Nova Scotia, was McKenzie's birthplace. He graduated from the Ontario Veterinary College in 1892, then practiced at Redwood Falls. It was in September of 1895 that he moved his practice to Northfield.

But in Northfield, McKenzie was just a beloved citizen, active in civic affairs as well as his profession. He served three successive terms as mayor, a record approached only by O. S. Jackson who served three full terms and part of a fourth (one term interrupted by military service) but the terms were not successive. They were two pairs of two in a row.

Relatives of McKenzie who still live here are a bit irked that while a group of Northfield streets have been named for mayors, there is no McKenzie Street. There is no street named for Jackson either, but there can't very well be one since a local street is already named for one-time United States

The early days of his practice were by necessity carried on by horse and buggy. Nevertheless he traveled over a wide area. We've heard that he was the only veterinarian who was willing to treat anthrax, then a dread disease of livestock, hence was called to farms in neighboring communities as well as this area.

It is recalled by family members that he would many times come back to Northfield from serving in the Farmington or Webster areas, hitch up another horse, put a hot stone in the buggy to help keep him warm in winter, and head out to some farm near

Dennison.

He was always eager to answer calls quickly and the family remembers his impatience in later years when his motorized vehicle would be hemmed in by double-parked cars. Several decades ago, before city officials exerted pressure, Northfielders would double-park their cars and go shopping. McKenzie would be parked in front of his office in part of what is now DuFour Cleaners and would find himself unable to take off when he wanted to answer an urgent call. Since he had suffered quite a hearing loss by that time, he probably didn't know what it sounded like, the family said, but he would press the accelerator down to the floor boards, roar up over the curb and down the sidewalk to Sixth Street and be on his way!

On the 50th anniversary of McKenzie's arrival here, Herman Roe, publisher of the *Northfield News,* saluted McKenzie in his editorial page column. He said in part, "During the five decades which have elapsed since he made that decision in 1895, this hardy Scotchman has not only filled the role of a pioneer veterinarian and acquired an enviable reputation as a consulting specialist on dairy cattle diseases, but he has the high distinction of being the only citizen in Northfield's history to serve three successive terms as mayor of the city. . . ."

Roe cited McKenzie's activities in veterinary circles and added, "Always an ardent sports fan, his favorite hobby is horse racing. He served as president and superintendent of the horse department of the Rice County Fair for 20 years."

(Not only did McKenzie enjoy watching horse racing, but he engaged in sulky racing himself. He particularly did this at Cannon Falls where sulky racing has been a tradition.)

Roe's column continued, "Now in his 77th year, 'Doc' McKenzie has had more than his share of illness in recent years. An auto accident brought a broken leg three years ago, but even at his age, this scrappy Scotchman licked that setback and returned to active practice, serving Northfield Community farmers during the acute wartime shortage of veterinarians.

"The past month he has submitted to operations at the Mayo Clinic, Rochester, for an ailment which has bothered him for many years. Not one to admit defeat, he surprises the MD's by staging comebacks when the average man would say he was licked."

Roe wished for McKenzie at least another decade of good health, but that was not to be.

His obituary a half year later revealed that he was active in Masonic orders — Social Lodge No. 48, AF&AM; Northfield Council No. 12, R&SM; Corinthian Chapter No. 33, RAM; and Osman Temple Shrine in St. Paul. He was a member of the Methodist Church.

After arriving in Northfield, he married Mabel Bierman Budd who survived him. He was also survived by three sons, a stepdaughter and grandchildren. Two of his daughters-in-law still live in Northfield — Evie McKenzie, widow of Lauren whose nickname was "Doc," and Marian Rolvaag whose first husband was Donald MacKenzie. (The latter son restored an "a" to the family name that had been dropped by earlier generations.)

19 January, 1989

1914: Two unusual Northfielders marry
Bride was first local woman to vote

"Miss Effie M. Stranahan and G.A. Santino of this city were married at Faribault Wednesday afternoon of last week," said a page one story in the Friday, Oct. 9, 1914, *Northfield News.* It was not all that unusual in those days for a wedding story to be placed on the front page. But this story, quite short, was significant because of the unusual couple.

The story continued that the ceremony had been performed by the Rev. F. E. Meierbachtol of the German Methodist Church at Faribault. Succeeding paragraphs said:

"The bride is well known in this city, having conducted an insurance office on Division St. for a number of years.

"Mr. Santino has been a resident of Northfield for about four years and was formerly conductor of the Woodman Band.

"They will continue to make their home in this city."

The couple was not young. Santino, who lived until 1930, was 76 at the time of his marriage. The bride, who lived until 1952, was 49 when she was married. It was the first marriage for both.

In Northfield, Mrs. Santino was the best known of the two for she had lived here since she was five years old. She was born in Leon Township, Goodhue County. She recalled being in school (in a little wood frame building at the current location of Longfellow School) at the time of the Northfield Bank Raid. The teachers dismissed classes and parents hurried to the school to take the children home and lock the doors. Although everyone was excited and afraid for a few hours, Mrs. Santino recalled in an interview many years later, almost everyone in town — including the little girl Effie — went down town later in the evening to see the bodies of the two bandits who had been killed. (They were laid out in an empty store building.)

Her family's boarder joined the posse that went after the gang and the Stranahans wondered whether they would ever see him again. Joseph Lee Heywood, bank cashier who was killed and who was the hero of the raid, was a near neighbor of the Stranahans.

Effie graduated from Northfield High School in 1884, one of a class of three girls. The principal suggested that since there were only the three, the school would not conduct graduation exercises and would simply give out the diplomas. But the girls demanded that they have a commencement just as nice and elaborate as any of the others had been. They all had silk dresses made for the event.

Effie taught school in Rice and Goodhue counties for awhile, but did not enjoy that and enrolled in a shorthand course in a business college in Minneapolis. She then went to work for Merril M. Clark, insurance agent whose office was in a small woodframe building with hip roof set back from the sidewalk in the current location of the Gundersen building, 319 Division. She became a notary public and in 1896 obtained her own license to sell insurance. She continued her career in that same building until it was razed in 1940.

Clark held the office of Northfield city recorder. Although he moved his insurance business to Duluth, he came to Northfield once a month to attend city council meetings. Effie not only took over the local insurance business when he moved, but she also did all the record keeping for the city — long before women were eligible to vote, to say nothing of hold office.

She joined the Northfield chapter of the Equal Franchise League, helping to circulate petitions. She was subsequently the first Northfield woman to vote. The first election in which women were allowed to vote, she was at the polls early in order to cast her ballot before leaving on a business trip to Faribault.

After many years of doing the city's business without salary, she decided to run for city treasurer in March of 1926. The first Northfield woman to be elected to municipal office, she defeated two male opponents with a comfortable margin. She continued in that office for 24 years. For a long time she was also secretary of the Northfield Cemetery Association.

After the building on Division was torn down, she moved her business and the treasurer's office to the Lyceum building, 109 E. Fourth (now Dr. Elvin Heiberg's dental office). Finally she moved the business to the building that now houses Dr. David Garlie's veterinary offices at 512 Division. She gave up her city career in 1950 when she suffered a stroke. Also at that time she gave up issuing driver's licenses which she had done for some time. She continued to sell insurance until her last illness.

A story that appeared in a *Northfield News* centennial issue said that "strangers found Mrs. Santino a bit brusk and were prone to laugh at her Queen Mary type of black hats. (Although we remember her as always wearing a hat from morning till night, she must have removed them for pictures — we can't find a hatted picture of her anywhere). But she really had a rapier sharp sense of humor. She knew everyone and their problems and fell a great deal of sympathy for those who were having a rough time. She had many loyal friends all of her life."

Her husband was ill for ten years and bedridden for 2½ years, paralyzed from a stroke, but with the help of good friends, she was able to keep up her career and give him care at home.

While not as important locally, Gustaf A. Santino's career was even more colorful. He was the son of an Austrian nobleman, an officer in the Austrian army who was killed during revolutions that swept Europe in 1848. Santino was born in 1838 in Austria (in an area that is now part of Italy), but grew up in Germany. As an older teenager, he attended military school in Vienna. There, according to his obituary in the *News*, "was cultivated a love for adventure and military manner that remained with him to the end of his life."

He came to the United States to visit an aunt in Philadelphia in 1862, but two days after his arrival — before he could speak English — he enlisted in the Union Army and fought until the close of the Civil War. He then reenlisted and served for nearly 11 years as field musician, principal musician and drum major in the 6th U.S. Infantry. Most of this time was spent in the West where his regiment was engaged in warfare with Indians.

He came to Minneapolis in 1876, organizing the first drum corps of Morgan Post of the Grand Army of the Republic. In 1885 he received a medal from General John A. Logan for having the best drum corps at the GAR encampment that year.

Later he was a band instructor in a number of cities including New York, Detroit, Minneapolis, New Orleans, then in southern Minnesota cities such as Rochester, Spring Valley, Claremont and Red Wing. He organized a military band at Kenyon. He came to Northfield as leader of the Woodman Band

and, according to his obituary, "was interested in band work here until ill health forced his retirement."

A former publisher of the *Kenyon Leader*, reminiscing about Santino several years ago, said that the musician had at one time been a member of John Philip Sousa's famous military band.

The late Gerhard Ellestad recalled that he had lived in house next door to the Santinos while he was a student at St. Olaf College. "We enjoyed his (Santino's) stories which came to us with a pronounced German accent and sometimes with a jumbled syntax. As I remember him, there was a touch of the aristocratic, occasional evidence of military discipline and a sense of humor all blended together to give us a unusual and entertaining neighbor."

Santino's obituary stated, "During his residence in Northfield, especially before his retirement because of poor health, Santino was a well-known and picturesque figure in the life of the city. His was an unusually imposing presence, and he had the unmistakable air of an old-world aristocrat. Although he liked to recount the adventures of his youth and the experiences of his long and varied career, he seldom talked about the title which he had renounced to become a citizen of the United States."

5 October 1989

1916: John Nutting wed in bride's home in Vermont
Couple assumes civic duties through half century

"Adams Home in Vermont Village Scene of Pretty Wedding," was a headline on page one of the Oct. 20, 1916, *Northfield News*.

Carrying a wedding story on the front page was not so unusual in those days, especially if the people involved were prominent in the community. John D. Nutting, the bridegroom, was then vice president of the First National Bank. The bride, Elizabeth Steele Adams, had been an instructor in German at Carleton College the previous year. According to the *News*, she had "made many friends in the community who will welcome her as a permanent resident."

The wedding story stated, "On Wednesday evening, Oct. 11, at 8 o'clock, occurred the marriage of Miss Elizabeth Adams and John D. Nutting at the home of the bride's mother, Mrs. Chloe Adams, in Peacham, Vt. The ceremony was performed by the Rev. J.K. Williams. Fred B. Gill acted as best man and Miss Amelia Kayes of Newton, N.J., attended the bride. Miss Frances Gill was the ringbearer and the bridal march was played by a classmate of the bride, Miss Lucy McClary.

"The bride was gowned in white messaline embroidered in silver, over silk net and chiffon. She wore a veil and carried a shower bouquet of white roses and lilies of the valley. The maid of honor wore lavender messaline and silk net, decorated with gold lace and gold and pearl beads. She carried yellow chrysanthemums. The house was charmingly decorated with autumn leaves, bitter-sweets (sic) and chrysanthemums."

The story continued, "The ceremony was followed by an informal reception where bountiful refreshments were served by young ladies, friends of the bride. Many beautiful and valuable gifts of silver, cut glass, linen, etc., evidenced the regard of many relatives and friends.

"The bride is a graduate of Peacham Academy and Mount Holyoke College. She has been a most successful teacher and has unusual musical talent. Mr. Nutting is the son of the late John C. and Calista Morse Nutting, formerly of Danville, Vt., and is vice president of the First National Bank of Northfield where they will make their home. . . .

Mr. and Mrs. Nutting arrived in Northfield Wednesday and will be at home after Nov. 1 at 209 Union St."

The Nuttings were to become beloved members of the community, undertaking civic duties and assuming responsibilities that would leave their mark in this city. Their marriage was to endure until Nutting's death in the summer of 1968. Mrs. Nutting died a year later.

Because he usually appeared to be very serious in nature while conducting business as president of the bank over a period of 40 years, Nutting continually surprised people with his delightful sense of humor when away from his desk. Excerpts from the funeral sermon for Nutting, given by the Rev. David Maitland, then Carleton College chaplain, and filed in the Carleton College archives, give an intimate picture of the deceased.

Maitland opened his remarks with, "Northfield has lost a man who loved his town dearly." A ways into his talk, Maitland said, "It is always dangerous to select any one thing to represent a long and good life. I choose, however, to run that risk today. At the First National Bank, where he went for the last time on Monday, there is an old toy which John liked. It is a purposeful toy, which makes it appropriate to talk about it at a funeral. The toy is a mechanical savings bank for a child. The insertion of a coin produces vivid, visual action which children of all ages enjoy. This says three things to me about John Nutting.

"First, he was obviously interested in money and banking. He was honored in 1960 with a plaque for 50 years of service to banking by the Minnesota Bankers Association. In one sense, banking was his life and he was well equipped for that vocation with a genuine conscience, a concern for the improvement of his community, and what many people have referred to as his 'utter honesty.'

"The second thing that the mechanical bank says to me about John is that he greatly enjoyed games. The more complicated the game, the more fascinated he seemed to be, which may be the basis for his admiration of the ingenuity of the toy bank's inventor. There is something about people who like games which is most important. Such people are not all seriousness. Certainly John was an intense player of games, particularly card games on his own back porch, but he knew and appreciated the difference between work and play. . . .

"Finally, the mechanical bank reminds me that John liked to share his pleasure with others. There must be many of you to whom he showed his mechanical bank. Is not our life permanently richer because of the delight which he conveyed? Such times were also often the occasion for a chat. It is said that he always had time for a bit of conversation. Perhaps that is the reason why another thing is said about him, which is particularly striking in view of the position he held. They say that he did not have an enemy in town — nor out of town either!"

Later Maitland said, "It would seem to me that Mr. Nutting did not receive much public acclaim for all that he accomplished and encouraged for the good of the community. The important point, however, is that he shunned any such acclaim. His life was apparently grounded on the conviction that good deeds are their own reward."

Maitland concluded his remarks by quoting a statement about John David Nutting that appeared in the Carleton "Algol" yearbook in 1906, "A kinder gentleman treads not the earth." And Maitland commented, "What more need one say?"

Nutting was born on Nov. 6, 1881, in a house at the present site of St. John's Lutheran Church. His father, John Claudius Nutting, was one of the founders of the First National Bank and served for many years as its president. Nutting's parents came to Minnesota in 1870.

The unusual house at 217 Union — now the home of Carleton presidents — was built by the Nuttings in 1890–91 and John D. Nutting grew up there. Although that residence has been listed on the National Register of Historic Places since 1970, Nutting enjoyed referring to it as "our Victorian monstrosity."

Nutting graduated from Northfield High School and in 1906 from Carleton. After attending a business college in Minneapolis, he became associated with the First National Bank in 1908. He was made vice president in 1916. He became fifth president of the bank in 1926.

He served in that post until the beginning of 1967 when he asked to be relieved of the responsibilities, but accepted the post of chairman of the bank's board. He still spent part of every day at the bank including the day before he died.

He was always interested in attracting industry to Northfield and was cited by fellow businessmen for his assistance at the beginnings of Northfield Iron Co. and Northfield Milk Products, neither of which now exists though they were important for many years.

Nutting always retained his interest in Carleton. His father had been a Carleton trustee from 1880 until 1910 and Nutting carried on that tradition, serving from 1924 until 1932. The Alumni Achievement Award which he received in 1956 noted that he lad served three terms as treasurer of the Carleton Alumni Association as well as a long-time presidency of the class of 1906. When the class held its 60-year reunion in 1966, part of the events were conducted at the Nutting home.

He joined the Northfield Lions Club during its first year and was still active in he club at his death. He had served as trustee and a deacon of the First Congregational Church (now United Church of Christ). Maitland told about Nutting's selling tickets at the door for a dinner the men of the church gave. "That it was a successful evening pleased him, but I doubt that he realized how much he contributed by his enthusiasm for the occasion."

Nutting worked in the Northfield Improvement Assn. He was a member of several Masonic orders — Social Lodge No. 48, AF&AM; Corinthian Chapter No. 33, RAM; Northfield Council No. 2, R&SM; Faribault Commandery No. 8, Knights Templar; and Osman Temple Shrine in St. Paul. He was honorary chairman of Northfield's Centennial Celebration.

His wisdom is currently being appreciated with the removal of the corrugated metal from the building into which the bank will expand.

As owner of the building at that time, he had insisted that the brick front and windows be left intact when the "improvement" desired by the tenant was installed.

His death was very unexpected. Taken ill during the night, he was found to be suffering from a perforated ulcer and was hospitalized in the morning. Death came in the evening. Providentially his two daughters had arrived in Northfield a few days before the death, intending to spend the summer, and the family had been together for some pleasant hours before the fatal illness.

Mrs. Nutting was born Jan. 22, 1881, in Peacham where she grew up. She graduated from Mt. Holyoke in 1902. She was a classmate of Frances Perkins, Secretary of Labor during the Franklin Delano Roosevelt administration, and her recorded mentions of Perkins have been welcomed by Mt. Holyoke archivists. Mrs. Nutting taught in Eastern schools, then for two years in Arizona. She came to Northfield to teach German at Carleton and to attend the college as a special student in the academic year of 1915–16.

She served as a bank director for a number of years and she was a director of the Northfield Cooperative Laundry which operated in the current location of the Rueb 'N' Stein. She served on the Northfield Board of Education for a number of years in the '30s.

She was active in Girl Scouting and at one time served as a Girl Scout regional camp visitor in Minnesota, North and South Dakota and Montana. She was a charter member of the Northfield Branch of the American Association of University Women. She was active in the Northfield Improvement Association.

She was an avid gardener and created most unusual flower arrangements for the flower shows of both the Improvement Association and the Rice County Fair when it was held in Northfield.

She was a member of Chapter N, PEO, and served in various offices of the PEO Sisterhood including president of the Minnesota State Chapter in 1953–54. She was a member of the Josiah Edson Chapter, Daughters of the American Revolution.

She served as a director of the Rice County Historical Society. She did exhaustive research during the time the Alexander Faribault House was being furnished, making many trips to obtain or special order items for the house. Her enthusiasm was credited with keeping the project on track.

Mrs. Nutting became a member of the First Congregational Church of Northfield in 1917 and served the church on various committees through the years. For a long period of time she was church historian, keeping the archival material catalogued and indexed. She had served as president of the Women's Fellowship of the church.

Besides gardening, Mrs. Nutting — with an enviable reputation as a hostess — was interested in china painting and refinishing furniture. When the Nutting home was shown in the Northfield Hospital Auxiliary's benefit Parade of Homes in 1966, it was noted that many pieces of walnut furniture from the Nuttings' original home on the West Side had been refinished by Mrs. Nutting "so expertly that they have the sheen of modern reproductions." Those who made the tour were fascinated to find that the house included 20 rooms plus halls, pantries, porches and two attics.

The couple observed their golden wedding anniversary with an open house in their home in 1966, the event arranged by their daughters, Helen of Chambersburg, Pa., now deceased, and Ruth of Menlo, Calif.

The *News* had hoped to feature a wedding picture with this story, but has learned from the couple's daughter Ruth that no photos were taken — an omission not all that unusual in that day.

18 October, 1991

1917: Frank Drake buys local variety store
Drake stays in business for 38 years

"F. E. Drake buys Evans Variety Store" was a page one headline in the March 2, 1917, *Northfield News*.

The story said, "Evans & Co. have sold their variety store on Division St. to F. E. Drake, formerly of this city but recently of St. Paul. Drake will take possession the latter part of next week.

"Mr. and Mrs. Evans and family have been in business here almost two years and state that they are very well satisfied with local conditions. They are selling out in order to go to Montana in quest of the outdoor life.

"Drake, the new owner of The Racket, is a son of Mr. and Mrs. Joseph E. Drake of this city. He has been employed for several years with the Snell Sash & Door Co. of St. Paul. After leaving Northfield about 11 years ago, he was located at Minot, N.D., and Saskatoon, Sask., Canada."

The store, which later was named Drake's Variety Store, was located at 323 Division, the north half of the building that the First National Bank is now remodeling for an addition to the bank. There was an open wooden stairway in the store and part of the stock was displayed on the second floor.

It was a true variety store with all manner of notions, housewares, school and office supplies, gift merchandise, toys, even work clothing for men and cotton housedresses for women.

When a feature story about Frank Drake appeared in a business series in the *News* in 1952, he had been in business here for 35 years. The story stated that Drake was a member of a pioneer family, was born (on Dec. 7, 1886) south of Northfield and attended a country school located near what was once the Ray Larkin farm.

"He attended the eighth grade in Northfield. Although his formal education ended there, his business experience the next few years provided him with adequate training for a business venture of his own," the story said.

The story revealed that while Drake was working at a sash and door factory at Minot, he met his future wife, Allie Wescott while attending a Minot church. From the Twin Cities area, she had gone to Minot for employment. Her sister's husband was employed at the same factory as Drake.

Those two men later went to Saskatoon to establish a branch for a Duluth sash and door factory. Drake's duties were as foreman of the outside work. Later he was shipping clerk, checking materials and merchandise in and out. He said that "he couldn't help but learn a little of carpentry during this period ... and did master the complicated art of laying out a stairway."

Drake returned to Minot for his wedding, but the couple established their first home in Canada. Some while later they moved to Minneapolis where Drake was employed by the sash and door firm that maintained the Minot branch. Later he transferred to its new branch in St. Paul.

The story about Drake said that "about this time he wanted to have a business of his own and began shopping for a grocery store on the outskirts of the Twin Cities. 'Am I glad I didn't find one!' he said, realizing that his Northfield business has been much better suited to the kind of life he wanted to lead.

"He purchased the variety store in 1917 from an Evans family who had been here for two years. Though built by the Mergen family, the store building has always belonged to the Nuttings since Drake began in business.

"The nature of his stock hasn't undergone too great a change in 35 years, Drake revealed, although the necessity to provide a greater selection in a single line has meant cutting out some types of merchandise.

"He now carries more notions, school supplies and gifts; less dry goods and clothing than he did a few years ago. Some of the small items require an unbelievable inventory; for instance, the store has on hand three of each kind of more than 400 zippers. In the line he carries there are available more than 500 shades of sewing thread, but he stocks only the colors he thinks will be most popular. He estimates that he buys from about 50 suppliers.

The story continued, "Though clearance sales don't work well in a variety store — the merchandise has to be priced to clear in the first place — Drake did have one gigantic sale in 1938 when a fire broke out during the night in the back room. There was little damage from the flames, but smoke from a supply of oil for the building's oil burner managed to smudge everything in the store.

"A picture of Drake that night would have made a good insurance company testimonial," the story said. "He remained perfectly calm, unlocking the front door for the firemen so they wouldn't need to break the lock. The reason for his calm — one of the components of Drake's recipe for good business is to carry 100 percent insurance coverage.

"Another ingredient of the recipe is to take the two percent discount for cash payment within 10 days. He found that the practice not only saves considerable money in the year, but he also firmly established an excellent credit rating early in his business career.

"Drake determined to prepare his three children for successful living. He gave them college educations — they are all graduates of St. Olaf College — but he insisted that they manage the money and the college expenses themselves. . . .

"Drake thinks his hobby is probably mowing the lawn at 712 E. Fourth St., but club and lodge work has filled a good deal of his life. He has been a member of the Rotary Club for 26 years, serving as treasurer for 20 of those years. . . . He has gone through all of the chairs in Social Lodge No. 48, AF&AM; Corinthian Chapter No. 33, RAM; Northfield Council No. 12, R&SM. He has also held all chairs in which it's possible for a man to serve in Sheba Chapter No. 73, OES. The Drakes are members of the Northfield Methodist Church."

Half a year after this feature appeared, Drake suffered a fall that resulted in serious injuries. A very short time later his wife died unexpectedly. Finally, in the spring of 1955, he decided to sell the store. He continued to live in his house on Fourth St. and remained active in both Rotary Club and the Masonic orders.

Ten years later, in the fall of 1965, he collapsed near the public library while on his way to the Thursday noon Rotary luncheon. He died two lays later, on Oct. 2, at Northfield Hospital.

Later in the month the *College City Cogwheel*, weekly news letter of the Rotary Club, paid tribute to Drake, noting that he had belonged to the club 39 of its 40 years of organization. His record of 28 years of perfect attendance had been broken only when he suffered the injuries from his fall. "Had it not been for the fact that Frank held the office of treasurer for more than 20 years, he doubtless would have been elected to every other office of the club at one time or another. His vacant chair will remind all of us of his faithfulness."

Your writer, who knew Drake all of her young life, remembers him as a substantial presence in the store, a quiet, dignified person with a dry sense of humor. Although he normally had a very competent staff, he was usually in the store during business hours.

Like Drake, his merchandise was substantial, likely to remain useful for quite some time. Much of his gift merchandise would now be highly collectable.

28 February, 1992

1918: Northfielder's leadership rescues Dan Patch Line
Whittier, self-made man, pursues many enterprises

"Dan Patch Line Saved for Sure" was the headline on a page one story in the July 19, 1918, *Northfield News*. The subhead on the story said, "It's the Northfield Line after this. Will give real service between Minneapolis and Northfield."

The story about a railroad that had been nicknamed for a famous race horse began, "It's not the Dan Patch Line any longer! Nor is it the more long-winded Minneapolis, St. Paul, Rochester & Dubuque Electric Traction Co. It's the Northfield Line hereafter and so let it be known. If you wish to use the full corporate title, here it is — The Minneapolis, Northfield & Southern Railway Co."

The name of the railroad remained "Minneapolis, Northfield & Southern" until recent years when the line was purchased by the Soo Line. But all those years, many longtime residents of the area still referred to the MN&S as the Dan Patch. The horse had belonged to the founder of the railroad, Col. M. W. Savage.

The 1918 story continued, "While the reorganization committee, of which H. A. Whittier of this city was a prominent and active member, did not have all of the $175,000 needed for the final payment to the bondholders on the purchase price of the road on Thursday, June 11, a few days of grace were secured and the required amount obtained. While the road, which has operated trains continuously from the 54th street station south to Northfield, will continue such operation only for the immediate future, it is expected there soon will be resumption of traffic on the cutoff from the Minnesota River to the Seventh Street terminal in Minneapolis.

"'When we get to running, we expect to give such good service that people cannot help but give us their freight service,' said Whittier, acting manager of the new company, in speaking of the situation Tuesday evening. The plans for the immediate future include an early day freight from Minneapolis, which will give business houses in Northfield and in the villages along the line better and quicker service than anything they have had in the past.

"Although the reorganization committee has raised enough money to buy the property, more funds will be required in order to give the company working capital. To supply these funds will be the immediate task before the officials of the company.

"The success of the new company in saving the Dan Patch Line is due largely to the untiring efforts of Whittier who has devoted much of his time the past few months in an effort to interest Twin Cities businessmen in the line. Whittier in active charge of the road, efficient and careful management is assured and advantage will be taken of every opportunity to increase the business of the line and make it a financial success."

In a story in the previous week's *News*, which was published on the day of the initial deadline, the possibility that the railroad line could be wrecked was described as little short of a calamity. "With the facts that the line can be bought as a going concern at a fraction of its actual value and less than its value as junk, and with assurance of the high investment value of its stock as basis, the local committee was hopeful that if granted a few more days, it could interest a sufficient number of people to make up the necessary amount."

There were decades when the railroad struggled and others when it was very successful, but it did survive until purchased by the Soo Line. The MN&S discontinued passenger service in 1942 and became a freight-only railroad. As a freight line, the MN&S was profitable because its trackage bypassed various bottlenecks and the short line could provide comparatively rapid service to area terminals.

The railroad was only one of the many activities of Whittier. But despite his successes and wealth, little ever appeared concerning him in the *Northfield News* because of his modesty and the private feelings of his family.

Mention of Whittier's saving the railroad appeared in a 1979 interview with Dana Sharp, engineer with the railroad for three decades. He was hired in 1918 when the MN&S was organized. He recalled "the man who was responsible for saving the Dan Patch line when it was ready to fold in 1918 — Bert Whittier. . . . 'Whittier was the one who really saved the Dan Patch from the scrap pile. He stepped in when they were going to scrap it when passenger trains weren't paying off. He negotiated the sale of the Dan Patch to MN&S.'"

In 1916, the late W. F. Schilling wrote about Whittier in his "Tales of the Town" column. He said in part, "Look at H. A. Whittier, another of our townsmen. Twenty-five years ago, Bert was digging rock out of the hills south of town and hauling it to town for a very few dollars a cord. He was later a teamster on the street, driving an old horse and an older mule, and was tickled to death to get $3 a day.

"He always worked well. He always hauled

the limit of a load and his employers saw it. The city saw it too and made him street commissioner and in this capacity he put in the big sewer system down Division St., much of which was dynamited through solid rock. He found he could handle men and then went sub-contracting, building big grades for railroads. He pushed things and though still a comparatively young man, he is on easy street."

The most ever written about Whittier in the *News* was his obituary in January of 1932, pulled together by the editor, Carl Weicht, before the Whittier family arrived in Northfield from the West Coast. Whittier had died in Long Beach, Calif., where he and his wife had been renting an apartment.

The story stated in, part: "Although he had not felt well on the Thursday evening preceding his death, Whittier was seriously ill only one day. Friday afternoon he was stricken with a serious heart attack and was removed from the Schuyler Hotel, Long Beach, where he and Mrs. Whittier had had an apartment since going to California a month ago, to Seaside Hospital. Death came to him there at 4 o'clock Saturday morning. Bursting of a cardiac artery was given as the cause of death.

"News of Whittier's death came as a great shock to many friends in Northfield and cast a pall of sorrow over the community which had been his lifelong home.

"Herbert A. Whittier was born in Northfield Nov. 5, 1863, the son of Charles F. and Margaret (Wilmarth) Whittier. He attended the city schools and grew up in this community. His first business experience was in the operation of a milk route, which he conducted for a year when in his early 20's.

"In 1884 he leased land in Bridgewater Township, south of Northfield, and opened a stone quarry which he operated for a number of years. Much of the stone used in foundations for buildings in Northfield came from Whittier's quarry during the late '80s and early '90s. At the same time he was for a number of years street commissioner in

Northfield.

"In 1896 Whittier took his first contract in railroad construction for the Great Western Railroad in Iowa, and began the work in which he made a fortune and became known throughout the state and the Northwest. He had many important contracts with different roads during the next 25 years, among them the building of lines for the Northern Pacific, for the Great Northern at Towner, N.D., and Devils Lake, N.D., as well as work on the coast line of the Milwaukee Railroad in Montana.

"When the Minneapolis, Northfield & Southern Railroad was organized, Whittier became one of the vice presidents, and he had built part of the old Dan Patch line. During the same period he carried on several highway projects, including a large road building job near Canby.

"Retiring from the railroad construction work about the time of the World War (World War I), Whittier became deeply interested in the development of the lignite coal industry in North Dakota and operated at Columbus one of the two largest mines of its kind in the world. He sold his entire interest in this enterprise in the fall of 1927 to the Truax-Traer Coal Co. for a consideration of approximately $400,000 (a large amount of money at that time).

"Whittier had been interested in the lignite industry in North Dakota for nine years, while for the latter seven years of that period he had been in active management of the project. In partnership with E. R. Crockett he first experimented with strip lignite coal at Columbus in the fall of 1918. Starting with a small steam shovel and a few dump wagons, this company uncovered 8,000 tons of coal the first year they were in business. Under Whittier's personal direction, the enterprise developed year by year until the production amounted to 150,000 tons annually. The Whittier mine at Columbus, N.D., was one of the best equipped in the state.

Whittier bought out his partner's interest in 1925 and at the time of the sale in 1927 the Northfield man was the sole owner of an exceedingly valuable and unencumbered piece of property, developed by his own foresight and aggressive management. Several grades of lignite coal were prepared, all of them of higher quality than is usually marketed, with the result that the volume of the company's business showed steady growth.

"Some folks laughed at him when he started operations in the lignite field at Columbus, but in less than a decade he built up an industry from virtually nothing to the place where he could sell it for $400,000."

The story does not tell about Whittier's ventures in gold mining or in the raising of ginseng. There were likely other ventures. Fortunately the Northfield Historical Society has the Whittier business papers.

The obituary continued, "Unusually successful in his various enterprises, Bert Whittier was in many respects a typical self-made man. In Northfield, where he spent most of his life, he was known for the generous spirit which he tried to hide under a more or less gruff exterior, and many a family in this community blessed the name of Bert Whittier for the quiet and unheralded kindnesses that he did. Independence was one of his strong characteristics, and while he seldom participated largely in the organized charities, he was unusually generous in his gifts to worthy people. He was particularly fond of young people, providing tickets for youngsters at the skating rink, entertaining the high school football boys, and doing similar things to show his interest."

Whittier married Stella Amoret Drake. They had three children, Grace A., Glen H. and Gladys R. (Mrs. Don Coleman). From the estate of the late Grace Whittier, the city's youth is currently benefiting from a recreation bequest. From the Colemans, also deceased, the Northfield Historical Society received the Northfield Bank Raid saddle that had been saved by Bert Whittier when he was a youth in 1876.

16 July, 1993

1919: Laura Baker School incorporated
Miss Baker recognized for pioneering methods

"Baker's School is incorporated" was a page one headline in the Jan. 31, 1919, *Northfield News.* "Good work done by this institution to be perpetuated," was the subhead.

The story began, "That Miss Laura Baker's School has won for itself a high reputation is evident from the desire of parents who have children in the institution to make sure that the good work should be perpetuated. The school has been incorporated and although it remains under practically the same management and supervision as heretofore, nine persons, including Miss Baker, are the stockholders and directors under the new organization. . . .

"The action is for the sole purpose of making the school a perpetual institution in order that the educational work which has been so successful thus far, may continue in the future.

"Only persons who have a child in the institution are permitted to hold stock and in case of the removal of the stockholder's child from the school, the parent must sell his shares to other members. . . . In this manner it is hoped to bring the sentimental interest in the welfare of the school up to the highest point, and to maintain the best conditions that can be secured to educate the children and make them happy while in the institution."

The school was the first of its kind west of the Mississippi, a boarding school for mentally retarded. Miss Baker's methods were very progressive in a time when facilities for the developmentally disabled were for the most part purely custodial.

Miss Baker was a native of Iowa, born April 10, 1859, in Chariton. According to a dissertation written by her great-grand-niece Laura Kay Allen (as part of her requirements for a degree of doctor of education), Miss Baker came from a family of activists, described by some as "liberal, open, even kind of wild-minded!" Growing up in that environment, she was an activist of sorts herself and, as she worked with the retarded, developed her own philosophy of how they should be educated.

She taught for seven years in the Glenwood Asylum for Feeble Minded Children in Iowa, then served for 12 years as principal of the school program at the Faribault State School for Mentally Retarded.

She came to feel that although these children were not functioning at a level at which they could be successful in public schools, they needed to be challenged.

When she decided, at age 38, that she would start a school of her own, she was aided by a man who had moved to Minnesota from Connecticut, hoping to find suitable care for his retarded daughter. To begin the school, they rented a large house in Minneapolis in 1897.

Feeling the need for a more spacious setting, Miss Baker searched in Glenwood, Iowa, Faribault and Northfield — she had been impressed by this city while riding through it by horse and buggy. They were able to buy a large house — in the present location of the school — for $5,000 and moved the school here from Minneapolis in July of 1898.

Miss Baker was a tall woman with regal carriage and, during many of her Northfield years, was crowned with snow-white hair. She was described as firm, desirous of perfection, yet patient and able to lavish love on her charges.

Despite the many hours of work she devoted to the children, she did an amazing amount of handwork — crocheted bedspreads, quilts, afghans. According to Allen's dissertation, she could even be seen hemming linen napkins for the school!

Articles that appeared in the *News* through the years emphasized that Miss Baker's aim was to help her students grow and develop and that she had no wish to hide them from society. In an age when retarded persons were commonly called morons, idiots, imbeciles or feeble minded, she named her school, "Miss Baker's School for Nervous and Backward Children."

Some of the children really were not retarded. With proper attention, they were able to blossom and transfer to public schools.

Miss Baker early realized the value of music and rhythm in the schooling of the retarded. She quickly introduced a rhythm band. Square, tap, folk and ballroom dancing were taught. She stated numerous times to the *News* that the mastering of percussion instruments, singing and dancing "invariably opens a door in their minds to further learning."

At the time of the incorporation of the school, there were about 35 students, boys under age 14 and girls of any age. In addition to academic subjects, girls were taught sewing, knitting, basketry, weaving and lace making. Boys were taught basketry, weaving, hammock making and net work.

Actually another reason for incorporation was providing a vehicle for fund raising — the school needed a new dorm. But the first brick building was not constructed until the late '20s.

Directly after the time of incorporation, Miss Baker had her hands full with a fight to prove that she indeed had established a school, not a profit-making residence, and that the property deserved to be tax-exempt. This was at the same time that the city had hoped to tax college property and the Minnesota supreme court had found for the colleges.

A *News* story in September of 1920 asked whether Miss Baker's pupils were making progress; if so, the school could claim to be an educational institution, it was stated. After taking testimony from parents, doctors and others who work with the retarded, the Rice County court found that this was indeed a school and that no taxes should be levied on the property.

Even before the dormitory was erected, the

school purchased cottages at Roberds Lake in rural Rice County so that the children could be at the lake in the summertime.

Dormitories that Miss Baker had seen had crowded a number of beds into one room and had provided large, common bathrooms. She designed her dorm with one bath to each two bedrooms and with a living area on each floor, hoping to provide a more homelike atmosphere. Unique for its time, this building was completed in 1928.

At about that time, for a few years, Miss Baker was associated with a woman who had taught with her at Faribault, in a school in Buckeye Hall in Faribault for lower functioning children. When she withdrew, she began working such children into her Northfield institution.

In 1938 Miss Baker's namesake, a niece, Laura May Baker Millis, and the latter's husband, Henry "Harry" Millis, moved to Northfield. They became associated with Miss Baker, who was nearing her 80th birthday, in the management of the school. Mrs. Millis became assistant director and her husband, business manager.

Mrs. Millis had attended St. Mary's School at Faribault and had obtained a degree in psychology from the National Kindergarten College at Evanston, Ill. In her dissertation, Mrs. Allen said that her mother "implemented with vigor Miss Baker's philosophy."

When the school celebrated its 50th anniversary on Sept. 1, 1947, there were 53 residents, nine teachers, eight housemothers and 11 other employees.

A story in the *News* at that time traced the beginning of the school to "many parents of children residing at the state institution (at Faribault) coming to her (Miss Baker) to discuss their problems. The general plaint was that they had children too capable to be confined in a home for the feeble minded and yet not possessing sufficient ability to compete with average individuals in public schools and to progress in the usual manner."

The story stated that the school's curriculum then included training in social skills, manners, arts and crafts, music, speech, reading, writing, mathematics, spelling, geography and vocational areas.

At the time of that anniversary, Miss Baker was still active at age 87 — and she was to live past her 101st birthday. When Miss Baker was 95, Mrs. Millis reported to the *News*, "She's just as interested in what goes on at the school as she ever was."

Miss Baker was in ill health for several years, however, and spent a year in the hospital, observing her 100th birthday there. She was at home for the 101st. She never had any thoughts of going to a nursing home; the Millises watched over her.

A story in the *News* regarding her 101st birthday said that "she remains interested in the school, continuing to ask frequent questions of her nurses and her niece regarding activities across the street."

Death came to Miss Baker on June 7, 1960, at home. Her friend, Nellie W. Phillips, *Northfield News* columnist, paid tribute to Miss Baker noting that the educator had said, "I have never had children of my own, but have been a mother to many."

Decades before, there was a Laura Baker School student who called the director "Old Hawkeye." This was partially because she came from Iowa, but also because she kept very close watch over her beloved charges!

28 January, 1994

The original Laura Baker School

1919: Rice prepares for ice skating season on Cannon
Northfielder devotes much time to young people

"Get your skates sharpened," was an unusual page one headline in the Nov. 14, 1919, *Northfield News*. The subhead read, "Dandy rink, portable band stand and warming house assured."

The story began, "Born — to the Northfield community another real live organization, prenatally christened the Northfield Skating Rink Club, with Ed Rice as guardian and godfather."

Rice's name was synonymous with Northfield ice skating rinks for a long time, possibly 30 years, according to his daughter, Peggy Grosser of Kerrville, Texas.

She recalled that during the skating season, her father scraped and watered the ice every night. During all of those years, the city's one skating rink was on the Cannon River ice between the Fifth Street bridge and the dam.

In a story about early rinks that appeared in the *News* in 1986, May Fremouw Shisler recalled that horses belonging to her father, Ed Fremouw (head of a company that cut river ice for year-round use in home ice boxes) were used to clear the rink of snow. She remembered that "after the rink was clear, a barrel on wheels and equipped with a spigot was pushed around the rink, distributing water. No one was allowed on the rink until that water was properly frozen. If it was too warm for it to freeze, we couldn't use the rink that day."

Shisler added that the young people didn't mind skating at 10 degrees, "We thought that was balmy."

Shisler also remembered that Shipstead and Johnson, whose Ice Follies later became world famous, were close friends of Rice. "One Saturday afternoon they came to Northfield and put on a good skating show on the rink," she said.

She remembered Rice, a six footer, as a wonderful skater who liked to waltz on ice if he could find an able partner.

Grosser remembered the Fremouw girls as being fine skaters, also Marlys Boone, now Formichella, who lives in Phoenix, Ariz.

Grosser recalled that her father didn't want anyone coming to the rink with double-runner skates in order to learn to skate. "He said that was like trying to learn to ride the bicycle with a four-wheeled bike." Instead, she explained, he would have beginners push a straight chair ahead of them on the ice, apparently something like using a walker.

In the 1986 story, Margaret Starks was quoted as remembering the pot bellied stove in the rink's warming house. She recalled that if you got within five feet of it, you were in danger of getting burned, it was so hot. "There were little benches in the house to sit on while you clamped on your skates," she said. "There were no one-piece boots and skates in those days."

Starks remembered that Rice kept amplified recorded music going for the skaters and the rink was lighted. Since it was the only rink in town, college students joined the local young people for an evening of action in the crisp cold.

Grosser spoke of the pot bellied stove and remembered eating Eskimo Pies in the warming house.

Rice had a number of other irons in the fire besides the skating rink, both in the nature of volunteer work and to make a living. Grosser recalled that he was an "eccentric" person who found it difficult to work for someone else. Therefore he needed to be self employed and often combined several things.

Rice was born in Northfield on Dec. 26, 1874. His family then lived where Florence (Canedy) and Roy Baker now reside at 1110 Division. His father was F. O. Rice, a substantial citizen who also had different irons in the fire. W. F. Schilling, *News* columnist (and once editor) at one time wrote of F. O. Rice that he was over six feet tall, a surveyor and candy maker, that he was occupant of a little store (apparently where VIP Travel is now located) where children could purchase many homemade chocolate drops for a penny. "No one knew exactly how tall F. O. Rice was, as when he was asked, he would always say, 'If I did not have so much turned up in feet I would be seven-foot-two.' He was city surveyor and justice of the peace for a long time."

Ed Rice is pictured and mentioned both as a football player and coach in *Northfield High School Athletic History*, a book compiled by the late C. E. Sandberg.

Grosser said that her father's independence asserted itself very early in his life. There is a family tale that he became angry with his grade school teacher, quit school and had to be home-schooled by his father. However since he is mentioned in the Sandberg book as an NHS gridder at the turn of the century, one would guess that he was back in school.

According to the Sandberg book, Rice began coaching and training the local team in 1905. He was coaching in 1906 when new rules became effective, designed to eliminate intentional injury and to bring about more open play. One of the rules changed the yardage for a first down from five to 10. That year the Raider gridders were Southern Minnesota champions.

According to the Sandberg book, Rice was still coach in 1907. It is not mentioned who coached in 1908. Rice is mentioned as refereeing in 1909 and a new coach is cited in 1910.

Rice bought a boat house near the Ames Mill, according to a *News* item on Feb. 6, 1914. The story said he would move the house from its present location and place it on the foundation of his boat house that had burned down, location not mentioned. The story said he also purchased the 10 canoes and two boats that had been stored in the boat house.

In August of 1914, according to a story in the *News*, he built another boat house, this one of sheet metal. It had a capacity for 12 canoes. Stating that Rice now had accommodations for 30 canoes, the story said that canoe rental was very popular on the Cannon.

On May 15, 1914, the *News* reported on the front page, "Edwin R. Rice, the well-known boat house and skating rink manager, surprised his friends the first of the week with the announcement of his marriage on Thursday, April 23, to Mrs. Mary Davis of Minneapolis. Mr. and Mrs. Rice will be at home at 515 E. Water after July 1." Grosser said this house was in the current location of the Grundhoefer, Neuville and Ludescher law office.

Grosser remembered that when she was a little girl, Rice had cold frames in the back yard and, also maintaining gardens, was able to sell vegetables to Northfield food stores. She recalled that he had a huge asparagus farm on the then southeast edge of town. She and her sister (now Rilda Johnson of San Antonio, Texas) picked the asparagus which sold to the stores for 10 cents a pound and was then sold to the public for 17 cents a pound.

Grosser also said that through the years her dad sold radios, cars, real estate and, with his father, insurance. Ed and Mary Rice cared for F. O. Rice, then a widower, in his last years. F. O. Rice's obituary in the *News* says that he was "tenderly cared for."

Grosser remembered her father hauling kids here and there for athletic contests, using his seven-passenger car.

When his arthritis was starting to be a problem, Ed and his wife moved to Donna, Texas, in the mid 1930s. There he had two fruit groves and packed fruit to sell all over the United States. "Lots of Northfielders visited my parents in Texas," Grosser said.

Her mother died in December of 1967 and her father in February of 1969. He was 95.

There are two exciting stories involving Rice in the *News* through the years that haven't as yet been mentioned here. Both times he had a hand in preventing a drowning.

In May of 1908 when the Cannon River was raging, Alson Blodgett, who later became a well-known Northfield businessman, and Vern Livingston were riding in a motor boat above the dam. As they approached the dam, something apparently went wrong with the steering mechanism and the craft went over the dam backward. Both boys were dumped into the swirling water.

The *News* said that there were a hundred onlookers, but no one made an effort to rescue the youths, excepting Ed Rice. He was standing by the First National Bank when the boat went over the dam. When he realized Blodgett was in the water, he recalled that the lad was not a strong swimmer and decided he would need help.

Rice tore through the Riverside Restaurant that was located where the walkway now is, alongside the current Riverside. He threw off his coat there and ran along the river until he reached the current site of the Nutting Mall. There he jumped into the river, taking with him a small board. That proved to

be inadequate, but he soon snagged a piece of lumber that was coming down the river. Blodgett was able to latch onto the board.

Rice told the *News*, "Just as I caught the plank, I saw Blodgett throw back his head and heard him call for help. He was about gone when I got to him."

Rice was so bogged down by his clothing and shoes that he was unable to haul Blodgett ashore. But he paddled with one hand and was able to grab some willow branches that leaned over the river. The crowd at that time sprung into action and hauled the two out of the water.

Meanwhile everyone had assumed that Livingston would be able to handle himself and he did until he was under the Second St. bridge. But then he disappeared and drowned.

Rice again participated in a rescue in June of 1916 when the Cannon was again on a rampage. This time it was a Carleton coed who was fishing off the river bank with two other girls. She lost her balance, fell in, was carried over the dam and lost consciousness.

While a number of people just stood and watched, a Norwegian immigrant who had been a swimming champ in his homeland and who was working on road construction here, leapt over the central bridge railing adjacent to the Riverside Restaurant and waited for the girl's body to sweep within reach. Again the current was too strong for him to haul her ashore, but Rice, having heard the commotion, called that he would come with a boat. He placed it in the river adjacent to his boat houses and was able to successfully shoot the dam at the east end without tipping. He took the girl to the St. Paul House, a hotel on the west bank, and apparently supervised first aid. She had little water in her lungs, but remained unconscious for four hours. The *News* commented, "Here Mr. Rice's knowledge of how to handle such cases was very helpful."

11 November, 1994

1920: Heibel to head harness dealer's state group
Life brings wide variety of activities to Heibel

"C.C. Heibel of this city was elected president of the Minnesota Retail Harness Dealers Association at their annual convention in the West Hotel, Minneapolis," said a story in the June 25, 1920, *Northfield News*.

The story also said that Heibel had been chosen to represent Minnesota at the national convention of retail harness dealers to be held in Detroit in September.

The story noted that the Retail Harness Dealers Association had affiliated with the National Horse Association of America, an organization that had been formed to advocate the breeding of more and better horses.

As horse breeders and harness makers hoped against hope, with the increase in automation, for continued need for their skills, the story ended, "A survey shows that more horses and mules are used per acre than 20 years ago."

C. C. Heibel was by then a well-established businessman in Northfield, constantly changing the nature of his business to match the trends of the times. He eventually became Northfield's postmaster and served in several civic capacities.

Carl Heibel had come to Northfield in 1912. He was born in 1890 in Marystown and grew up there, attending Catholic parochial school. He graduated from nearby Shakopee High School.

Heibel had completed his apprenticeship as a harness maker at Shakopee and had worked for three years at Belle Plain when he decided he wanted to have his own business. He asked a traveling salesman of supplies to watch for an opportunity.

Soon the salesman discovered that J. Deckelnick wanted to sell his Northfield business and building and go farming in Wisconsin. Heibel arranged the purchase and began his business in the small building on W. Third which he was to use for 10 years. Both this building and the large one that he was to have erected in 1922 were razed when the path of TH 3 through the West Side business district was established.

Heibel's sons, Robert and Richard who reside in Northfield, recall that not only was the first little building crowded, but it had a problem not unusual in that day when the city dump was at the edge of the business district. Heibel had to keep five rat terriers in the building at night to challenge the constant invasion of rats!

When he had been in business for about a year, Heibel married Blanche Mayer at Jordan in May of 1913 and they established their first home on Orchard St. in Northfield.

A 1919 story in the *News* revealed that Heibel had installed a new $1,200 Landis stitching machine in his shoe repair area, "The machine is of a modern type and insures the output of high class repair work."

Heibel had already branched out into various other lines. Basically he made from scratch several styles of harness, sometimes creating special harnesses to order. He repaired shoes and also sold new shoes, a special hand-made kind that was put together without nails in the soles and heels. He made buggy whips. Through the years he made leather billfolds that had no stitching to wear out.

Heibel was already advertising in the *News* in 1920 that he could bring about "one of the newest and most practical (car) top improvements ever introduced." He could replace "the unsatisfactory factory-installed mica window that you never could see through, with durable glass of crystal clearness. Now is the time to have these sensible windows installed in your present top." The illustration shows oval windows in the old flexible tops of the touring cars. ·

Heibel's new brick building at the corner of W. Third and Water streets (directly across the street north from the present-day Northfield Travel) provided room for a large line of luggage from brief cases to steamer trunks. In those days college students all carried brief cases, creating considerable business for Heibel. Heibel also provided luggage for the traveling choir and bands from Northfield's colleges.

The new building provided room for an unusual service that proved very successful. A driveway was established at the rear of the building that led to a basement workroom. Heibel precut the pieces of the standard leather tops of the Model T's and Model A's and had them ready to assemble. These tops had to be replaced periodically and Heibel could install a top in a half day. At that time it took more than a day to have this work done in the Twin Cities.

Always an inventive person, Heibel in the late 1930s designed and built a shoulder harness for the late Jim Lippert (uncle of the present-day Jim Lippert of Northfield). Lippert, an athletic champion, had difficulty with shoulders that slipped in and out of joint and Heibel solved the problem with the leather harness.

Heibel's sons remember a father who was willing to allow them to use shop equipment. Bob recalls making cowboy belts and holsters.

During the early summer some years later the St. Olaf College maintenance staff came to Heibel with a problem. A quantity of furniture from dormitories and public rooms needed reupholstering and the college had been unable to find any place in Northfield or the Twin Cities that would take on the project with the understanding that it must be done by fall.

Heibel, with the many contacts he had made in the state by that time, got a semi-retired master upholsterer to come, teach him the art of upholstering and work with him to finish the project by the deadline. Eventually Carl taught this art to his son Dick who operated an upholstery shop in Northfield for several years.

Meanwhile, when Heibel presided at the harness dealers' 1923 convention, a friend of his, W. F. Schilling of Northfield, was among the speakers. After he completed his term as president, Heibel became executive secretary of the organization for three terms.

In 1931, Heibel was elected chairman of the Northfield Retail Merchants Association. In 1934, the Commercial Club and the Retail Merchants joined forces and changed their name to the Northfield Association. Heibel, elected president, pledged "hard work and enthusiasm."

At a time when post office appointments were political in nature, in February of 1934, the *News* announced that "Carl C. Heibel, Northfield businessman and prominent local Democrat, has been named as acting postmaster in Northfield." He succeeded Anna Dickie Olesen, Democrat who was the newly-appointed state director of the National Emergency Council.

The story explained that there had been six applicants for the appointment. When the three with highest ratings in a Civil Service examination had been determined by the Civil Service commission in Washington, one name was to be selected by Postmaster General James A. Farley for recommendation to President Franklin D. Roosevelt. The presidential nomination would then have to be confirmed by the senate.

The story said that the Civil Service commission had not as yet certified its list of three, but that this was not necessary in the case of appointment of an acting postmaster. However, the story also said, "The appointment of Heibel as acting postmaster is regarded in well-informed circles as a forerunner of his appointment as postmaster for the full four-year term."

This proved to be true and he served as postmaster until 1960 when he retired.

In 1936 Heibel was elected president of the First Minnesota District of the National Association of Postmasters. In 1940 he became president of the Minnesota Chapter of the association.

He was elected president of the Northfield Lions Club in 1939. He was a charter member of Northfield Golf Club. He served for a time on the Northfield planning commission, on the city zoning board, on a city charter commission, on the advisory board of Greenvale Apartments. He was an active member of the Knights of Columbus. After his retirement from being postmaster, he became a member of the Association of Re-

tired Postmasters. He was an active member of the Church of St. Dominic.

Heibel sold his leather business in 1937, but when he retired from the post office, he became active in his son's upholstery business. He also enjoyed woodworking, building clocks and making models of horse-and-buggy era transportation.

Northfield history buffs enjoyed visiting with Heibel in his old age as he had a keen memory for what had occurred here though the years.

Soon after his 83rd birthday, he suffered a stroke. He died about three weeks later at Northfield Hospital on April 15, 1973.

His wife had died in 1960. He was survived by the two sons and a daughter as well as grandchildren and great-grandchildren.

23 June, 1995

1920: Lashbrook named county Farm Bureau director
Al Lashbrook known nationally as Holstein breeder

A front-page story in the Dec. 24, 1920, *Northfield News* reported that Alfred J. Lashbrook was one of three men elected to the board of directors of the Rice County Farm Bureau. Another Northfielder, Hagbarth Bue, was president of the county organization at the time.

Lashbrook was long active in the Farm Bureau, but he was for much of his adult life nationally known as an important Holstein breeder. He resided in Northfield all but a very few of his 86 years

He was born on Jan. 11, 1890, in Austin, Minn., where his father had a store. He was the oldest of three sons of Ulysses L. and Della E. Lashbrook.

He spent his early childhood on a farm near Waverly, Iowa, where the family resided through 1902 and where he began school.

The family moved to Northfield in January of 1903, Ulysses having purchased a farm at the northwest edge of Northfield from W. F. Schilling, editor of the *Northfield News*. Schilling had long urged Northfield farmers to concentrate on breeding Holstein cattle as he felt offering a wide choice of young stock of one breed would make Northfield a mecca for breeders. With the farm, Ulysses purchased a herd of 11 purebred Holsteins which were under contract to provide milk to St. Olaf College.

He also bought nine grade Holsteins from another local herd. But within two years the grades were gone. The Lashbrook herd was all purebreds after 1905. Seven-day testing was started in 1910. After 1919 the herd was on continuous yearly testing.

Meanwhile, Al graduated from Northfield High School in 1908 and attended Carleton College for three years. He then transferred to the College of Agriculture, University of Minnesota, receiving a B.S. in dairy husbandry in December of 1913.

He then received practical teaching experience in the high school agriculture department at Fergus Falls during the second semester. He returned to Fergus Falls in the fall but, a short time into the school year, was appointed a dairy specialist by the U.S. Department of Agriculture and was assigned to the state of Washington. For 1½ years he was headquartered at Pullman, Wash., engaged in dairy extension work throughout the state.

On Aug. 19, 1915, he married Edna Stake of Anoka whom he had met at the university. She had obtained her teacher's certificate there after completing a normal course. Before their marriage she taught home economics at Winthrop.

The couple moved to Pullman, but into the second year, Al's mother died. After the funeral, Edna stayed in Northfield to keep up the work Della had been doing on the dairy farm. After completing his duties at Pullman, Al returned to Northfield in the spring. He joined his father in the operation of the Lashbrook Holstein Farm.

Later he purchased the herd and spent 40 years breeding registered Holsteins. The first important herd sire that went into service

— Sir Walker Segis Homestead in 1918 — had been bred out of a world's record milk producer and put heavy milk production into the herd. Another sire, Dean Colantha Segis Ormsby, had several famous offspring. One of them, Lashbrook Pearl Ormsby, sold for an astounding price for that day to the Detroit Creamery Co., and made Holstein history through her son Woodmaster.

Through the years, Lashbrook Holsteins were sold into 23 states and three foreign countries.

Most of his life, Al was a member of the Northfield Holstein Club. After serving several terms as secretary to the group, he served as president. From 1918 until 1955 he served as a director of the Minnesota Holstein Breeders Association. He was president in both 1948 and 1949. For 40 years he was elected a delegate to the annual conventions of the National Holstein-Friesian Association. In 1938 he was named a director of the national organization and continued that work until 1946.

In 1956 Al decided to disperse his herd. In a story on May 3, 1956, the *News* reported, "The lack of competent help in these years when Al Lashbrook would like to slow down and enjoy some leisure makes it too difficult to continue the herd. His decision will make it possible for other breeders throughout the nation to take advantage of the 50 years of effort that has gone into the development of the Lashbrook Holsteins." The story also revealed that Al's two sons, Willard and Donald, both of whom had important agriculture-related positions, would be here to assist at the sale of 50 head on May 5. It turned out to be the fourth highest dispersal sale in the United States that year.

It was announced that Al and Edna intended to continue living in their farm home.

Al was not one to take it very easy. That fall he was elected to the office of secretary of the Minnesota Holstein Breeders Association. He was to attend meetings of the 27 county associations in Minnesota, carry on extension work, edit the state *Holstein Breed-*

ers News, manage state sales. And he would be attending interstate planning conferences.

He was continuously re-elected until 1964. When he announced in the fall of 1963 that he would like to retire from the position,

He and Edna were honored at a dinner at Mankato. A story in the *News* of Nov. 14, 1963, stated, "It was pointed out during the dinner program that Lashbrook has devoted much time and energy to the position. He in turn gave much credit to Mrs. Lashbrook who, he said, has greatly helped him with the big task of processing the mail that is involved in an organization of 1,300 members scattered throughout the entire state."

The couple was presented with a tray that was engraved, "For devoted service to the Minnesota Holstein Association, to Al and Edna Lashbrook, 1963."

In 1960, Al had been recognized by the Minnesota Livestock Breeders Association for his outstanding contributions to animal husbandry. More than 600 persons attended the event during the organization's annual meeting held at New Ulm. The organization also honored Al by hanging his portrait and a citation in Peters Hall at the Institute of Agriculture in St. Paul.

Al continued to attend national conventions of the Holstein Association as long as he was able. He was also a respected choice as cattle judge at county fairs. But in the meantime, he took many responsibilities in his own community.

He had helped to organize the extension work in Rice County from which the Farm Bureau grew. He was secretary of the Northfield local of the Twin City Milk Producers Association from 1918 to 1955. He served on the board of the Northfield Farmers Cooperative Elevator from 1933 until 1957.

When his two sons and two daughters were young, he served in PTA offices. In 1944 when there was a vacancy on the Northfield Board of Education, the board proposed to name Edna to fill it. She declined, but suggested her husband. Al accepted and continued to serve until 1956. He also served as a trustee of the Congregational Church. He served on the Rice County Fair board while the event was held in Northfield.

Edna was also active in the church and she received national recognition for her work with Girl Scouting. She was long extremely active in extension work. She was a delegate to the National Farm Bureau convention in 1938.

One of the Lashbrook daughters, Helen Olson of South St. Paul, recently recalled that St. Olaf College students frequently lived with the Lashbrooks, working for their board and room. "It meant the difference between being able to go to college or not," she said. "We would have both male and female students and they became close family members. Both Al and Edna understood what it was like to be away from home for the first time and truly accepted these students as family."

Al suffered a stroke in late December of 1972. He suffered a speech impediment and partial paralysis in his left arm. After receiving care at the Dilley Unit for four months, Al moved to the Minnesota Odd Fellows Home infirmary. Edna moved to an apartment in Three Links so that she could spend a great deal of time with him. She was later quoted in the *News* that "no matter how handicapped he was, he never complained about his lot, making it a lot easier to take care of him."

Although the couple had been able to celebrate their golden wedding anniversary with a big open house at their farm home, the 60th in 1975 was a quiet affair. But it was held at the farm, the new owners of the property inviting the family to fellowship in the familiar setting.

Al was able to attend a family gathering on Christmas Eve of 1976 at Edna's apartment and all nearby family members spent Christmas Day with him at the care center. The next day, he abruptly became acutely ill and died on Dec. 26, 1976. Edna died in May of 1979.

The couple has come to the attention of Northfielders again in very recent years. When it was proposed to build almost 100 townhouses on a portion of the one-time Lashbrook farm, the community protested, organizing Northfield People for Parks. As a result of their efforts the 11-acre parcel was named Lashbrook Park — with plans for development into a passive park with hiking trails. Parts of the area will be planted to prairie grass and prairie wild flowers. There will also be shrubs and trees. A dedication program is planned for spring.

22 December, 1995

1920: Tschann, builder of Central Block, dies

Tschann operated superb meat market

A picture of Louis Tschann appeared in the Sept. 3, 1920, *Northfield News*, along with the caption, "Louis Tschann, whose death occurred Aug. 23, was one of Northfield's pioneer businessmen, starting in business on Bridge Square in 1866. In 1893 he erected the Central Block, the largest business block in the city."

His obituary in the *News* commenced, "One by one the men who helped to make our splendid community what it is are slipping away and this week death has claimed one of our very best citizens in the person of Louis Tschann."

The story continued; "On Wednesday, Aug. 18, after running the lawn mower for quite a time, he came into the house and while sitting in a chair in the kitchen was stricken with paralysis. He dropped to the floor where he was found unconscious a few moments later by a daughter who summoned the doctor. It was found that nothing could be done to save him and after lingering for nearly a week in comatose state, he died on Aug. 23."

Obituary facts included, "Tschann was born in Roderen, Alsace, France, Aug. 12, 1844. He came to this country with his parents when he was 18 years old. The family lived for a time in Manlius, N.Y., coming west and stopping for a day or two at St. Cloud looking for a farm. Not being satisfied with that country, they came to Northfield where they settled. . . .

"Louis soon became interested in the butcher business and in the year 1866 started a meat market on Bridge Square."

This market was located on part of the current site of the Northfield post office.

The story continued, "In a few years he took in as a partner his brother-in-law (a sister's husband), Frank DeGross, and they remained in the market business for about 30 years until DeGross retired. Tschann continued the business for another five years when he too retired."

In 1879, the *News* printed a large group of short stories about Northfield businesses and the meat market of Louis Tschann & Co. was included. The sketch stated, "The meat market is an establishment most worthy of a piece in this review. That Tschann has been successful none will deny who have seen his superb establishment of today.

"They have just completed a new building, a brick structure 50 by 23, two stories high plus basement and which would do honor to the business circles of the largest city in the state. The building is provided with plate glass front and is constructed in the most approved and convenient method.

"We venture to say they have the best refrigerator in the state. This is so constructed as to supply the ice from the ice house with very little labor. It is surrounded with a double air chamber and while a cool and even temperature is maintained, it is entirely free from moisture.

"The second floor is devoted to office uses. . . .

"The stock carried is in keeping with the handsome surroundings and it is perfect in every respect and is the model feature of Northfield business interests."

In 1890, the *News* carried a similar feature, this time written by a veteran newspaperman, George W. Harrison.

After tracing Tschann's early years and arrival in Northfield, Harrison wrote, "In 1871 he built the handsome two-story brick building he now occupies as a meat market. Shortly after going into the meat business, a partnership was formed with Frank De-Gross, also born in Europe, but in Luxembourg. . . .

They carry meats of all kinds, also sausages, bolognas, etc., made fresh every day. Hides, games, etc., are also bought here. They do a free delivery business to all parts of the city."

A story in the July 21, 1875, *Rice County Journal* tells of the fire that destroyed Tschann's slaughter house. It was located on a Bunday farm about a mile south of Northfield, the story stated. It described the loss as consisting of "the building, one beef creature just dressed, a barrel of tallow, etc. No insurance. It was a clear case of incendiarism as they have no fire about the premises."

The Jan. 10, 1891, *News* told of another fire that plagued Tschann. "A building on W. Water St. owned by Louis Tschann was burned early Sunday morning. The fire department did excellent work in preventing the spread of the fire." The story did not state who or what occupied the building.

Tschann's retirement was announced in the March 2, 1907, *News*: "After 36 years (it was really 41) of active and continuous business in Northfield, Louis Tschann has decided to retire. He is one of Northfield's prominent and successful businessmen. During his long business career in this city, he has enjoyed the confidence of all his business associates and has left a record for business integrity worthy of emulation by younger merchants. Tschann retires on account of ill health from which he has suffered for the past two or three years." However he lived another 13 years.

The obituary continued, "Perhaps the biggest business undertaking of the firm of which Tschann was senior member was the building of the Central Block in 1893.

"This was the year of the panic and in the spring Tschann went into the First National Bank to consult with G. M. Phillips, who was then the cashier, and told him he would like a sum of money to help in this venture and was told that he could have all that he wanted. But a little later in the year, money tightened and Phillips called on Tschann and told him it would be doubtful if he could spare the money. Tschann reminded him of the promise and told him he would have to make good and the money came forth. This block cost the firm about $35,000 and to this day is the largest business block in the city."

In light of the panic of 1893, it is interesting to note that J. C. Nutting, the president of the First National Bank, was at the same time erecting the building that is now the Nutting Mall. He stated at the time that it represented his faith in Northfield and was an effort to bolster the economy.

The Central Block was erected on the site of the former Central House, a wood frame hotel that had previously been called the Dampier House. It was also at one time called the American House, the same name but not the same business as John W. North's hotel.

A search of the 1893 bound volume of the *News* revealed that "the Central House has been entirely taken down," reported in the March 18 issue. The April 22 issue announced that "work commenced on the Tschann building Monday last."

It was a cold, rainy, snowy spring and the May 6 issue said that work was rushed whenever there was an hour when weather permitted. By June 3 the bricklayers had reached the third story and by July 1, "the interior of the Tschann building is ready for plaster, the cornice is here and as soon as the roof is on, the work will be finished in a short time."

The *News* of July 15 announced that the staging had been removed and the building was now being plastered. That same week, Dr. E. G. Riddell announced that he would have an office in the Central Block as soon as it was completed. He did move about the first of September.

The Aug. 26 issue (just three months after the building was started) announced that the Central Block, "nearing completion, will soon be ready for occupancy. The first two store spaces (from Fourth St.) will be occupied by C. R. Griebie & Co. (a general store). D. D. Turner will have the room on the south end for his drug store." The Griebies mowed in at the end of September.

Finally on Nov. 4, the *News* stated, "The Central Block attracts the attention of all strangers and the general verdict is that it is one of the finest to be found in the state."

The obituary concluded, "The very best that can be said of any man can be truly said of Tschann. He is a true Christian gentleman who lived every day a life that could with profit be emulated by every citizen of the community. If he had any troubles or sorrows in his life, he kept them where his friends never heard of them. He helped every worthy enterprise all he could and has left a host of friends and neighbors who will miss him."

He and his wife, the former Mathilda Kaus, did lose a daughter in infancy. They had seven other children, all of whom survived their father. One of them, Helen Tschann, still survives, celebrating her 100th birthday anniversary last December here in Northfield. Probably the best known of the children was Father Fred Tschann. Another son, Frank, who died relatively young, was vice president of the State Bank of Northfield.

Louis Tschann's widow was a fascinating person in her own right. She was born in New Ulm where her father was the first postmaster and also owned a lumberyard. During her childhood they moved to nearby Lafayette where he built and operated a hotel. That was burned by Indians during the 1862 uprising.

The father stayed in Lafayette to try to protect the hotel while his wife and children, including Mrs. Tschann, took refuge in St. Peter. When he finally took off on horseback to join them, he was shot through the hat. He had presence of mind to fall off the horse and pretend to be dead. He crawled on his hands and knees two miles to New Ulm and was then able to reach his family.

They resided for a time at Faribault, then at Fergus Falls. During that period Mrs. Tschann taught at Elizabeth.

Next the family lived for a short time at Dundas. During that period, Mathilda met Louis Tschann and many years later admitted that it might have been love at first sight.

The couple was married in 1882 at Parkdale where her parents had by that time moved, her father having bought a mill there. The Tschanns lived on N. Division until they bought the house at 316 E. Fifth in 1906. Mrs. Tschann lived there until her death in 1948 at the age of 92. She was active and of clear mind until her unexpected death from a heart attack. Her mother had lived to be 93 and Mrs. Tschann had a sister two years older than she was who survived her.

Nellie Phillips, Northfield newspaperwoman, wrote of Mrs. Tschann on her 92nd birthday that she was beautiful, looked to be in her early 70s, didn't wear glasses except to read, knit or crochet — of which she still did a good bit. She made the bread for the family, assisted with the rest of the cooking and the housework.

Both Mathilda and Louis Tschann were active in the Church of St. Dominic.

1 September, 1995

1922: Frank Curren on ballot for Northfield's mayor
Curren serves city 'loyally and ably'

"Only two contests for city office — the one for mayor and the other for municipal judge — will have to be settled by the voters of Northfield at the municipal election Tuesday," said a story in the March 10, 1922, *Northfield News*.

The story continued, "The petition of Frank Curren for mayor (he was 'drafted' by a group of friends) was filed with city recorder R. H. Moses Saturday. Alex MacKay, the city convention's choice for the nomination, filed last week.

"Political dopesters, taking cognizance of the fact that both MacKay and Curren can muster a great deal of support, are looking for a close race, no one venturing even a guess as to the probable outcome."

The *News* of the following week declared in its headline, "City chooses Curren mayor." The subhead said, "Close race in mayoralty contest revealed by ballot count."

The story stated that Curren had won by only 18 votes. In the first ward where MacKay, a prominent merchant, was a resident, he rolled up two votes to every Curren vote. But Curren led substantially in the second and third wards.

The following week when the *News* reported on the reorganization meeting of the city council, it was stated that "to make Northfield one of the best towns in the state is the object of the new city administration as voiced by Mayor Frank Curren Tuesday night."

But the March 31 *News* carried the headline, "Vote for mayor to be contested," and the subhead, "Errors in counting alleged."

John E. Murphy, a resident of the second ward, had filed an appeal in district court. The story reported that MacKay had stated that he was in no way behind the action, that he had tried to discourage any such action when the matter was called to his attention. The *News* story said that MacKay was "plainly surprised when he learned that ac-

tual legal steps had been instituted."

Meanwhile Curren said he would make no effort to fight for the office which he said had been "handed to me."

"Count leaves Curren mayor" was a headline in the April 14 *News* — but by a majority of only one vote! The count was now Curren, 494, and MacKay, 493. Previously it had been 503 to 485.

In his motion to dismiss the contest, the attorney for Murphy moved that Murphy should assume the costs of the recount.

Several years later, in 1936, MacKay was elected mayor. Both men had served on the city council.

Before the recount motion, the *News* published a story about Curren, the headline stating that the new mayor had been "a prominent citizen for a half century." The story began, "By electing Frank Curren to the office of mayor, the citizens of Northfield Tuesday honored a man who for half a century has been prominent in the upbuilding and development of the city."

The story stated that Curren's widowed

mother, her five sons and a daughter had come to Northfield in 1855, buying a farm seven miles southeast of Northfield. When he was 17, Curren enlisted in the Union army and served until the close of the Civil War.

"He joined Company F, Seventh Minnesota Regiment, served first in the department of the West and later in the department of the Gulf. He took part in the battle of Tupelo, Miss., in the second battle of Nashville, Tenn., and in the siege of Fort Spanish — across the bay from Mobile, Ala. — where he was under fire for 13 days. The regiment was on its way to Montgomery, Ala., when the armistice was signed.

"After the close of the war, Curren returned to Northfield, living here until 1872 when he moved to Windom. He took up a claim there, but returned to Northfield in 1874 and since that time has been a resident of this community. His business was contracting and railroad work until 10 years ago when he entered the real estate business. He was in partnership with the late I. D. Wilson for a number of years.

"Curren has been prominent in community affairs in Northfield for many years, serving the GAR (Grand Army of the Republic), of which he is now commander, in various capacities."

The story stated that he had served as alderman for five years. While on the city council he was chairman of the water, street and finance committees and was elected vice president of the council during his second term.

While he was serving as mayor, Curren was the subject of a questionnaire in a series carried by the *News*. The same questions were asked of all persons interviewed. The feature reveals that he was born in 1847 at Raymond in Racine County, Wisconsin. To the question, "When did you come to Northfield?" he answered, "Northfield wasn't here when I came in 1855." (That was the year of the arrival of John North, founder of Northfield.)

When he was asked about the first thing he could recall in his life, Curren said, "When I was a little fellow and had the mumps, my mother made me wear a great big hood when I went out of doors, and I was mad as blazes about it."

Another question was, "If you were counseling a young man about to start out in life, what would be your advice?" Curren answered, "A young man's first ambition should be to get an education. If I were young I would want to be a soldier. If I had a boy I would send him to West Point."

Then he was asked, "What aided you most in attaining success?" Curren answered, "The question is, did I make a success? Common sense is mighty important."

Each of the interviews ended by asking the individual, "What one thing does Northfield need most?" Curren answered, "It is hard to say, we need so much. But the thing we need most is to get busy and pull together."

When Curren observed his 81st birthday anniversary in January of 1928, he had been confined to bed by illness for several months, but the *News* reported that he was in his usual good spirits and keen mental alertness. "Better still, his birthday found him feeling better than he had for some weeks and making a New Year's resolution that he would be up again as usual."

The story further said, "Many years of activity and interest in public affairs were climaxed by Curren's able administration as mayor of Northfield. He served a chief executive of the city from 1922 to 1926 at a time in life when most men would have retired to their own firesides."

Curren died almost two years later, on Nov. 10, 1929, at his home on Union St. "The end came peacefully, following an illness of nearly four years' duration and brought on by the infirmities of advancing age," the *News* said.

The obituary stated that Curren's father, John Curren, was an immigrant from Ireland while his wife was a native of New York state. Her grandfather had served in the American Revolution. The Curren family went to Wisconsin in the early 1840s and

Curren's father died there before the family came to Minnesota.

"Although then but a lad of eight years," the obituary said, "Curren remembered vividly the pioneer surroundings into which the family came. There was then little of Northfield to be seen and the Currens experienced the hard work and self-denial typical of the early settlers who laid the foundations for the progressive community of today."

The obituary revealed that Curren had taken an active part in the formation of the Ware Auditorium company which brought under local control the building that later housed the Grand Theater.

A few years after the death of his real estate partner, he became associated with L. W. Huestis who survived him.

The monetary amounts seem strange today, but the obituary commented in some detail about Curren's service as mayor: "When Curren entered his first four-year service as mayor, the city treasury showed a balance of $138 with $5,000 borrowed and outstanding warrants of $9,000. At the close of his service there was not an unpaid bill and the treasurer's report showed a balance of more than $4,000.

"Inherited from the previous administration were a large number of court actions against the city, the city during this period being involved in more litigation than during any like period of time in its history. The cases included the Carleton College tax exemption case, numerous damage cases growing out of the construction of the viaduct and an accident shortly after it was completed, detachment proceedings and others. The city, represented by W. W. Pye, who was city attorney during the Curren administration and special counsel a few months previously, won all of the litigated civil actions excepting that the judgment of the district court in

the Carleton College tax case was reversed by the supreme court."

The obituary stated that Curren was deeply interested in Freemasonry and belonged to the several Masonic bodies that were chartered in Northfield.

Curren was married in 1872 to Elizabeth Bennett, a daughter of early settlers of this community. She died in 1882. In 1912, he married Mrs. Anna Mikkelsen who survived him. He was also survived by two daughters, six grandchildren and three great-grandchildren.

The *News* commented editorially about Curren at the time of his death. The editorial said in part: "Another link with pioneer days is broken by the death of former Mayor Frank Curren. Here was a territorial pioneer and veteran of the Civil War who knew the Northfield of an early day as intimately as he knew that of the present. His was a large part in the building of the community structure, and at the end his zest for 'doing something worthwhile for Northfield' was undimmed.

"Frank Curren was a fine citizen. He worked harder than most men and he built a comfortable competence for old age, but he was never unwilling to share in the common tasks of the community. 'I like to get out and hustle for the city,' he often said. At 75 . . . with a spirit and energy that belied his age, he undertook the task of serving his city as its mayor for two terms. His election was a tribute to the character of his citizenship. His singularly able and effective administrations indicated his grasp of municipal problems and the alertness and energy with which he discharged the duties of his office.

"There is inspiration in the sturdy spirit of Mayor Curren, and the record of his life reveals him well worthy of a place among the builders of Northfield."

7 March, 1997

1922: Henry A. Boe sells hardware store after 43 years
Boe known for public spirit, community leadership

"Retires after 43 years in business," was a headline in the March 31, 1922, *Northfield News*. The subhead said, "Henry Boe, pioneer hardware merchant, sells out to Donaldson & Hall."

The story began, "One of the pioneer business firms of Northfield passed into history Tuesday when the sale of the H. A. Boe hardware store was announced. The new owners are Donaldson & Hall, the partnership consisting of Oscar Donaldson who for six years has been employed in local hardware stores, and William F. Hall who for nine years has been employed at O.A. Lysne's West Side Hardware. . . .

"For 43 years Henry Boe has dispersed hardware on the Square. This is a record for continuous service in business exceeded by only one other man in Northfield, John Morton (a jeweler and watchmaker). At that, Boe is recognized as the youngest and most active man on the business street in spite of his 43-year record. Always cheerful and willing to serve, he has won a host of friends who will concede that he has earned a rest, but who will miss his familiar figure and cheerful greeting on the Square."

Born in Norway, Boe came to the United States in 1864. He spent a year at Washington Prairie, Iowa, then came to Northfield. Since there was no railroad available at the time, he walked from Decorah, Iowa, to Northfield.

The retirement story revealed that he spent the next few years as a clerk in various stores here — the Rork grocery store on the West Side, the J.B. Harper dry goods and millinery store in the Mansion House on the West Side, the Thorson & Bjoraker store, then for nine years at Skinner & Drew's general store on the East Side. During that time he also attended public school here and for a year attended Carleton Academy.

Because of poor health caused by a severe bronchial ailment, he discontinued his work and, at the suggestion of his physician, in 1877 made a trip to Norway to visit his father. There he regained his health and he returned to America after a year and a half.

He entered into partnership with A. R. Manning, the Northfield Bank Raid hero, in hardware business. A few years later he became sole proprietor of the store and moved the business into the Scriver Building. He occupied the so-called inner section of the building so that he had entrances on both Bridge Square and Division St. The post office was located in the corner of the building, the space now occupied by the Northfield Historical Society's gift shop.

The retirement story said that Boe was one of the organizers of the Commercial Club that preceded the Community Club of that time. Both are forerunners of today's Chamber of Commerce. At the time he retired, he was a member of the club's board of directors.

The story also reported that he had in the past been a member of the board of education for several years. He was serving at the time the "new high school was erected." This would be the oldest section of the current

Middle School.

Boe must have been known for his sense of humor because a sketch regarding him in William F. Schilling's book, "Up and Down Main Street 40 Years Ago (1895–1935)," was in the nature of a roast. It started out with a salute: "Henry in my judgment is surely one of God's chosen people. He was always one of the finest men that ever trod in leather, and I have yet to hear of a man who could discount that statement. His good nature and square dealing never were sidetracked for an instant and when it came to doing things for the good of the community, Henry was always, although unostentatiously, busy doing his part."

But then Schilling got informal: "Henry never had much hair to my knowledge but he wanted a supply as in his sparking days, it would have been more appropriate to have had a swish to have dragged over the center as some do to make believe anyway. (Henry was not married until he was 45.) Henry tried almost everything to get the hair to grow and someone told him if he would rub a raw onion on his scalp every night before retiring, he would soon have hair. Well, he tried this and after several applications he had to give it up as the odor from the onions was much worse than being bald. After a time he was very much encouraged for a good crop of fuzz did come out, but this never metamorphosed into hair. In Henry's case, at least, the expression, 'Marble tops are rarely put on poor furniture,' is literally true."

Schilling continued, "One of Boe's big troubles all through the years of his occupancy of the Scriver Building was to tell the story of the James-Younger Raid. The First National Bank was located in this building at the time of the raid and when strangers came to town, quite naturally they wanted to know all about the raid, and sure, it was Henry who could tell it with flowers, for he was working as a clerk in the Skinner & Drew store across the way at the time of the raid.

"Some were even so mean as to say that Henry lost his hair from fright at the time the robbers were shooting up the town. He assured me, however, that this was not a particularly hair-raising adventure for him as many times in the mountains of Norway while herding goats did he have encounters with bears when he had only a jackknife to defend himself. That looked worse to him."

When St. John's Lutheran Church observed its 60th anniversary in 1929, Boe was the only living charter member. He was especially honored during the anniversary celebration. The Rev. Lawrence M. Stavig congratulated Boe, according to the *News*, "and cited his unique record of faithful service to St. John's in many different capacities. . . . Boe was elected a trustee in 1886 and served on that board for nearly 40 years. He was elected treasurer in 1888, an office he filled for 18 years. From 1881 to 1884 he served as secretary of the congregation and in the late 1880s he served as Sunday school superintendent. During his 60 years of membership in St. John's, Boe has faithfully served in many other capacities and has in his quiet way been setting a worthy example of loyal church membership."

A week shy of his 88th birthday, Boe died on July 10, 1937, at his home at 818 South Division. He had been confined to his bed since January and had been in frail health for several years, according to the obituary.

The story said, "To all of his friends and to generations of Northfield citizens, Boe was known as Henry Boe, but his real name was Helge A. Boe. He was born July 17, 1849, in Vang, Valders, Norway. He was a lad of 14 when he came to this country along with a brother Osten and a sister Berit."

A year later, the three of them made that 120-mile walk together from Decorah to Goodhue County in a few days.

His marriage to Mary Lajord took place May 16, 1896, in St. Paul. They had four children, one of whom died in infancy. His wife survived him as did three children, Dr. Aslak M. Boe, Bertha Thorson (Mrs. Lawrence) who lived for many years in the house where Boe died, and Anna VanPool (Mrs. Gerald).

In addition to civic activities already mentioned, Boe had served on the city council. As a young man he had joined the volunteer fire department. The obituary stated, "He belonged to various civic and business organizations and was a leader in all of them.

"Although he had had no formal musical training, he was deeply interested in music, was a member of the Northfield Choral Union and sang in several of the oratorios presented by that group. He played the violin and was in demand as a vocalist. He was the first director of the church choir of St. John's Church.

"Personally, Boe was a delightful companion, cheerful and happy in his outlook, a good story teller, and generous almost to a fault. His helpfulness, his civic-mindedness and his earnest effort to live the good life will long be remembered in Northfield."

In an editorial column, the *News* — presumably Carl Weicht, the editor — said, "Henry Boe, who passed away Saturday, was truly one of God's noblemen. I think I have known Boe as long as I have been conscious of knowing anyone, and from the first childish confidence in him to more mature judgment, I have never had any reason to change my mind. He was an admirable, lovable, thoroughly fine man."

28 March, 1997

1923: Baldwin, confirmed gardener, cites value of rain

Horace Baldwin known for fresh produce, great kindness

There were people who gossiped that Horace Baldwin resembled Andy Gump of the comic strips — so much so that a newcomer to Northfield innocently addressed him as "Mr. Gump" — but no kinder person could be found here at the turn of the century and until his death in 1934.

Contributing to the "Views and Interviews" column in the *News* on Aug. 10, 1923, he spoke of rainfall, something of prime importance to a truck gardener. He had conducted a market garden since 1890.

When Baldwin died, Carl Weicht, editor of the *News*, wrote the following tribute:

"Few of the many fine men and women who have lived out their allotted span of years in this community and have passed on to that 'undiscovered country' from which no traveler returns, have left a place in the affections of neighbors and in the life of the community that will be as difficult to fill as has Horace Baldwin. Friend of all, benefactor of many, exemplary citizen, his singularly useful career, spent in quiet avenues of devoted and helpful service to others, bears eloquent testimony of the worthwhileness of the good life. Baldwin was a good man, no less so because he always sought, and found, good in others. For 45 years he supplied vegetables from his garden for Northfield homes, but he also planted another garden where homely philosophy, good humor, kindly deeds and generous service were nurtured day by day. He loved the soil, growing things, the trees; but he loved human beings best. Of him it may truly be said that he always plucked a thistle and planted a flower where he thought a flower would grow."

Baldwin was born Nov. 13, 1860, at Columbus, Wis., the son of a couple who had come from New England. When he was a small child, his parents brought their family to a farm in the Plainview community. There Baldwin grew up and attended high school.

For a few years he operated the home farm, but after his father's death, his mother brought her family to Northfield, and this remained Baldwin's home for most of the rest of his life.

He did spend five years in Connecticut where he was associated with an uncle in operating a fruit and truck gardening farm. After he returned to Northfield, he attended the normal school at Winona and taught school for several years.

In 1889, he bought eight acres at what was then the southeast edge of Northfield. One corner of the property was at Woodley and Winona. The following spring he established his market garden, the produce of which he sold both directly to householders and to local stores. His obituary stated, "Astride his bicycle or riding behind his old white horse, he was a familiar and beloved figure in Northfield."

He developed into an authority on gardening and horticulture, in demand as a speaker at local meetings and throughout Minnesota.

He was for many years a member of the State Horticultural Society, serving as a director for some time. He spoke at meetings of the society, at farmers' institutes and at sessions at the University Farm that were devoted to the interests of gardeners. For several years he judged the market garden exhibits at the Minnesota State Fair. He contributed articles on gardening to various publications.

His obituary stated, "It is doubtful if any man has done more for charity in Northfield than has Baldwin, not only in taking an active part in organized welfare agencies of the community, but by private visitation and from his own means.

"He originated the idea of the Christmas basket distribution here, which he carried on for many years, and he started the united program in this respect that was later taken over by the Community Chest (a forerunner of the United Way and United Fund). Many families owe much to Baldwin's kindliness, his help and his friendly advice and goodwill."

He was a faithful member of the Congregational Church for years, active as an officer. He taught a men's Bible class for many years and was especially active in the Sunday school department. He also taught a rural Sunday school at the Cannery schoolhouse in Greenvale Township for 25 years.

He served on the city council for five years. He served as an officer of Social Lodge No. 48, AF&AM, and was a member of other Masonic bodies. He was active in the Pioneer Club and farmers' clubs.

On Dec. 30, 1908, he married Bertha Park of Denmark, Iowa. She had attended Carleton College and for a number of years had taught mentally handicapped children at the state school at Faribault. A daughter, Elizabeth, died in 1921 when she was 11 years old.

Baldwin died on March 13, 1934, at his home at 615 E. Second. He had not felt well for a couple of days, but his death, caused by an embolism, was very unexpected.

According to his obituary, he had lain down to rest after lunch and his wife was reading to him when he died, "peacefully and without warning."

The obituary stated that the death came as a shock to the community. Everywhere where groups of people were gathered, "his many kindly deeds, his unassuming charity, his homely philosophy, and his vital religious spirit were spoken of, and in every walk of life in the community were friends who thought of is passing as a personal loss."

Referring to the funeral, the obituary stated, "Not only in Samuel Johnson's (the minister) eulogy, in the beautiful flowers, or in the large attendance at the funeral was the sense of a community loss evident, but the people who attended testified to the wide range of Baldwin's interests and helpfulness. There were friends from town and country and from other communities, associates in church, lodge and civic groups, those from families Baldwin had helped, boys who had worked for him, college professors, businessmen, city officials, customers — a most unusual and representative gathering."

While Baldwin was only 73 when he died, his widow lived until she was only a month short of 96. She had, after her husband's death, helped care for sisters in Michigan and Iowa.

She took up playing pool when she was 91 and became quite famous for her "mean cue." She even appeared on the nationally viewed Mike Douglas TV show, demonstrating her pool playing ability!

7 August, 1998

1925: Guy 'Barney' Wells helps sheriff enforce Prohibition

Wells serves as chief of police almost 20 years

The liquor raid in which Guy "Barney" Wells participated as a patrolman on the Northfield police force, recounted in a story in the Feb. 26, 1925 *News*, was one of many that took place both in Northfield and rural Rice County from the time Prohibition became the law of the land until the repeal of the 18th amendment.

Most were routine, but one Aug. 28, 1926, more than a year after the aforementioned incident, had dire effects on the life of Wells.

A family that lived on what is now County Road 1, about midway between what is now TH 246 and what is now TH 3, was believed by their neighbors (some of whom were friends of your writer's family) and authorities to be engaged in moonshining. Sheriff C. M. Livingston had tips that moonshine was being transported along that road every Saturday night, bound for dance pavilions on Rice County lakes.

On this fateful Saturday, a private detective working with Rice County authorities went to the home in question and purchased a pint of liquor. While there he asked whether the occupant intended to be at Circle Lake pavilion that night and whether he would have a supply of liquor. The detective said he received an affirmative answer.

Therefore authorities took up posts at both ends of that segment of road, armed with search warrants and criminal warrants. Livingston and a private detective were adjacent to the brick Drake schoolhouse that was once located at the intersection of the east Cannon City Road and 1. Northfield Chief of Police W. D. Smith, Wells and the detective who had purchased the liquor during the day were at the other end near what was then the L. B. Smith farm.

At the latter location, the detective parked his car in the middle of the road, expecting that it would slow down anyone driving along. They stopped one car, finding that it was no one connected to moonshine. A second car rushed by and did not stop. Close behind was a truck known to belong to the suspected moonshiners.

The truck did not stop; in fact, its speed increased. A crash of glass was heard. The truck

brushed so close to Wells that he stumbled over backward to avoid being run over. As he recovered his balance, he shot twice, hoping that the driver would stop. Wells testified that he shot toward the road and aimed at a spot short of the truck. It was believed that one bullet ricocheted from a stone in the road and struck a 12-year-old boy, one of three children in the rear of the truck. The children had not been seen by the police. There was another child in the seat next to the driver.

Although the boy cried out that he had been struck, the driver did not stop. The truck proceeded to a nearby farmhouse where the boy was carried inside and a Northfield doctor was called. But the child died before the arrival of the doctor.

Meanwhile the authorities had stopped a passenger car that closely followed the truck and found a bottle of moonshine inside. The people in the car were members of the family in question. In one of the ditches along the road, a canvas bag containing bottles of moonshine, some intact and some broken, was found, apparently explaining the noise of broken glass that authorities had heard just before Wells fired.

The sheriff had already heard that the carriers always packed the booze in bags so that it could be thrown out of the vehicle quickly in case of an encounter with officers. Another bottle of moonshine was also found in the ditch. None of this had been in the ditch before the passing of the truck although the driver tried to claim that it must have been there previously. Occupants of the second vehicle accused the detective of planting the moonshine that he reportedly found in their car.

When the authorities traced the truck to the farmhouse, a woman claimed to have been driving the truck although the detective thought it was the man he had talked to in the afternoon. She said she had worn a man's jacket and cap. When Wells heard that the child had died, he was horrified and formally turned himself over to the sheriff.

At the coroner's inquest, the jury found that the child's death was due to "gross negligence on the part of Barney Wells in shooting the way he did." The jury, was made up of four men from Dundas, one from Bridgewater and one from Northfield.

The mother of the child, a Minneapolis woman who was not at the scene that Saturday night, appeared in Faribault during the coming week and made a formal complaint charging Wells with manslaughter.

Northfield Mayor K. J. McKenzie held that the shooting was accidental and directed Wells to continue his work as patrolman. McKenzie said, "Mistakes are likely to happen at any time, but if public officials do not stand behind the officers of the law even under unfortunate circumstances such as those existing here, how can we expect the law to be fearlessly enforced? Patrolman Wells has been a conscientious officer and I stand back of him in his misfortune in this tragedy which no one regrets more than he does."

The sheriff and Chief Smith also endorsed Wells. The city council exonerated him by resolution, stating that at all times he had exhibited due patience, courtesy and consideration in pursuit of his duties and "has always served the city faithfully and well." The resolution indicated that the council held him "blameless for the accidental death." Members of the council at that time were the cream of Northfield — A. O. Lee, F. J. Fairbank, C. E. Bill, F. M. Babcock, A. C. Hauer, Alex J. MacKay, O. S. Jackson, C. J. Johnson, A. W Bierman and R. H. Moses.

The preliminary hearing to determine whether or not Wells should be bound over to district court for trial on a charge of murder in the third degree was held in the Northfield Community Building with A. B. Blodgett as judge. When he heard that Wells would like him as his attorney, W. W. Pye volunteered to represent Wells without charge. He had successfully applied for change of venue from Faribault to Northfield.

Seventeen witnesses were questioned including Wells himself although he could have pled immunity from testimony. He said that he wanted to tell all he knew about the tragedy. He noted that he was 34 years old, had been a policeman for 4½ years and had used firearms all of his life.

The hearing ran all day until 6:30PM when Blodgett stated that the hearing had not indicated probable cause to believe Wells guilty of the crime of third degree murder and that there was no evidence of depravity of mind or wanton, reckless disregard of human life as alleged in the complaint.

Wells issued a statement printed in the *News*, "I am sincerely grateful to the many people in Northfield who have shown such sympathetic interest since the shooting accident. The support of Mayor McKenzie and other city officials, the generous help of W. W. Pye, and the sympathy expressed by many citizens and friends are all things I know I can never repay."

Guy Richard Wells was born April 5, 1892, in Waterford. He attended local schools and for several years assisted his father, George Wells, in operating a threshing machine. From June of 1918, during World War I, until February of 1919, he served in the U.S. Army.

About a year after his discharge from service he became a member of the Northfield police department.

He became chief in 1934, continuing to serve in that capacity until the fall of 1953. During that period he received training, three terms each, at the police school of the University of Minnesota and the FBI training school which was conducted at Faribault.

He died in his sleep on April 25, 1955. He had suffered a mild heart attack several months before, but had seemed to make an excellent recovery. The day of his death he had not felt well and had gone to bed at the suggestion of his doctor. He was 63.

Your writer felt that she knew the chief well, although he was a quiet person, not given to making statements to the press. For some reason she had never seen him out of uniform. One day she met a man along Division, clad in a tan hat, red plaid shirt, tan corduroy pants. She didn't recognize him though he looked at her with a twinkle in his eye. Suddenly after he had passed, she recognized his somewhat unusual walk, ran after him and explained she hadn't known who he was in his civilian clothing. He seemed to enjoy the incident.

In 1948, when Wells did submit to an interview with a student intern at the *News*, he said that the scope of an officer's duties had broadened tremendously. He said that the modern police officer must not only apprehend criminals "but they must also be experts in law, first aid and psychology."

He recalled apprehending as many as 30 bootleggers in a single year during Prohibition.

He complained that upstanding citizens had now become habitual violators in continually breaking what they considered insignificant traffic regulations. He noted that there had been 70 traffic accidents in Northfield during the past year, bearing out his contention that there should be more "intersection etiquette."

4 February, 2000

1937: Prominent businessman dies
Johnson seen as community leader

"Neighbors pay high tribute of affection to W.E. Johnson" was a headline in the *Northfield News* of July 30, 1937. A man who had been prominent as a Northfield businessman and in community service had died.

The story said that St. John's Lutheran Church was "filled with friends and neighbors whose presence (at the funeral) testified to the high esteem in which Mr. Johnson was held in this community.

"Dr. Nils Kleven, president of the Southern Minnesota District of the Norwegian Lutheran Church, conducted the service, paying a touching tribute to Mr. Johnson's high Christian character, his kindly spirit, his generous friendship for the church, for St. Olaf College and for neighbors in Northfield, and his helpful citizenship over a long period of years."

Johnson had died July 22 at Mineral Springs Sanitorium near Cannon Falls where he had received care for a week. *The Northfield Independent* commented, "Mr. Johnson, never robust in spite of his incessant application to work, had been in steadily failing health for several months." The story added that Johnson had been ill at home for several weeks before being taken to Mineral Springs.

Johnson was the father of David E. Johnson who was to become a St. Olaf College vice president and a man active in the Northfield community. (W. E. Johnson also had a daughter Margaret who has not lived in Northfield in adulthood, but who has many friends among *News* readers.)

Walter E. Johnson was born May 13, 1878, at St. Peter, the son of pioneer residents. Af-

ter attending Gustavus Adolphus College at St. Peter, he tried his hand at farming near Little Falls. However he soon entered retail business at Spiritwood, N. D.

It was in November of 1909 that he bought the St. Olaf Store in Northfield. The "Ole Store," as it was even then familiarly known, dated back at least to 1897; some say many years before that. The obituary in the *Independent* states that Johnson "built it up to one of the largest in the city and conducted it until his death." The *News* commented that he made the store "the center of broad civic interest, of friendship for generations of St. Olaf students and faculty members, and of wide helpfulness to many Northfield neighbors." Mrs. Johnson, the former Anna Marie Christofferson of St. Peter (the Johnsons were married a month after he purchased the Ole Store), was also active in the store.

In February of 1921, W. E. Johnson & Co. bought the stock of the D. D. Springsted department store on Northfield's West Side. The substantial brick building in which this business was located, was taken out by the relocation of TH 3 many years and several businesses later. The store had long been owned by Jacob Fink, but had been bought in 1920 by D. D. and R. E. Springsted. Henry B. Kump, many years later to become a mayor of Northfield, had been working with Johnson at the Ole Store, had a financial interest in the new store, and was named its manager. Much later, he operated his own grocery store on the West Side.

In October of 1927, the firm W. E. Johnson & Co., opened a third store, this one in Merriam Park, St. Paul. A Northfielder, Edroy Hegland, was named manager. The *News* reported that this business would operate strictly on a cash basis and that it took in $400 the first day. Eggs sold at the St. Paul store were trucked from Northfield.

The following June saw W. E. Johnson & Co. establish two other stores, one in Farmington and the other in Cannon Falls. Norval Malchert of Northfield was named manager of the Farmington store and Robert Brynstad of Northfield, manager of the other. The *News* stated that it was Johnson's aim to centralize purchasing power and management.

The *News* obituary for Johnson stated, "Noted for many benefactions, quietly given, Mr. Johnson was one of Northfield's most generous and public-spirited men." The *Independent* said, "Many of his benefactions were anonymous, but on occasion he would give substantial gifts to bear witness of his own allegiance to a cause." Both cited as typical of the latter kind of gift, the purchase of the bell for St. John's Lutheran Church on the congregation's 60th anniversary in 1929. Part of the inscription on the $1,500 bell is, "Come to me all ye that labor and are heavy laden and I will give you rest."

In its initial story about Johnson's death, the *News* noted that "the bell, whose notes have drawn worshipers to the church and have symbolized both sad and happy events in the lives of the members of the congregation, will send forth its summons Monday afternoon to those who would pay a last tribute to a true Christian gentleman."

It was noted in *News* stories that Johnson was very interested in welfare work, "giving not only generously from his means, but devoting much time and energy to benevolences, both private and organized." It was not surprising then that he served as president of the Community Chest, forerunner of the United Way. He became a director of Northfield Hospital (then at Eighth and Water) in 1935 when it was taken over by the City of Northfield. He was a member of the Northfield Rotary Club and of the

Northfield Association, forerunner of the Chamber of Commerce. He served St. John's Church in many capacities and was "a loyal friend of St. Olaf College."

In her centennial history of St. John's Church, Edna Hong reported on the "amazing and unprecedented testimonial to a member of the congregation that was inserted into the book of the records of the congregational meetings" of St. John's. She continued, "One understands why a congregation was moved to do so when one reads the astonishing and humbling account of one Christian man and wife's quiet and unostentatious work in the congregation."

The resolution, written by J. F. Grose, secretary of the board of deacons, said in part: "It has pleased God in His infinite wisdom to remove Deacon Walter E. Johnson from our midst by death. Looking at his departure from us, we have a feeling that, humanly speaking, he was one of the persons we could least dispense with in St. John's Church.

"By word and deed he showed himself to be deeply interested in the welfare of the congregation, with which he identified himself immediately upon his arrival in the community. Only circumstances over which he had no control would keep him away from its services and important meetings. He was a member of the board of deacons for a score or more years. Due to a standing invitation from him, the board would nearly always hold its meetings at his home.

"For years he presented each member of the confirmation classes with a Bible on confirmation day. He often furnished gratuitously eatables to various church activities and church organizations whenever eatables were also a part of their program.

"He was kind to the erring, sick and needy. By his wise counsel he helped many a child to walk in the paths of rectitude and uprightness. By his innate desire to bring cheer to the sick, he would give them good things that they would relish and he would sit at their bedside bringing them comfort and strength by reading to them appropriate Bible passages, by offering prayer and by speaking words of encouragement and comfort otherwise.

"He aided the poor and needy in various substantial ways. He performed a number of charitable acts of which none but the beneficiaries and God were aware. . . ."

Because of his initials, W. E., Johnson had the nickname of "We," used affectionately by young and old. Lest the reader think of him as a man who always went about his work soberly as well as diligently, your writer has been told in years gone by that "We" loved practical jokes.

I was once entertained at length by a person now deceased with a collection of stories of jokes that emanated from the Ole Store. Only one can I remember enough about to relay some parts.

It seemed that there was a man in the Ole Store neighborhood who always strove to have the earliest homegrown potatoes of anyone. When it came near time for the potatoes to form, he hovered over the plants every morning to check their progress. He bragged about his results over coffee at the Ole Store. Imagine his surprise and cause to crow one fine summer morning when he found wonderfully well developed new potatoes under his vines. I can't remember when or whether he found out that the potatoes came from the Ole Store, carefully buried under the vines by "We" Johnson.

16 July, 1987

1940: Jackson elected to one of four terms
Jackson serves in two world wars

"A candidate for second term as mayor of Northfield, Mayor Jackson is unopposed in the municipal election next Tuesday," said a story in the March 7, 1940, *Northfield News*.

Appearing with the same picture used here, the short story which ran as a sidebar to a story about the other candidates, concluded, "His Honor's first term of two years is thus uniquely endorsed — or will be — by the voters of the city."

Jackson was to serve Northfield for nearly four terms as mayor, a unique public record here. The second term to which he was elected in 1940 was unexpectedly terminated in February of 1941 when the National Guard Headquarters Company, 68th Infantry Brigade, of which he was captain, was activated and left for Camp Claiborne, La. He therefore had the unusual experience of serving in two world wars.

A few years after he returned to Northfield, he threw his hat into the ring again, filing for mayor in the spring of 1952. He was unopposed. When he filed for re-election in 1954, he was again unopposed. However when he filed yet again in 1956, he was defeated by George Zanmiller.

The issue most emphasized in that election was whether the city should issue $25,000 in bonds to splice out publicly gathered funds to build a $90,000 swimming pool and field house. The bond issue was defeated, 1103 to 835. Zanmiller had outspokenly opposed the bond issue. (When it eventually appeared that the city never would build the pool, the school district did so.)

Another unusual aspect of the election was the total of five candidates for mayor! In addition to Jackson and Zanmiller, candidates were W. L. Bryan, John Fremouw and Al Friest. Jackson received the second largest total of votes.

When Jackson tried again for the mayor's seat in 1958, Zanmiller was re-elected.

Jackson served the community in other

ways. He was a member of the city council for many years. He was a long-time member of the volunteer fire department. He was chairman of the Rice County selective service board for a time. He served as president of the Rotary Club in 1953. He was a member of Northfield Lodge No. 50, IOOF, Social Lodge No. 48, AF&AM, other Masonic orders including Osman Shrine Temple, St.Paul. As any prominent citizen, he served as chairman of this and that through the years.

Jackson, who was known to his friends as "Jack," was born Oct. 18, 1889, in Hamilton, Ohio. He came to Northfield as a child with his parents, graduating from Northfield High School where he was prominent in athletics. He attended Carleton College. During World War I, he served in the Air Corps with 18 months of duty in France.

Becoming an electrician, he established Jackson Electric Co. here after returning from World War I. He continued that work until his World War II service, and re-established the company when he returned to Northfield after that war.

After he arrived at Camp Claiborne during World War II, he transferred to the Army Air Corps and was sent to Fort Benning, Ga., for battalion staff school. He was there when the United States actually entered the war. While still serving stateside, he was commissioned major. He became commanding officer of the 419th School Squadron at Sheppard Field, Texas, an Air Corps reception training center for men coming from all parts of the United States.

From November of 1943 until August of 1944, he was stationed in England as a plans and training officer. He and his wife Nora had visited England 20 years before and he found many remembered landmarks destroyed by bombs.

On his return to the United States, he was slated for a desk job when he wanted to remain in the field. He secured his release from Air Force duty and signed up for civil service employment. Although he was delayed by illness — he spent three months in the Veterans Hospital at San Francisco — he was soon on his way to Honolulu, Hawaii, where he spent 18 months as engineer in a power plant at Pearl Harbor. Mrs. Jackson was able to be in Honolulu with him. All of that period, he was in the active reserve and reported once a week for duty at Hickam Field. He returned to Northfield in September of 1946.

In the early 1960s, the Jacksons traveled to Japan, the Philippines, Hong Kong and made an extended visit to Hawaii.

With failing health, the couple decided to move to a warmer clime and established their home in Carmel Valley Manor on the Monterey peninsula at Carmel, Calif., in January of 1964. Jackson died there of cancer on Feb. 1, 1968. Mrs. Jackson died there on Jan. 26, 1974, after a lingering illness.

Shortly after Jackson's death, the *News* published a tribute that had been paid him at Carmel Valley Manor: "Since his illness we have come to realize how much we took for granted his many contributions to our comfort and safety. We missed his quiet presence at many times and places. That's the way he wanted it — no praise or honor or award.

"We noticed here the extension of his life of public service. In Northfield, Minnesota, where he lived nearly all of his life and owned the Jackson Electric Co., he was a member of the city council for many years and mayor for four terms. There, as here, he had an instinct for being where help was needed and giving without hope of reward.

"Oakey was a military man, serving in two world wars, but not a militarist. As chairman of the selective service board of Rice County, he wept then as he did today over the loss of youth and the waste of war. He was a humanist, interested in the welfare of others, enjoying people of every walk of life, race or creed, and in giving of himself at the last to medical research, he fulfilled all his earlier contributions and affirmed that there is more to life than living. Now we can only say thanks, again, to one who never stayed for praise."

Having known Jackson practically since her birth, your writer thoroughly approved of the tribute, finding only the phrase about his "quiet presence" a bit strange. Jackson had a keen sense of humor and his happy laugh was one of his most attractive qualities.

22 February, 1990

1940: MacKay establishes store in 1890

Marshalls on Division for many years

"All Northfield Joins in Feting Local Business" was a major headline on page one of the May 4, 1940, *News*. The subhead read, "Alex MacKay, Sr., founder, still active president of company."

This unusual drygoods store, founded here in 1890, was to continue in business in Northfield until 1973. It had a colorful history.

The story said, "For half a century this firm, now one of the oldest businesses in Northfield, has held a leading place in the commercial life of the town and its personnel has taken a constructive part in the life of the community. The golden jubilee is especially significant for Alex MacKay, Sr., head of the firm, for he has been associated with the company since its beginning and has taken an active part in the life of Northfield."

The story stated that MacKay "began his experience in the drygoods business in his native Scotland about 63 years ago. As a young man in Forres, Scotland, he entered an apprenticeship of five years in a drygoods establishment." He had done this when he decided he didn't like living and working in the country, another story in MacKay's file states.

The 50th anniversary story continued, "In 1882, after he completed his apprenticeship, MacKay came to America to seek his fortune. He first lived in Cleveland, Ohio, later in Chicago, and then came to Northfield. Here, in partnership with Alex Marshall, his father-in-law, he organized a drygoods firm, MacKay & Company, which later became known as the Alex Marshall Co. when MacKay was away to engage in other business ventures at Windom and at Cleveland."

The May 6, 1890, *News* reported that MacKay and Marshall "expect to open up the finest line of goods ever brought to Northfield. They will occupy the Mergen Building, four doors north of Fourth St." This building is now part of Northfield Variety Store. The drygoods store remained there until 1900 when it moved to the building now known as the Nutting Mall.

It was in 1902 that MacKay left for Windom and then Cleveland, although he retained his financial interest in the Northfield store. The local business was incorporated as the Alex Marshall Co. in 1905. MacKay returned to head the business upon the death of Marshall in 1907.

The store spread into three stories of the Nutting building and for a time, a department of men's clothing occupied the nearby building at 314 Division. Much later that space was to become the first section of Perman's in Northfield.

MacKay remained vigorously active in the business. In 1933, he erected a new building to house the store, the building now occupied by the Dahl House.

A story that appeared on the 75th anniversary of the store — after MacKay's death — recalled that always a speciality of the store "was dress goods by the yard, as MacKay had a rich background for this, dating from his experiences in Scotland." Fabrics remained an important feature of the store although ready-to-wear items — clothing for women and children — and housewares became increasingly important through the years.

MacKay, in addition to developing a successful business and remaining active in it until his death in May of 1944, was a community leader, serving in a number of civic and organization posts. He was vice president of the First National Bank for a number of years. He served as mayor of Northfield in the late '30s.

Several members of the family became active in the business at various times. Alexander J. MacKay assisted his father and succeeded as president of the firm. He had stayed in Cleveland when the family returned to Northfield, employed by a coat manufacturing company. After serving overseas in the U.S. Army during World War I, he was associated with the Northfield store after 1919. He suffered a stroke in late 1949, but was able to remain active in the business until a few months before his death in August of 1956.

His sister, Jessie MacKay, a 1915 graduate of Carleton College, was long active in the store. She succeeded her father as a member of the Northfield City Hospital board in 1944, active in that capacity for many years, and she engaged in many other civic activities. She died in March of 1958, president of the store at that time.

Through the years her other brothers had been active in the business. A brother Norman who died in 1947, had been manager of the men's store. In 1929 he was elected second vice president of the Minnesota and North Dakota Retail Clothiers and Furnishers Assn.

Allan MacKay also stayed in Cleveland when the family returned to Northfield. He was employed by the New York Central Railroad. However he returned here and was associated with the store after World War I. He long served as Northfield's fire chief. He died in 1956.

By the time Alexander J. MacKay became ill, Allan's son, Allan A. "Sandy" MacKay had become active in the business and he headed the company after his Aunt Jessie's death. During his years in the store, he was particularly active in the Northfield Area Chamber of Commerce. He and his wife, Lois, still live in Northfield community in retirement.

Northfielders who have lived in Northfield for many years have warm memories of this store that was always modern for its day. They may recall the tall wood and steel stools that were spaced through the store to allow a patron to sit down while considering fabric or trying on gloves. But most of all they would remember the network of change machines.

When a Marshall clerk would make a sale, she would send the charge slip or payment record and the currency or check rendered in a little metal cup that would scoot along a cable across the store to the desk of the cashier. Change would be returned to the clerk and customer by the same means.

The store had a stable sales staff with favorite people assisting the public for long periods of time.

May 1990

1942: Carl Weicht enters service at age 41
Career takes many unexpected turns

"Carl Weicht expects call to serve Uncle Sam — Resigns as president of school board, other civic groups," was a headline on page one of the Sept. 3, 1942, *Northfield News*.

The story explained that "Carl L. Weicht, president of the Northfield Board of Education, has resigned his position in anticipation of induction into the United States Army in September.

"Weicht has also resigned as president of the Rice County Historical Society, as president of the Northfield Golf Club, as chairman of the Nerstrand Woods committee, secretary of the Charter Commission, and district supervisor of the Masonic Grand Lodge of Minnesota."

The story continued, "Until Weicht's resignation in 1940, he had been editor of the *Northfield News* since 1926 and a member of its staff for 21 years. For the past two years he had conducted the Paper Shop (stationers) which he closed about two weeks ago, also selling his home at 319 Nevada St. at that time.

"During his lifetime in Northfield, Weicht has taken an active part in community and social affairs. He was one of the organizers of the Community Chest, has been president of the Lions Club, secretary and master of the Masonic Lodge (Social Lodge No. 48, AF&AM), a director of the former Community Club (forerunner of the Chamber of Commerce), and a member of various other civic and community organizations."

Weicht had lived in Northfield since early childhood. He was born in 1901 in Westchester County, New York, the younger son of Charles H. and Marianne Weicht, natives of Germany and Austria respectively. The family's move to Northfield came when Weicht's father was named superintendent of the Minnesota Hemp Company's mill here, part of a developing flax and hemp fiber industry in Minnesota. Farmers were encouraged to grow these unusual crops. But in his latter years, Weicht wondered at the propriety of admitting this bit of history; hemp is now grown to produce marijuana!

Weicht's mother was a teacher of piano and German in Northfield. His father died in 1912 while Weicht was still very young, and his mother, in whom he delighted, died in 1931. Both his brother and his sister preceded their mother in death.

Weicht attended the public schools here and studied at Carleton College before joining the *News* staff in 1919. In addition to the activities mentioned in the 1942 story, he had been active in the Northfield Improvement Association; presiding officer of Corinthian Chapter No. 33, RAM, and Northfield Council No. 12, R&SM, Masonic orders. He had been president of the First District Editorial Association and of the Rice County Publishers Association. He was a member of Sigma Delta Chi, national journalistic fraternity.

He wrote thoughtful papers for the Rice County Historical Society. He also spoke on a variety of subjects on WCAL radio.

Weicht was at his best when relating anecdotes — he was an entertaining story teller with a sophisticated sense of humor.

By the time he resigned as editor in 1940, the *News* under his leadership had won singular honors — state and national honors for weekly newspapers for community, service, editorial excellence, typography and makeup and newspaper production. The paper was cited by outstanding schools of journalism and designated by Inland Printer as "one of the finest small-town newspapers in the United States."

His editorials were often quoted in the press of the state. He was one of the first Minnesota editors to advocate a state income tax for support of public schools. He won recognition as an advocate of highway and traffic safety and during a time when isolation was strong in the Midwest, sounded a prophetic appeal for acceptance of America's international obligations and responsibilities.

He supported many movements in Northfield and was one of the strongest supporters of the city hospital when the new building was built in 1938–39. The *News*, under his leadership, raised about $4,000 (a tidy sum in those days) to furnish hospital rooms.

He led a movement for establishment of a swimming pool, particularly interested because his sister had drowned in a swimming area in the Cannon River during childhood. When he returned to Northfield in the mid-50s, he once again adopted that project and had much to do with fund raising for the current outdoor pool.

He was particularly active in the movement for preservation of the Nerstrand Woods as a state park.

In 1927 he was one of 14 young men and women to receive highest honors in the Woodrow Wilson Foundation essay contest which attracted 10,000 entries. He was one of 20 nominated for an original Nieman Fellowship at Harvard from among 300 applicants, but did not receive the appointment. The Harvard Committee decided not to make a selection from among weekly newspapermen at that time because of the limited circulations of their publications.

When he entered military service in 1942, he was 41 years old. But he said he "wished to serve in the same way as the young men being drafted for World War II service."

After basic training, he attended officer candidate school. Upon receiving his commission in the Transportation Corps, he was assigned to the Boston Port of Embarkation which served the European Theater of War. Much of the time he was staff personal affairs officer of the port. As a security officer, he made three trips to England, once on a crippled ship which was traveling without escort near the icebergs of the north Atlantic.

In August of 1945, Lt. Weicht was released from active duty to become secretary to the new governor of Minnesota, a Northfielder, Edward J. Thye. He continued this relationship with Thye when the latter was elected United States Senator.

In 1953 he made a trip to the Orient with Senator Thye in connection with the latter's assignment by the Senate Committee on Appropriations to study the foreign aid program. They traveled to Japan, Korea, Formosa, Hong Kong, Indo-China, Thailand, India, Pakistan, Saudi Arabia, Cyprus, Rome and Madrid.

Weicht resigned the Washington position in the fall of 1955 and returned to Northfield in the summer of 1956 as editor of the *News* and secretary-treasurer of the Northfield News, Inc. He then bought the house at 700 E. Fourth. He never married.

The last part of his life continued to take unexpected turns, but contained many difficult experiences. Northfielders had long advocated the union of the city's two weekly newspapers, the *News* and the *Northfield Independent*. Weicht was able to purchase *The Independent* and its printing plant. Both papers were then in the 300 block of Division, across the street from each other.

For awhile the papers were published as "twin weeklies," one on Monday and the other on Thursday. Negotiations to merge the two businesses took several years. After the death of Herman Roe, for more than 50 years the publisher of the *News*, in the fall of 1961, Weicht was named in the following March as president of a newly organized Northfield Press, Inc., which published both newspapers.

There were serious financial problems and then a disastrous fire in the fall of 1964 destroyed much of the *News* plant. Weicht's feet were for many hours soaking wet that day, a condition that aggravated a circulation problem that had been building. For a time the condition was stabilized through use of an experimental medical program.

Weicht resigned from his newspaper post in April of 1965. Later, after the *News* had relocated on Fifth St., he did some writing for the paper and in other ways aided publication.

But in 1968 he suffered a broken arm in a fall at his home which by that time was in Northfield Apartments. While he was in the hospital to have the bone set, he suffered a stroke that paralyzed the other arm. The following year, the circulatory problem had worsened so much that amputation was made above his right ankle.

In 1975 he began receiving care at the Dilley Unit of Northfield Hospital and on March 9, 1977, he died in the hospital. Even in those last uncomfortable days, he read extensively. His obituary stated, "Always fond of young people, he was a favorite of the staff — aides, male and female, were often to be found at his bedside visiting or joking with him."

The obituary also stated, "An acute illness of 3½ days brought to a close 12 years of ill health, but before that a vital career that had made a difference in Northfield and Minnesota."

Although most of his family preceded him in death, Weicht has close relatives in Northfield — his niece, Elaine Weicht Lyman and her family.

4 September, 1992

1942: George Bickel named to city council
Service to city continues 21 years

"Council elects George Bickel new alderman," was a headline on the front page of the *Northfield News* on May 7, 1942.

Bickel was chosen by the city council to fill the unexpired term of John E. Fremouw who had accepted a wartime defense industry job in Duluth. (Fremouw would serve on the council again after his return to Northfield.) Bickel was recommended to fellow councilmen by two second ward aldermen, L.F. Beytien and L.M. McKenzie. He was to serve the city as a councilmen from the second ward for 21 years.

When he was chosen, Bickel had lived in the city of Northfield for 14 years. Much of that time he had been employed by Rice County as a motor patrolman in maintenance work on Rice County roads. Because of that background and other similar interests, emphasis in his council career was on the street department and improvement of Northfield streets.

George Herman Bickel was born Jan. 10, 1886, in Northfield Township, the son of Ferdinand and Kathrine Bickel. He grew up in Northfield community and attended the schools of the area.

Following his marriage to Agnes Koester on Thanksgiving Day in 1908, the couple farmed in this area. From 1919 to 1930, they lived away from this community, farming first at Havre, Mont., and then near Ada, Minn.

His Rice County employment was from 1930 until 1953. From 1953 until his retirement in 1958, he owned a hearse service in Northfield.

In 1950, while he was a member of the city council, he ran unsuccessfully for county commissioner from the second district which then included the city of Northfield, the village of Dundas, the townships of Bridgewater and Northfield.

At that time he reminisced a bit about his county highway work. He said that his

first piece of equipment had been a grader drawn by a truck. His second outfit was a hard-tired, gasoline-motored tractor-grader. Bickel said that when he started the county work, grades of the rural roads sloped steeply into the ditches and the grader operator was often in danger of tipping over while working. The roads were gradually widened and the ditches sloped more gently. Grades were built up to allow the wind to help clear the roads of snow in winter.

From the beginning of his council membership, Bickel served on the street committee and very soon he became chairman, to serve in that capacity until the end of 1963. At various times he also chaired the sanitation, water, fire, park and ordinance committees.

But the streets of Northfield were his "first love." When he was running for re-election in 1961, he said that "through years of continuous effort we have brought our street department to a position where we can meet the demands of tomorrow. Our new city shop enables us to house and to keep in good repair a fine assortment of the latest equipment. We can all say, without reservation, that Northfield's street department and personnel is surpassed by no other city of comparable size in the state.

"I am in no way attempting to take full credit for such accomplishments as they come only through the excellent cooperation of our mayors and city councilmen. Having served under seven mayors and with an undetermined number of councilmen, I have never encountered difficulty in having them recognize that building and maintaining our streets is one of our major obligations to our citizens.

"To keep pace with our rapidly expanding development areas and to provide adequate and safe accesses to our new school area (Sibley), I feel that we are now faced with one of the greatest challenges in the history of our street department. It means many hours of careful planning and more hours than should be expected of the department chairman. However, I have more or less dedicated myself to the work and I would gladly give the time required to assure sound and speedy completion of all projects."

Your writer, who covered city council meetings during many of the years that Bickel served, remembers the pride and interest in the streets evidenced by his monthly reports. He was a quiet person, but his face reflected his pleasure as he spoke of knotty problems that had been solved. He was frequently to be seen on the scene when major construction was taking place.

Bickel actually won two elections in 1961. It was that year that city elections were held as they always had been in March, then were switched to November, to take place at the same time as state and national elections.

Again in 1963, Bickel promised, "I can and do devote my entire time to city affairs. I give city business the full and undivided attention that it deserves." However there were many in the city who believed that Bickel devoted too much time to the streets and not enough to other city matters including planning for the future. He was defeated for reelection by Dr. David Remes.

He served until the end of the year and early in 1964 was presented with a shield-shaped plaque in appreciation for his work as a public servant.

Five years later, suffering no previous illness, Bickel suffered a heart attack and died while watching the all-star baseball game on television. His death occurred on July 9, 1968. He was 82.

Mrs. Bickel lived until March of 1973.

8 May, 1992

1943: H. O. Dilley, long-time cashier, dies
Estate Dilley built used at hospital

H. O. Dilley, with a record of 63 years of service at the First National Bank, died Feb. 7, 1943, according to a story in the Feb. 11, 1943, issue of the *Northfield News*.

The story stated, "Contracting a severe cold in December, Dilley had recovered sufficiently to resume his duties as cashier of the First National Bank. But early in January he was stricken with a cerebral thrombosis, resulting in paralysis of the left side, to which he succumbed — at his home — following five weeks' illness."

The funeral service was held at the Congregational Church (now First United Church of Christ) of which Dilley had been a member for 60 years and treasurer for 40 years.

Dr. Robert Rasche, minister of the church, paid tribute to Dilley's "sterling qualities of kindliness, honor and integrity for which he was known, admired and respected by the citizens of Northfield," according to the story.

Rasche said, "The history of the First National Bank is the story of his life — a story of integrity and fidelity that has few equals. The handling of other people's money he considered a trusteeship that he held sacred. He was a good banker, a student of banking, and was the oldest banker in active service in Minnesota at the time of his passing, with a record for the longest continuous service to one bank of any banker in the state."

Attending the funeral in a group to honor their departed brother were members of Northfield Social Lodge No. 48, AF&AM, and of Faribault Commanders, Knights Templar. Dilley was also a member of Osman Temple, Order of the Mystic Shrine, St. Paul.

Dilley had become a Master Mason in Social Lodge on June 1, 1892, the story stated, and for several years before his death he had been the oldest initiate of the lodge. He presided as master in 1898 and 1899 and was the oldest past master. From Dec. 28, 1900, until his death he had served as treasurer of Social Lodge.

Harry O. Dilley was born Jan. 27, 1865 in Dakota County, west of Farmington, to William C. and Margaret (Hagerty) Dilley. His father's family had moved to Minnesota from Ohio, settling first at Hazelwood and moving later to Farmington.

The family moved to Northfield when Harry was a young child and he attended Northfield public schools. It was while he was in high school that he accepted a position as collection clerk in the First National Bank. This was in 1880 when he was age 15. After serving as assistant cashier for several years, he was elected cashier in 1916. He succeeded G. M. Phillips who had been cashier since the bank was organized in 1872. In addition to his banking duties, Dilley conducted an insurance agency in the bank.

In 1889 when the family lived in the Third Ward, Dilley was elected a member of the Northfield City Council. He served one term and could not be reelected to that seat because he then moved to the East Side and the First Ward.

Dilley served as treasurer of several civic organizations in which he took an active interest, according to the story. "Not only as a banker was he a helpful advisor and counselor to many, but he was imbued with a heart interest in his community and was a supporter of and contributor to every worthy cause."

Dilley did not marry and made his home with his sisters, Minnie and Ida at 417 Winona. It was stated in the obituary of Minnie Dilley that the house was "a center of warm hospitality to many friends and associates."

Many present-day Northfielders know of Harry D. Dilley only through the name of the H. O. Dilley Unit of Northfield Hospital, the convalescent unit that was dedicated in the summer of 1963. The addition to the hospital was in large part made possible by a bequest of Minnie Dilley, last of her immediate family, with instructions that the unit be named for her brother.

The dedicatory address was given by Carl L. Weicht, editor of *The Northfield News* and a close friend of the Dilleys. He said in part: "Remember the words, 'The gift without the giver is bare.' Do you think that Harry Dilley ever did anything in his life, whether it was meeting his obligations of trust as an officer of the bank or discharging the debt which he felt he owed to the community in which he lived, without giving himself? Do you think Minnie Dilley, the distinguished citizen, the gracious lady we have known, ever made a gift of talent and leadership, or of any kind, wherein she did not give herself with that gift? Or did the sister Ida, who helped build this competence and whose hospitality so many of us have shared?

"The 'chalice of this holy grail' began with a fund of money which Harry Dilley earned and brought together, and then with wisdom, integrity and foresight invested. I believe that he looked upon this competence which he built up just as he looked upon all money which was a tool of his vocation. To it he applied a question:

'What will this money do?' He wanted it to do a very reasonable thing, to attain an end which should be the proper objective of everyone — a competence if the productive capacity were to end that would provide for himself and his family, and maybe a little luxury here, and possibly a favorite charity there. It was well put together, and it served well the purpose for which it was intended during the lifetimes of all who were to be served.

"Then after his death as the years passed with their inevitable economic effect, plus the remarkable husbanding of this great asset by Minnie Dilley and her associates at the bank (she was a director of the First National Bank for many years), the principal fund became a very substantial amount. . . . It now became for Minnie Dilley not simply a possession, the mere ownership of which might have given some people a unique pride, or a fund to be spectacularly conveyed for some dramatic and unusual purpose when the owner no longer needed it. Minnie Dilley looked upon the 'chalice' and placed a new inscription thereon. It read: 'What will this do for those we love?'"

Dilley had a ready laugh when he encountered moments of good humor, but your writer recalls he was not a "hale, hearty, well-met," back-slapping type. He was quiet and sober in conducting his business, his demeanor creating uneasiness in those not accustomed to borrowing money, but who needed to do so during the Great Depression.

Dilley apparently loved to ramble around the countryside in his auto on Sunday afternoons and when he would slowly pass a farm which was being kept afloat by money he had helped to provide, the occupants tended to suspect the worst. It did not occur to them that he might merely be looking for signs of progress. Subsequently we didn't hear tales of harshness. Dilley personally and Dilley the cashier apparently treated the community evenhandedly.

12 February, 1993

1945: C.L. Brown long a Northfield industrialist
40 years devoted to Northfield Iron Company

Fifty years ago, in 1945, C. L. "Chan" Brown celebrated his 35th anniversary as head of the Northfield Iron Co. A story in the March 22, 1945, *Northfield News* traced his career.

He was to continue as head of the industry for another five years. When he was 71 in April of 1950, he resigned and his son Richard became president and general manager.

The 1945 story recalled that it was on "March 10, 1910, that Brown assumed the management of the business, coming from a good position as secretary-treasurer of A. Y. Bayne & Co. and the Algoma Steel Bridge Co., bridge contractors of Minneapolis and Winnipeg.

"Northfield Iron Co. was a small institution at that time, occupying the property of the Fox Foundry Co. on the corner of Second and Water streets where the Mader Tire Shop and Branes-Johnson Garage are now located." Today, Schultzie's Bike & Ski occupies much of that site.

The story continued, "It (the Iron Co.) had an invested capital of only $8,000, and $5,000 for the patents on a special metal culvert pipe. Also 1910 was a discouraging year, Brown recalls, but during 1911 the business earned a net return on capital invested of 13½ percent.

"In 1912 the company enjoyed a marvelous business with net earnings of nearly 39 percent. This enabled the company to finance the erection of its present building." This was in approximate location of the Country Inn before TH 3 ran anywhere near the area but there was good rail service.

"The Iron Company's products," the story continued, "include metal culverts and a varied line of road and bridge supplies and highway equipment." Your writer recalls that some farm equipment, such as tanks and troughs, was also produced.

The story continued, "A letter expressing appreciation for the Iron Company's effective cooperation in the war (World War II)

effort was received recently from Lt. Col. A. V. Stallard, Ordnance Dept., of the Twin Cities regional office of the War Production Board."

The story also stated that "among the veteran employees are A. T. Peterson, secretary-treasurer, who joined the company as bookkeeper and stenographer in September of 1910, and L. F. Beytien, plant superintendent, who first started with the firm in 1908."

Ten years before, when Brown had been with the company for 25 years, he wrote a story for the *News* about the progress of the Northfield Iron Co. (NICO) and its meaning to the community. Figures quoted in the story would mean little today after years of inflation, but some of Brown's thoughts would be applicable to the present.

For instance: "The company's name, containing the word, "Northfield," and the products most all being sold under the brand, "Northfield," and the address on such advertising being Northfield, Minn., this town of Northfield had been pretty thoroughly stamped on the minds of all who were probably prospects for NICO goods. We did not want them to forget where to get those goods.

"For many years the company has mailed out annually approximately 100,000 mailing pieces to the trade throughout the states of Wisconsin, Minnesota and the Dakotas as well as considerable quantities into other adjacent states. Today, there is scarcely a road official, from the state highway engineer down to all the road bosses here in the Northwest, who is not well acquainted with the fact that they can get mighty good 'Good Roads Machinery and Equipment,' even if I do say it, right here in this good old town of Northfield."

. Brown also expressed the thought that community reputation is a decided help in "breaking down sales resistance."

Stressing the importance of industry to a community, he quoted some payroll totals and noted, "This payroll money, most of it, I believe, has found its way into the channels of trade right here in this community."

Having passed through the gravest years of the Great Depression, Brown said that in June of 1933 the company employed 25 people while in June of 1934, 40 people were at work.

Brown also mentioned that there were at present 59 field sales agents under contract. "Most of these men, during the selling season at least, look to Northfield for their livelihood."

He called attention to the "fuel we buy here, the crating and other lumber we use, the taxes we pay (I believe we rank third or fourth from the top in that item) and the money we pay out to local truckers for moving our products, the dray bills for delivery to the depots, the freight we pay to the railroads here, and a lot of other expenditures too numerous to mention."

Brown predicted good times for the future and opined that "the best times, I believe, will come to the rural communities instead of the concentrated centers."

Directly after his retirement from NICO (he was chairman of the board for that year), Brown accepted the appointment of the National Association of Soil Conservation Districts to act in an advisory capacity. Along with Herbert G. Miller, chairman of the Rice County district and a prominent Northfield farmer, he was to attend various national meetings.

In a story in the *News*, Miller described Brown as a long-time "enthusiastic supporter of the soil conservation movement. We are very glad to have his help in this important work as we have long needed the advice of a practical businessman."

Miller emphasized that no one in the movement, excepting the program planner, received any compensation for their services. "Brown will receive no compensation . . . other than the satisfaction of helping the growth of conservation in this land. The movement is for the sole purpose of conserving the nation's top soil and for developing better farming methods."

That Brown had long been interested in farm problems is born out by a 1933 *News* story which reported that he had received "scores of letters from farm organizations, members of Congress and others interested in agricultural problems, all approving 'his proposal.' The text of his plan had been published in the government's report covering the hearings before the House committee on agriculture."

The *News* attempted to summarize in a few words Brown's idea which he had titled the "Northfield Plan of Farm Relief: To raise farm prices by fixing a minimum price on agricultural products in which a surplus is normally raised and limiting the farmer's sales for domestic consumption on any field crop regulated to his acreage share of the national consumption." This was at a time when much innovation was needed to combat the deepest depression in the history of this country.

Following retirement, Brown suffered from arthritis and a year before his death, had a heart attack while on a trip to Arizona. His death, at Northfield Hospital, was attributed to a cerebral hemorrhage suffered several hours after he had been admitted to the hospital. He was nearly 79.

The lead paragraph in his newspaper obituary stated, "In the death of C. L. Brown Sunday afternoon, Jan. 12, 1958, Northfield lost a citizen who had devoted more than 40 years of his life to the building of one of its leading industries, the Northfield Iron Co., and who during his active years gave generously of time and effort to many civic and community causes."

The story stated that Chauncey Lewis Brown was born on a farm near Sioux City, Iowa, on April 26, 1879, and grew up and attended school in that area. Following a business education, he came to the Twin Cities in 1900. . . . Then began the interest in bridge building and road construction which became the central interest in his business life for a period of many years.

"He was credited with having built the first all-steel welded bridge in this country, erected in Wisconsin, and was known as an authority in this field.

"A pioneer good roads enthusiast, Brown was responsible for a number of inventions and developments in culvert construction and other highway needs, and was the inventor or me well-known 'Blizzard Buster' snow fence which was in use in many parts of the country. He was also an ardent soil conservationist."

The obituary stated that Brown married Mary Louise Skogerson of Sioux City, Iowa, on June 10 1903, and "after the establishment of their home in Northfield, both Mr. and Mrs. Brown took an active part in the life of the community. After Mrs. Brown's death in 1943, and in the years of his retirement, Brown continued to live at the family home at 501 Nevada St. There his daughter, Ruthella, was with him during the months of his failing health.

"Brown continued his active interests in later years and enjoyed traveling, including trips to South America, to Hawaii and various parts of the United States.

"He was long active in community and civic affairs and in the work of the Congregational Church (now United Church of Christ), and was interested in Masonic activities. He and Mrs. Brown together served as presiding officers of Sheba Chapter No. 72 Order of the Eastern Star. A charter member of the 36-year-old Lions Club of Northfield, 'Chan' Brown was its second president and only a week ago attended the club's luncheon downtown, being escorted by a fellow member of the club.

"He was a well-liked friend and neighbor to many in Northfield, honored for his fine civic spirit, and respected for the high sense of integrity and constructive effort which characterized his entire life.

"Asked once to define how he would counsel a young man just starting out in life for himself, he said: 'To train himself to smile, no matter how blue his opportunities may seem, because the world has no use for a grouch.' His formula for his own success tells in a sentence a great deal about him: 'Working faster, better and longer than the average person does — at no matter what I had to do — and keeping up a cheerful front.'"

Among his survivors were the daughter Ruthella MacDonald, and three sons, Robert, Richard and Dr. E. L. "Ned" Brown.

Four years before Brown's death, the Iron Co. was purchase by a Jensen family. A year before Brown's death the company was again sold — to the Wheeler Lumber and Bridge Supply Co. of Des Moines and the name was changed to Northfield Iron and Culvert Co. Somewhat later — after Brown's death — the company was moved from Northfield.

24 March, 1995

1945: Goodhue named to committees
Northfielder a respected senator

"Rice County's Senator Ralph B. Goodhue will be kept busy attending committee meetings during the second legislative session he is attending during his four-year term in office," began a story in the Jan. 11, 1945, *Northfield News*.

The story continued, "Important committees to which Senator Goodhue has been appointed for this session include agriculture, dairy products and livestock, elections, labor, motor vehicles and motor tax laws, public institutions and buildings, railroads, town and counties."

Goodhue was well known in the state's agricultural circles before he ever sought election to office. He farmed in Dennison community until moving into Northfield in 1955.

He was born in Northfield, however, on Jan. 27, 1878. His father, Horace Goodhue, was the first dean of Carleton College, serving on the Carleton faculty for 40 years. Senator Goodhue's mother was Sarah A. Bigelow Goodhue.

The senator grew up in Northfield, attended Carleton Academy and Carleton College, then the School of Agriculture of the University of Minnesota. From 1901 to 1914, he owned and operated a livestock farm near Herman in Stevens County.

In 1914, he returned to the home community, moving onto a 170 acre farm six miles east of Northfield, very near the Goodhue County line. That county, incidentally, had been named for James M. Goodhue, third cousin of Horace Goodhue.

The farm to which the couple moved had been purchased by his father as an investment in 1888. In 1920 Ralph Goodhue bought out the other heirs and became the sole owner of the farm.

He had married while living at Herman. His wife, the former Emily May Rice, taught school at Herman for five years. The couple was married in 1903.

The Goodhues became active in Dennison affairs after moving to this area. He became manager of the Dennison Cooperative Dairy Association, manufacturers of butter and cheese, prior to the association's becoming affiliated with the Twin City Milk Producers Association (TCMPA). He was elected by the Dennison patrons to attend the organizational meeting of the TCMPA on Sept. 1, 1916. He became director of the Dennison Local and served on the TCMPA executive committee until 1922.

In 1929 he was again elected to the five-member TCMPA executive committee. A story that appeared in the *News* at that time stated, "As the representative of Northfield community on the board, Goodhue brings to its service not only the benefit of an active and loyal participation in the work of the association since it was formed and of previous experience of years on the executive committee, but also the good judgment and the sane viewpoint, the high standards and the vision for which he is known and respected among his neighbors in the home community."

He served on the executive committee until 1953 and as a director until 1955 when he was succeeded by Albert H. Quie, then a member of the Minnesota Legislature.

He was first vice president of the TCMPA for 20 years. The association became one of the leading dairy cooperatives in the United States.

Goodhue was a Holstein breeder, one of the builders of Northfield's long reputation as one of the important Holstein centers in the United States.

His obituary stated, however, that he was perhaps even better known in the field of dairy marketing because of his TCMPA leadership. "Revolutionary changes occurred in the marketing of dairy products during the more than two score years that he was active in this field," the story said. "From the pioneering period in producers' cooperative organizations, when acceptance of this type of marketing organization was widely opposed, to the day when the strength and success of the producers' cooperative is widely recognized, Goodhue's quiet leadership, good judgment and keen understanding played an important part.

"His neighbors at Dennison thought so much of his leadership that after he had served for 25 years as director of the Dennison Local, 200 of them gathered to present him with a handsomely inscribed gold watch and a testimonial letter of appreciation."

In an interview with Goodhue that appeared in the *News* at the time of that anniversary, Goodhue recalled that as new manager of the Dennison creamery, he had called on the commission men in the Twin Cities in an effort to interest them in choice dairy products. But World War I was just breaking out and they were more interested in beans than milk. "The commission men knew, even ahead of the doughboys, that beans were needed in every army," Goodhue explained. He was successful in his efforts in behalf of dairy products, however.

In 1942 Goodhue was elected state senator from Rice County. He was re-elected for a second four-year term in 1946.

He was continually appointed to important committees. A 1949 story reported that he would serve as chairman of the railroads committee. His other assignments were to agriculture, motor vehicles and motor tax laws, public institutions and buildings, rules and legislative expense, taxes and tax laws, towns and counties.

About his career as a legislator, his obituary stated, "He became one of the conservative leaders of the legislature, known for his studious attention to state affairs, but he was proudest of his authorship of several state laws relating to livestock health measures and improvement of dairy standards. He was active in developing plans for preservation of the Nerstrand Woods as a state park."

Another story in the Goodhue biographi-

cal file at the *News* states that he had worked extremely hard for a compulsory milk pasteurization law.

The obituary further stated, "Indicative of Goodhue's forward-looking interest in betterment of farm life is the fact that he was the first farmer to sign a contract hiring a county agricultural agent in Minnesota. He was an organizer and director of the Rice County Farm Bureau, an area vice president of the National Dairy Council, president for two years of the Minnesota Frozen Foods Association, Northfield township treasurer for a period of years, and a director of the state association of township officers. Goodhue was a lifelong member of the Congregational Church and contributed in many ways to the church. He had belonged to the Masonic Lodge for nearly half a century and was a member of Social Lodge No. 48, AF&AM."

After 42 years on their Rice County farm, the Goodhues sold the farm and moved into Northfield, buying the house at 207 E. Third.

He was experiencing a heart condition that forced him to be much quieter than was his want. He was to live five more years, dying on Jan. 18, 1960, at Northfield Hospital. He had suffered a stroke at his home three days earlier.

One of the pallbearers for the burial in Oaklawn Cemetery was Edward J. Thye, Northfielder who had served as United States senator and as governor of Minnesota.

Thye's statement of appreciation of Goodhue was as follows: "My first introduction to Ralph B. Goodhue was when he addressed a community gathering at a farm club meeting in my early years of farming. I was impressed with his message. In later years I was privileged to serve with him on the TCMPA board of directors and in other community activities. While serving as governor of Minnesota, I again was privileged to serve with Mr. Goodhue. He was then a state senator serving in the Minnesota Legislature.

"Mr. Goodhue was one of the finest persons it has been my good fortune to have known. His devotion to public service to his state and nation I admired and respected. He was a gentleman of the old school. Minnesota has lost one of her best sons. Senator Goodhue will be remembered by all who knew him as a neighbor and a public servant."

Carl L. Weicht, editor of the *News*, paid the following tribute: "To all of his activities during his long and useful life, Goodhue brought not only an active and loyal participation, but also the good judgment and sane viewpoint, the high standards and vision, the kindly goodwill and friendly spirit for which he was always known and respected among the neighbors and friends in the home community. Possessor of a name famous in Minnesota and Northfield history, he added luster to it by his own leadership and accomplishment for the common good, but best of all he made the name Ralph B. Goodhue stand for sterling citizenship, kindliness and goodwill, and a character above reproach."

Mrs. Goodhue survived her husband by nine years. He was survived by three children including Alice (Mrs. Lloyd) Berg of Northfield.

13 January, 1995

1945: Orval Perman to return to civilian life here
Businessman also serves Northfield, community

"Orval Perman returns from service in Africa, Italy and France" was a page one headline in a November, 1945, *News*.

The story began, "Arriving in Boston on Oct. 19 from France, M/Sgt. Orval Perman has returned from overseas duty and received his honorable discharge at Camp McCoy, Wis.

His wife, who has spent the past several months in Denver, Colo., doing Red Cross work, met him in Milwaukee and they returned to Northfield last week — in time to attend Market Week in Minneapolis. Orval will soon resume his work in the men's department of Perman's Store."

The story continued, "Leaving Northfield in May, 1942, Orval went overseas in February, 1943, serving with . . . the finance service in Casablanca, Marrakech and Oran in Africa; Caserta in Italy; and Marseilles in France for the past year."

The story noted the lack of fuel and food in France. "In comparison, the variety, quality and quantity of food in America seems quite unbelievable to Orval and rationing for a few more months here will present no problem for him."

Orv was not a long-time Northfielder at that time. He had moved to Northfield with his parents, Martin and Mathilda (Odegard) Perman, in the spring of 1937. Mr. and Mrs. Perman and their two sons, Stanley and Orval, at that time established the Perman clothing store here and were quickly accepted into the Northfield business and social community.

Orv's parents had married in 1913 and soon after, Martin became associated with his brother-in-law, Oscar Odegard to form the Odegard & Perman general store at Santiago. This relationship continued until the Permans moved to Northfield.

A story that appeared in the *News* on the 14th anniversary of the beginning of Perman's in Northfield, told of the opening of

the store: "The Permans recall that 1937 was marked by a backward spring. On the opening date, April 7, snow fell all day. But more than 500 Northfielders called at the new store."

The story also said, "The Permans reveal that they came to Northfield not only for business opportunities and for the availability of college educations for their sons, but because they thought Northfield would be a fine place in which to live.

"The two sons, Stanley and Orval, had worked in the Santiago general store which stocked everything from davenports to milk pails. They began immediately to work with their parents in the new clothing store in Northfield, attending St. Olaf College intermittently. Since their graduations, both have become financially associated in the business."

The story added that the store had started in a single store space, the part of the building that now houses most of Ramona's. Men's clothing was at the front; women's directly behind and drygoods at the rear. In 1940 Perman's obtained the portion of the building now occupied by the corridor of the mini-mall that has been established in the Perman building. At that time men's clothing was moved to the new portion of the store and the drygoods department was discontinued.

A story that appeared in the *News* in 1987 shortly before Valentine's Day told of the romance of Orv and his wife Jean: "Orv Perman was a junior at St. Olaf College that fall. He remembers a young woman on campus, a freshman, standing out from the crowd. 'I just spotted that girl in the brown and white coat, called and arranged a blind date,' Orv Perman remembers almost half a century later.

"That girl was Jean Hillestad of Des Moines, Iowa. If it was blind for Orv, apparently it was not for Jean. Orv remembers that she later told him that she had called around to some friends to see if Orv was 'O.K.'

"The first date? Orv's not sure, but he thinks it was probably a movie at the Grand Theater and then Cokes at the old Gates Cafe, a frequent St. Olaf hangout.

"The courtship lasted for two years. Orv finished at St. Olaf in June of 1941. They were married in the fall of that year, shortly before Orv entered service.

"He returned to Northfield after serving in North Africa, Italy and France and he and Jean raised their five children and worked at the family's apparel store in Northfield." (One of the five children, Scott Perman, died in an auto accident when he was 19.)

The entire main floor of the store was modernized and redecorated in 1946, not long after Orv's return. The basement was obtained for the children's and infants' departments.

Stan Perman, the older brother, left the family business in 1955, moving with his wife and children to California where he engaged in retail clothing business.

With a black and white colonial theme, the store was remodeled inside and out in 1963. The portion of the building that now houses Authors' Ink was purchased in 1965. Men's wear moved there, but not for long because the Permans bought the final portion of the building, on the north end, in 1971 and the men's department moved there. (Under new ownership, the Men's Store is still there.) The Lower Deck, devoted to young men's fashions, was developed at that time.

(When Martin Perman died in January of 1968, Orv became president of the company. Orv's mother died in 1974.)

The move into the new spaces was completed in time for the annual anniversary celebration in 1972. Orv said, according to the *News*, that an effort had been made to give the store an open look so that patrons would not have a hemmed-in feeling, something that he said is hard to avoid in small-city stores. At that time the exterior of the building was painted a shade of gold with blue accents.

The company added stores in other towns in the early 1980s, peaking in 1986 with stores in Winona, Cannon Falls, Hastings and Red Wing in addition to Northfield.

Just as the Winona store was being added, in September of 1986, a major change occurred in the management of Perman's. Orv was named chief executive officer of the privately-held company and his son-in-law, Paul Klinefelter, was named president and chief operating officer. Carol Cowles, a daughter of the Permans, was named secretary of the corporation, succeeding Jean Perman who was named executive vice-president.

Klinefelter, husband of the former Anne Perman, had been with the firm since 1972. He had served as comptroller.

Orv told the *News* reporter that he was not retiring at that time. He still planned to be actively involved in the corporation and the Northfield store.

Remodeling and redecorating occurred again in 1989. There was also tuck pointing and redecorating of the exterior. The *News* story at the time of the "grand opening" noted that Permans had started with 2,200 square feet and today had 14,000 square feet of selling space with 88 feet of Division St. frontage.

But then came a sad day for the Permans and the entire community. A story in the Nov. 18, 1992, *News* began, "Perman's Family Apparel owner Orval Perman looks back on 55 years of clothing retailing in Northfield with fondness, and laments giving it up. But Perman's officials announced this week that the women's and children's clothing departments will close sometime after the first of the year ....

"I want retirement. I'm 73 years old. And nobody in our family wants to take it on,' Perman said." (Klinefelter was changing careers at the time.)

The story also said, "Perman emphasized that Perman's is not closing because it is losing money. 'We have a group of very loyal customers that we consider close friends.' He said he and Jean plan to do some more traveling now that they are retired, but will miss the day-today contact with customers and employees. 'We leave with real sadness. It's been very traumatic for our whole family because it's more than just a store. It's been a part of our lives,' he said."

Although he was especially known in the community through the store, Orv was long active in other phases of community life. He has been an active member of St. John's Lutheran Church. He has been president of the Northfield Arts Guild of which Jean was a founding member. He has been president of the Northfield Rotary Club of which he has been a member since 1946. He was active in the Junior Chamber of Commerce (now Jaycees), has been president of the Northfield Area Chamber of Commerce and active in the Northfield Industrial Corporation.

He has served as president of the St. Olaf Alumni Association and was a regent of the college for 12 years. He is a charter member of the St. Olaf College Associates.

He served on the Northfield Board of Education for two terms, as chairman part of that time. He was named to the First National Bank board of directors in 1968. He has worked in the United Way and has raised funds for the Community Swimming Pool, the Northfield Retirement Center and the Northfield Historical Society. He has volunteered for Meals-on-Wheels.

He addressed the Northfield High School graduating class at the 1968 commencement, his son Graig being a member of the class. Because Jean Perman has been similarly active in the community, the couple was jointly honored, receiving the Heywood award during Defeat of Jesse James Days in 1993. The award is given to persons who have demonstrated outstanding service to the community — in the tradition of Joseph Lee Heywood.

At the time, Orv said, "It was not easy for us to accept this. We're representing a large group of wonderful people. Northfield is filled with giving people. We don't feel at all special as far as making a contribution."

As they were presented with the award, Orv said, "We have received much more than we have given." He recalled the family's move to Northfield in 1937 and said, "What greater place could they (his parents) have brought us?"

This past summer, Orv was given Northfield Rotary's Service-Above-Self award. He had in years gone by received Rotary's Paul Harris Fellowship award.

Because they now spend the cold months in California, the Permans are not as active in the community as they once were. Orv's somewhat less than robust health has also caused them to be less active and they have probably traveled less than they had hoped. They've had some fine trips through the years, however.

With the Ken Althoffs of Cannon Falls, they once spent seven weeks in Mediterranean countries and Scandinavian countries, among other things visiting the International Trade Fair in Milan, Italy. Orv was able to see in peacetime places he'd been in wartime. This was also true when the Permans toured Morocco with the Ed Soviks and the Althoffs.

In more recent years, the Permans participated in a University of Minnesota safari to Kenya. Orv's cousin, a vice-president of the University, and his wife were also members of that tour group.

Certainly the couple's children and grandchildren are a joy to them. The children include Anne Klinefelter, Carol Cowles (of Kids on Division in the Perman building), Craig Perman and Lucy Arneson.

24 November 1995

1945: Sales secretary sends Holsteins far and wide

Nels Parson long active in Northfield community

"Carloads of Northfield Holsteins head for Illinois and overseas buyers" was a page one headline on Dec. 6, 1945.

The story began, "Nels Parson, sales secretary of the Northfield Holstein Club, shipped a carload of 21 Holsteins Monday to Frederick G. Schmidt, Freeport, Ill., banker. This buyer of foundation stock from Northfield community Holstein herds is a repeat customer, so well pleased with previous purchases here that he returned for more of Northfield's Holsteins.

"Two weeks ago," the story continued, "Parson received a phone call from Washington, D.C., asking if he could fill another order for two carloads of Holsteins for shipment to Europe. This order called for heifers, plus a good bull with each load. Parson assumes that this shipment is for Poland. Previous shipments of Holsteins totaling 90 head were destined for that war-devastated country."

Stories about shipments of Holsteins, arranged by Parson, were not uncommon in the *News* during the days when Northfield was one of the most important Holstein centers in America.

Parson was saluted in the "Who's Who in Northfield" feature in the *News* in August of 1924, the picture that appears here having been used with that column. Parson was called a "Northfield farmer and Holstein breeder who has been active in cooperative enterprises."

Included in the information in that column were Parson's date and place of birth, April 1, 1870 near Christianstad, Sweden; the earliest event he could recall, the death of Charles XV, king of Sweden and Norway; boyhood ambition, to be a merchant; favorite sport, hunting.

He was asked, "If you were counseling a young man about to start out in life for himself, what would be your advice?" His reply was, "Choose the work he wants to do and

stick to it, work hard and be honest."

When asked what aided him the most in attaining success, he replied, "A good wife."

Finally he was asked what one thing Northfield needed the most. His reply was, "More cooperation among business people, among citizens of the community and among educational institutions."

Many facts about Parson's life appeared in an interview conducted in April of 1951. During the 75th anniversary year of the *News*, a number of senior citizens were interviewed for the "Diamond Club." Parson had just celebrated his 81st birthday and his wife, Hannah, would be observing her 82nd birthday in October.

Both were born in Sweden where their families knew each other, but Nels and Hannah met here in the Hazelwood community.

Hannah Ackerson had come to the United States in 1879 when she was 10 years old. With her parents, she lived at first in Chicago where she had an uncle. She learned

English from her cousins and started school in Chicago. In 1881 she came with her parents to the Webster-Hazelwood area where they farmed.

Nels came to America with his parents in 1886 when he was 16. They settled first at Stillwater where they found employment in the thriving lumbering industry. But after 1½ years they moved to the Union Lake area west of Northfield to begin farming.

Nels attended Carleton Academy for a year, taking a special interest in YMCA activities. As a young farm lad, he continued to lead YMCA activities for several years.

While he was working at Stillwater, he lost part of a thumb in an accident with a saw, the Diamond Club interview revealed. The couple recalled that when he first visited the Ackersons at their farm, the daughter Hannah felt very sorry for him because of the thumb. They didn't start to date for two years, however. They were married on Feb. 27, 1892, at her parents' farm.

Their first home was on a 90 acre farm on the east shore of Union Lake, located on the old Dodd Road. After five years, they sold that farm and bought a 200 acre farm a mile north. Fourteen years later they bought a farm on the Wall Street Road east of Northfield — the farm where their son Harry lived for many years and more recently their grandson, Phillip lived for several years. Parts of it are now settled as Mayflower Hill.

There were no buildings on the farm when Nels bought it. The house was completed and they were able to move in 1911.

Nels bought his first Holstein in 1908 from W. F. Schilling, enthusiastic breeder who had urged farmers of the community to concentrate on one breed of cattle. From then on, Nels maintained a Holstein herd.

A stroke of luck for him — Mrs. F. B. Hill, probably Northfield's wealthiest and most influential citizen, was advised by her doctor to provide Holstein milk for her children. He said that Holstein milk included better protein and less hard-to-digest fat than other milk. So she stopped Nels while he was on

the way to the creamery and asked that he bring her milk for her children.

Nels said that his dairy business boomed as her friends demanded Parson's Holstein milk for their children also. Because he didn't want his dairy business to expand beyond what he and his family could handle, he confined his route to the first ward where Mrs. Hill and her friends lived.

Hannah recalled that she spent five hours a day in the milk house, keeping the equipment spotless and following the instruction of the inspector. She remembered proudly that the family established a reputation for pure and tasty milk.

But after the business had thrived for five years, the sons left for World War I service and the parents, swamped with work, found it necessary to close down the dairy.

They retired when Harry took over operation of the farm and moved into Northfield. At various times they lived at 503 College, 411 Union, 215 Elm and 610 E. Fourth.

Both loved to travel and in their old age made several trips to Arizona and California. They sometimes spent the winter at Santa Ana, Calif.

Possibly Nels's first adventure with a cooperative came when the telephone company serving the city of Northfield refused to install rural service. Area farmers formed the Farmers Telephone Co. Nels was secretary and manager for 20 years until the equipment was sold to Tri-State Telephone Co., a forerunner of Northwestern Bell.

Ever since he owned his first Holstein, Nels was active in the Northfield Community Holstein Club. He served in all of the offices and was sales secretary for 24 years. He relinquished those duties in the fall of 1950 because of ill health.

Nels estimated that during those 24 years he sold some 15,000 head throughout the United States and in many other countries.

For a number of years he was a board member of the Northfield Farmers Cooperative Elevator — forerunner of Cannon Valley Coop — and he was president some of those years. He also managed the business for a time.

He was active on the Rice County Fair board during the years the fair was held in Northfield. He served as trustee, secretary and treasurer of Oaklawn Cemetery, giving up those duties in the spring of 1951, again because of ill health.

During the Diamond Club interview, he recalled a couple of other activities from a long time before. He was elected justice of the peace while living in the Union Lake area, but said that he never needed to perform a marriage. He was also for a time manager and president of a farmers' cooperative general store in Northfield's West Side business district. The store was eventually sold to William Ebel who was in business for many years.

Both Ness and Hannah were active in the First Congregational Church, now First United Church of Christ.

The Parsons had a big open house celebration on their 50th wedding anniversary. A large family gathering celebrated their 57th anniversary. At that time the late Nellie Phillips, *Northfield News* columnist, saluted the couple. She wrote, in part: "Mr. and Mrs. Parson have contributed much to the Northfield community both in civic and rural affairs. They have lived a quiet life and have brought up a fine family of girls and boys of whom they can be proud. I have known Mr. and Mrs. Parson for many years and have always been happy to call them friends. Mrs.

Parson has such a sweet smile when I meet her, and Mr. Parson always greets me with some special word of greeting."

The couple was able to observe their 59th anniversary on Feb. 27, 1951. They were entertained at luncheon at the Stuart Hotel, now the Archer House. The *News* story said, "Although both have suffered some ill health this winter, they were well for the anniversary celebration." Of course, they were looking forward to celebrating their 60th anniversary, but that was not to be.

It was fortunate that the Diamond Club interview was conducted in the spring of 1951 for Nels died very unexpectedly on Aug. 28, 1951. Although he had resigned from major responsibilities, he was active until the end.

The couple had eaten downtown at noon. They and their daughter Myrtle who was residing with them at the time had visited together on the porch before supper. Nels, responding to the call to supper, suffered a heart attack and died.

Hannah died almost exactly a year later — on Aug. 25, 1952. She had been ill for 10 days and died at Northfield Hospital from a cerebral hemorrhage. Besides her farm and church duties, she had been active through the years in the Women's Christian Temperance Union and in the Town and Country (Study) Club.

Three of the couple's children had died. But they were survived by three daughters, two sons and a number of grandchildren and great-grandchildren.

8 December, 1995

1945: Turkeys become important crop

Haugen always involved in many activities

"More than 60,000 turkeys in flocks near Northfield" was a headline in the Nov. 1, 1945, *Northfield News* as the *News* staff looked forward to Thanksgiving.

Sixteen different flocks were listed, among them that of Sanford L. "Sam" Haugen who was growing 7,000 turkeys at the time. A picture of Sam feeding the turkeys accompanied the story — possibly chosen from the 16 growers because the *News* photographer, the late Kirk Roe, and Sam were good friends.

This was only five years after the Armistice Day blizzard had wiped Sam out. He recalled in recent years that "I owed money all over town. But hard work and discipline paid off."

Present-day Northfielders think of Sam as the 1995 Heywood Award winner, a man who with his family has traveled extensively, who as a Turkey Growers Association official has presented turkeys as gifts to Presidents Harry Truman and Lyndon Johnson in the White House, who has a nice home in town in addition to turkey raising land near Northfield, but it wasn't always that way.

Sam was born in 1912 at Harmony where his father was editor and publisher of the *Harmony News* and postmaster. But his father died in 1916, right while he was running for a seat in the state legislature.

Sam's mother had come from Norway as a very young woman and had worked in a Minneapolis home as a maid and cook while she learned the English language. She was one of 12 children in her family and four siblings came to the U.S.A., inspired by her adventure.

The new widow took her youngest child, Sam, with her to Staten Island, N.Y., to live with her bachelor brother who had become a Lutheran clergyman. It was there, while Sam and other lads were playing outdoors, that a stone hit him and blinded his left eye.

Another uncle had a good connection with the Norwegian-American Steamship line and when Sam's maternal grandfather was becoming quite old, Sam and his mother were able to go to Norway. Sam began school there and when he and his mother returned to the United States a year and a half later, he remembered no English!

While Sam's brother Abner was attending St. Olaf College, Sam and his mother moved to Northfield in 1924. They lived first in two rooms with bath on the East Side, then moved to a second floor in a home on St. Olaf Ave. They moved up and down St. Olaf Ave. seven times while Sam's mother, a wizard at stretching a dollar, tried to find a place more financially advantageous. They took in student roomers and sometimes the mother slept on a cot in the kitchen while Sam slept in a closet.

His youthful adventures included hopping freight trains to New York to consult with his eye doctor (he had surgery then). His mother knew nothing about the freights, she thought he was hitchhiking in motor cars. Sam learned what to do from transients he met in the rail yards.

Later Sam left St. Olaf to drive to New York in a jalopy, hoping to find work. He became a deck boy on a small Norwegian freighter headed for the Caribbean. Sam treasured this experience, but decided that the next time he went to sea, it would be as a comfortable passenger.

Before matriculating at St. Olaf, Sam had graduated from Northfield High School and played football, winning a letter.

As a teenager, Sam dreamed of raising some kind of fowls and he started with chickens in the back yard. This led to the purchase of a hilly piece of land west of Northfield and a beginning in the turkey industry in 1936.

The next time a picture of Sam and his flock (by now changed from bronze to white turkeys) appeared in the *News*, Sam had been the subject of a story, "Look What the Pilgrims Started," that appeared in the November 1959 Northern States Power Co. employee magazine. By that time, Sam was raising 53,000 birds on three farms.

The story explained that white turkeys were by then in general demand because they could be processed at the smaller size that families were preferring. The bronze turkey needed to reach a weight of 25 pounds or more before it would "taste like a good turkey should," the story said.

Sometime during that period, John Mackie, former minister of agriculture in Great Britain, visited the Haugen farms while studying poultry diseases. He became close friends with the Haugens and while Sam, his wife, Kay, and daughter Susan were visiting Europe in 1961, they were guests at the Mackie home. They were in England to attend the Royal Show at Cambridge, a huge display of farm equipment. Mackie, a member of the House of Commons, took the Haugens to visit both that house and the House of Lords.

After the English visit, the Haugens toured in Scotland, Norway where they visited Sam's relatives, Denmark, Germany, Switzerland, Italy and France.

In 1963, Sam was back in Europe, this time as a member of the Minnesota Agricultural Leaders Goodwill People-to-People international exchange. Members of the group paid their own way and visited farms and cities in England, Belgium, Russia, Poland, Hungary, Austria and Germany. After the tour, Sam visited Holland, Denmark and then visited his relatives in Norway.

Sam was most fascinated with conditions in the countries behind the Iron Curtain —

East Germany, Poland and Russia. He tried wherever possible to visit with the youth of the countries.

He told the *News* on his return, "We tried to give them facts and not brag about our country. They were interested in what we had to say, but we found that they simply cannot believe in God. They trust in their intellect and their hands, believing that they must give all for their country and that others will carry on when they are unable to do so."

Sam was elected president of the Minnesota Turkey Growers Association in 1964. The story about his election that appeared in the *News* said that he was elected during the 25th year of the organization which he helped found. He had already served as vice president and secretary-treasurer. Later he was to serve several years on the board of the National Turkey Federation.

In 1965 he was elected to the board of the Poultry Egg National Board. He was subsequently named to the executive committee of the organization for promotion of poultry and egg sales.

Sam took his daughter Mary along when he attended the World Turkey Federation Congress in London and the World's Poultry Congress in Kiev, Russia, in 1966. They also visited Gibraltar, Italy, France, Germany, Romania, Hungary, Austria, France, and of course, Norway where they visited family.

While in France, our Northfielder had the distinction of being kicked out of the Louvre — for taking a couple of flash pictures.

It was on that trip that Sam fulfilled a longtime desire — he purchased a London taxicab and had it shipped to Des Moines. He and an employee, Lawrence Moe, drove the diesel-burning auto to Northfield for 90 cents worth of fuel.

In 1970, Sam attended the World's Poultry Congress in Madrid. He and Kay and their daughter Kathy spent a month in Europe, visiting France, Germany, Holland as well as Spain and spent time with family in Norway.

In 1973, Sam and Howard Holden, fellow Northfield turkey grower, accompanied by a representative of the U of M extension department and a person from Jennie-O turkey products, went to England to observe positive environmental control for turkeys. Sam had met a specialist in the field at a national turkey meeting in Dallas, Texas, and was inspired to observe the man's work.

While the group was in London, Sam looked up Mackie who took the group on a tour of London in his Rolls Royce. The four also went to Scotland where a turkey grower who had served on an international committee with Sam took them on a "royal tour" of the area.

Sam long ago discovered how and when to keep his "nose to the grindstone," but he did a bunch of other things too.

He was elected president of the Northfield Rotary Club in 1955 and has always kept up his interest in the activities of the service group. In 1976–77, he took a special interest in the club's project related to Operation Bootstrap Tanzania. The local club raised money toward building a school in the African nation. Sam and Kay visited the site and came to admire the Tanzanian government's attitude in wanting the people to construct the school themselves.

In 1963 Sam was installed as president of the congregation of St. John's Lutheran Church. He has also served on the church board. He was named to the board of directors of Northfield National Bank (now Community National Bank) in 1964. He served on Northfield's Community Development Program (CoDeP) in 1966–67. He has long been a member of the Waldorf College board of regents and has served as national co-chair for the college's fund-raising campaign.

In 1974, St. Olaf's centennial year, Sam was among 10 alumni of the college to receive the distinguished alumni award.

Back in 1948 when Sam was an active member of the Jaycees, the group that sponsored the earliest of what's now known as Defeat of Jesse James Days, Sam was general chairman of that first celebration. He can remember meeting almost every night that summer to hammer out details of what was really an elaborate festival. It included the first reenactment of the James-Younger Bank Raid.

Sam was grand marshal of the Defeat of Jesse James Days parade on the 30th anniversary of the celebration in 1978 and now this year, he was the recipient of the Joseph Lee Heywood award given annually to those who have been good to and for Northfield.

With typical modesty, Sam said he was "shocked and embarrassed" to get the award. "There are too many other good candidates in town." But he thanked the committee for a special blessing — getting all of his family together at once.

All of his friends were in service and Sam was feeling kind of depressed during the early World War II days — when suddenly he met Kathryn Anderson — he has described that meeting as a godsend. He had recently been turned down when he had tried to enlist in service. He had originally been deferred because of his farming status, but he tried to enlist anyway — and was sent home because of his blind eye.

He has described Kay as "beautiful, intelligent, very creative, with more finesse than me" and as his best friend who has always encouraged him.

Kay came to Northfield to serve as secretary and bookkeeper at the Federal Land Bank. She had attended the University of Minnesota and Mankato Commercial College.

Kay and Sam were married in 1943 in a small country church at Hanska, Kay's home territory.

They have brought up the three daughters, Susan, Mary and Kathy, all of whom have now married and moved away. Sam has expressed the hope that he "was there when they needed me."

He also frequently expresses the thought, "If you want your ship to come in, you had better send a ship out first!"

He admits to loving feathers! But he has stated, "I've learned one thing, don't count your turkeys until they are hatched."

3 November, 1995

1946: Alvin Houston returns from Newfoundland

Houston pursues many interests through the decades

"Alvin Houston, who has been serving as field director with the Red Cross in Newfoundland for the past year, will be relieved of duty," *Northfield News* readers learned at the beginning of February, 1946. The item stated that after a short stop on business in Washington, D.C., Houston would return to Northfield.

Houston was 45 years old at that time, going on 46. He is still with us, remarkably active, and nearly 96.

He's had a remarkable career, serving for many years as a Northfield mail carrier and active in the National and Minnesota Rural Carriers associations; active at many sites on behalf of the American Red Cross; active on the home front in helping solve environmental problems; always interested in preserving and calling attention to local history.

A story prepared by Bill Cupp for the *News* this past fall shed further light on his work in Newfoundland. After a friend had persuaded Al to apply for a position as Red Cross Field Director, he was called and was loaned by the Postal Service to the American Red Cross to serve in Newfoundland. Cupp wrote, "There he served as a liaison officer, Military Welfare, simultaneously at Ft. McAndrew and the Argentia Naval Base. As Red Cross director, he dealt with matters for the 300,000 U.S. and Canadian troops stationed in the area, plus the naval and air traffic that passed through.... Most frequent were concerns about family matters such as illness or the death of a dear one."

The story revealed that Al's own son, Paul, was wounded in the Battle of the Bulge and declared missing in action during this period. He was actually imprisoned in a German hospital and when liberated, was taken to England for nourishment and treatment. From his mother he learned of his father's whereabouts and plotted to meet Al when his plane — by which he would be transported to America for further hospital care — would stop in Newfoundland for refueling. With the help of several people, they did get together and then dense fog prevented flights for four days while the two had a joyful reunion!

Although he's been an enthusiastic Northfielder for many years, Al was born in Iowa in May of 1900. He was one of 11 children of Ralph and Minnie Houston. With his family he moved to Northfield in 1910 and attended Northfield schools.

He began work at the Northfield post office directly after attending Northfield High School and was appointed to a rural route in May of 1920. At that time the route was 30 miles long and he used a horse and buggy or sleigh to carry mail.

With the exception of 15 months that he served as a postal clerk in Milwaukie, Ore., in 1927–28 and the months that he was on leave for Red Cross duty during World War II, he always served a mail route in the same area. However by the time he retired in 1957, the route had grown to 65 miles.

When he retired, Al told a *News* reporter that the work had been very pleasant through the years, his relationships with the patrons very congenial. "Strangely enough," he said, "there are few people living on my route that were there 37 years ago, although some of the farms are being operated by their children or grandchildren."

One of the unusual features of Al's mail-carrying days was his use of the snowmobile — he built his own in 1926. He removed the body of a used Model T Ford, cut and re-welded the front and rear axles to the width of a farm bobsled, made hickory skis that were strapped to the front wheels. Special tires and chains went onto the rear wheels. With that machine he could follow the rural "trails" that the farmers had broken with sleighs. Later he bought a Snowflyer, made in Wisconsin and also mounted on a Model T chassis, and still later a Eskimobile mounted on a Model A chassis and equipped with steel skis.

These vehicles sometimes served other purposes than delivering mail. Sometimes Al took doctors out into the country on emergency calls during blizzards. After Al sold his first snowmobile to a Webster mail carrier, a baby was born in it while the mother was being taken to the hospital!

During the years that Al served on boards and in office in the rural letter carrier organization, his picture once appeared on the cover of the magazine of the national group. With it was the following caption: "Alvin Houston of Northfield, Minn., member, executive committee, N.R.L.C.A., whose efficient and energetic service on behalf of his fellow carriers has stamped him as an independent thinker and one who stands firmly against a majority sentiment stifling minority opinions. Alvin is the antithesis of a 'yes man.' He is not easily swayed by what appears on the surface, preferring to plumb to the bottom of every association problem before subscribing his approval."

When he retired, Al said that he would probably do first aid instruction for the Red Cross and putter around his rural home two miles northeast of Northfield. But in the reserve disaster service of the Red Cross, he was soon reporting here and there. He recalled later that he hardly got home at all

in 1961.

When Al and his wife Peggy (her real name is Myrtle) were among five citizens honored for their community service by the Northfield Historical Society in 1988, the *News* story revealed that he had been active in Red Cross efforts since 1942. "His emergency efforts took him as far away as (the aftermaths of) a dramatic earthquake in Alaska and a destructive hurricane in southern Texas. Closer to home, Houston helped with the relief efforts due to spring floods and a night of tornadoes in the Twin Cities in 1965. At times his wife Peggy accompanied him on missions. She would help with the Red Cross records and other support activities at the scene." She is a nurse.

A *News* story in January of 1962 revealed that those places Al was called in 1961 were in the wake of ice jams, torrential rains, tornadoes and hurricanes in such points as Nebraska, Iowa, Kentucky, Mississippi, Alabama, Oklahoma and Texas.

Al was quoted, "I could list disaster after disaster, but the names and places would not really convey the magnitude of some of them, or the smells, the mud, the lack of sanitation, the confusion, the shock and numbness of survivors, the misery, the dashed hopes, the eternal questions of 'Why? What can we do?'"

After working at a number of disaster scenes, Al was given special training in Virginia as a building adviser. First of all he would survey the disaster area, then he would study local building materials, labor prices and practices, and building codes. Then he would do the actual estimating of the cost of repairs or replacement of individual homes. Finally he would assist the caseworker who worked with a family in the letting of contracts and the buying of building materials. Al said that every effort was made to spend the Red Cross funds fairly to individuals, fair to all affected by the disaster.

Al also revealed that he saw dramatic and awesome sights in arriving very early at the disaster sites. Then after a few days, the area would "reek from dead fish and animals. One has to have a fairly hardy constitution to work in a disaster area the first week or two, especially in warm weather."

In the 1960s, Al served as Northfield Civil Defense director.

He has worked diligently on causes on the home front. In 1971 he organized opposition to the plan of Northern States Power Co. to store natural gas in the ground in this area. He recommended that NSP store compressed gas in tanks above ground and the company ultimately built such a facility near Rosemount.

Al also took a leadership role in a battle against a plan of Koch Refinery to lay a crude oil pipeline in the ground from St. Louis to St. Paul. That plan was eventually abandoned.

During that period, Al was volunteering time to nine boards. But after he suffered a heart attack in 1977, advised by his doctor, he lightened his work load.

In 1976, Al was chosen Dakota County's Outstanding Senior Citizen and participated in Senior Citizen Day events at the State Fair.

While his children were growing up, Al lived in Northfield. Then for 35 years he lived on Canada Ave. in Waterford Township. He and Peggy moved back into Northfield in 1982. They have an apartment in the Northfield Retirement Center complex.

Al's first wife, Gladys, died in 1948. He and Peggy, at one time superintendent of Northfield Hospital, were married in 1949. Al has a daughter, Margaret Nevins who lives in Washington state. His sons Paul and Bruce have died.

When interviewed by the *News* a couple of years ago, Al described Northfield as both pretty and nice. He said he likes the friendly Northfield people who "you don't even have to know to greet."

9 February, 1996

1946: Dr. Bernard Street arrives in Northfield
Busy physician serves community as well as practice

"Dr. Bernard Street, grandson of John Street, and nephew of Mrs. Joseph Moses and Mrs. Ralph Henry, all of Northfield, will enter into partnership with Dr. Joseph Moses and Dr. Warren E. Wilson," the *News* announced at the beginning of 1946.

The story stated that Dr. Street had been in the army for four years, attaining the commission of major. "He is a graduate of the University of Minnesota School of Medicine. In addition to his practice as a physician and surgeon, Dr. Street has also had experience as an oculist."

The *News* in addition reported that Dr. Street was having a difficult time finding housing for his family — his wife, Mary Lou, and three children "who have been residing in Minnetonka Beach during the war. Dr. Street is staying at the Joseph Moses house temporarily."

When Dr. Street observed 35 years of practice in Northfield, he reviewed for a *News* reporter the history of the medical firm he joined and the nature of his coming to Northfield.

He said that the firm (now part of the River Valley Clinic) was started in 1898 when Dr. Warren Wilson, Sr., purchased the medical practice from Dr. A. J. Schmidt.

The story stated, "After the war, Dr. Street came to Northfield as a temporary replacement for Dr. Moses who was recovering from an illness. Dr. Moses was never able to resume his former role and Street returned permanently in June of 1946."

At the time of that interview, Dr. Street was 66, but he said he had no notion of retiring. He planned to spend more time with his family and at traveling and fishing, but he wanted to continue seeing his patients. However, retire he did in September of 1984 when it became evident that it would not be practical to work part time and pay the tremendous insurance premiums that are now necessary for doctors.

When he retired, Dr. Street expressly ordered that there was to be no elaborate farewell event for him. But a top-secret project was underway for months in advance of the retirement. "The Quilt that Love Built" was made of 48 blocks, each one designed and embroidered by a person who had been associated with Dr. Street in some way at Northfield Hospital. Some of the blocks recalled humorous incidents, some kidded about the doctor's handwriting, some recalled instances of healing.

A poem accompanied the quilt with the beginning:

A quilt's been made for you,
It comes from those who care,
From those whose lives you've touched.
Here, there, and everywhere.
Each block was made with you in mind,
A certain meaning for a certain time.
Its colors are bright, tried and true;
In fact, it's a lot like you.
It's warm and gentle, it's tough as hide.

The quilt was presented to Dr. Street at a Northfield Hospital picnic and the doctor admitted it was an overwhelming experience.

Some people thought of him as crusty, but he had a keen sense of humor and those who knew him realized that he had a deep love for humankind. One of his daughters once called him "a sheep in wolfs clothing."

Dr. Street always had a heavy practice and he was known for taking time with his patients. In one interview he said that patients are all old friends and it takes twice as long to take care of them!"

But he had many other activities. After separation from active duty in the army, he served in the army reserve for many years, attaining the rank of full colonel. In 1989 he was honored for 35 years of service to the American Red Cross. He was an active supporter of the Northfield Rescue Squad.

He served on many committees and boards and as moderator of the First United Church of Christ. He worked with the Northfield Arts Guild, the Northfield Historical Society, the A Better Chance program. He was a member of veterans' organizations. He was named Employer of the Year by the Northfield High School Office Education Association in 1979.

After his retirement he became active in the Northfield Lions Club. He headed the club's Quest project, a program to help students in middle grades to build a positive self image.

Dr. Street continued to study throughout his career and in 1973 was elected president of the Southern Minnesota Chapter of the American Academy of Family Physicians. He served as a preceptor for the Mayo Medical School, guiding students from the school in periods of observance of a small city practice of a general practitioner. He was subsequently appointed to the faculty of the school in 1974, serving until his retirement.

His wife, Mary Lou, was through the years and still is active in many groups and has originated some action organizations and committees to meet Northfield problems. When the two, Bernard and Mary Lou were given the Hometown Spirit Award by Community National Bank in 1989, Dr. Street said that the award was earned mainly

through his wife's accomplishments. However, she said, "Maybe I was more visible, but he was always there to support it with both labor and money."

Among those who nominated the Streets for this award was Betsy Maitland. A long-time patient of Dr. Street, she said she remembered that he always made an accurate diagnosis. "He put things together," she said. "He had a good mind and would figure out what was wrong. It was very easy to have faith in him."

Maitland also said that the Streets could "best be described as 'participants,' and their energies always have been directed toward making the community a better place."

Earlier, in 1987, the Streets were honored on the Fourth of July, being among the couples chosen to represent Northfield's senior citizens during Heritage Day events.

Because his relatives lived here, Dr. Street was familiar with Northfield before beginning his practice here, but he had never before lived here.

He was born Sept. 20, 1914, in Las Vegas, Nev., fourth of the five children of Bernard and Ella (Richardson) Street. Both of his parents had grown up in Northfield and both graduated from Carleton College in 1906.

When Dr. Street was two years old, the family moved to Huntington Park, Calif. The father, a school principal, died in a hunting accident two years later.

The mother then supported her family by teaching. To ease the burden, Dr. Street went to live with maternal grandparents in Sutherlin, Ore. When he was 12, he moved to Keewatin in Minnesota's Iron Range country where his mother was teaching.

There he grew up with Mary Lou Loofbourrow who was to become his wife. He was greatly influenced by her father who was a physician. Dr. Street once told a *News* reporter that he had never wavered in his desire to become a doctor.

After graduating from Keewatin High School, Dr. Street attended Hibbing Junior College for two years, then earned his B.S.

and M.D. from the University of Minnesota medical school. He did his internship at Minneapolis General Hospital.

When he graduated in 1937 with education debts, "No one was looking for bright, young doctors," he told the above-mentioned reporter. "Those were still depression years. Most of us were in debt and it would take three to four years to develop a practice."

So he accepted employment from the state of Minnesota. He was medical officer at Stillwater State Prison for a year and at the state reformatory in St. Cloud for 1½ years.

He was married June 24, 1939, at Keewatin.

He was ordered into active military duty in 1941. After serving stateside at several locations, he was sent to the European Theater as executive officer of a general hospital.

Returning to the states in November of 1945 he was on terminal leave when he came to Northfield, until February of 1946. Just before coming here, he took a refresher course and practiced for three weeks at Minneapolis General Hospital.

When he joined the practice here, the offices were in a Bridge Square building that has since been razed. The location is now part of the site of Community National Bank. When the doctors learned that the building was slated to be razed sometime in the future, the firm moved in May of 1949, to the Medical Arts Building at Division and Second.

Dr. Street and Dr. David Halvorson organized Northfield Physicians and Surgeons in 1964. That firm moved in 1983 to 500 S. Water. Dr. Street was no longer practicing when the firm's doctors joined River Valley Clinic.

The Streets traveled widely after their children were grown. For many years they also enjoyed a summer cabin on Woman Lake in northern Minnesota. Dr. Street especially enjoyed gardening, fishing and woodworking.

During the winter of 1989, ill health overtook Dr. Street. It was found that he was suffering from an aneurysm at the base of his brain. At first it was thought that nothing could be done, but surgery in the fall did bring relief and he seemed his old self until February of 1990.

Dr. Street died at his home April 2, 1990. He was survived by his wife, two daughters, one son and grandchildren. One son preceded him in death.

5 January, 1996

1946: Stanley 'Tiny' Johnson moves to Northfield

'Tiny' participates in many community efforts

"Smoke Shop sold; new owners move here from Renville" was a page-one headline on Nov. 7, 1946 — 50 years ago. The new owners were Stanley "Tiny" and Ethel Johnson who were to be important Northfield citizens.

The story stated, "Mr. and Mrs. Johnson moved here last Friday and opened the shop Monday morning. They plan to redecorate as soon as possible. The pool hall and a full line of tobacco and accessories will be continued. They are residing in the apartment over the shop.

"Mr. and Mrs. Johnson operated a restaurant in Renville for two years. Their older daughter, Shirley, is residing in Morris where she is completing her senior year in high school. (She was named valedictorian at the end of that school year.) She plans to attend St. Olaf College next year. Their other daughter Carol began classes Monday at Northfield High School where she is a sophomore."

The Smoke Shop was across the street from its current location, in one of the buildings that was razed when the Community National Bank's present home was erected. Before the arrival of the Johnsons, the business had had its ups and downs, sometimes considered an unhealthy place for teen boys to hang out.

In those days, women had not darkened its door. But through the years the Johnson girls became very adept at pool and had fun whomping surprised males at what was considered their game.

Early on, Tiny, who was anything but tiny, became involved in Jesse James Days, later Defeat of Jesse James Days. At times he grew wondrous beards for the celebration.

In the early 1960s he served for the first time as fireworks coordinator for the Northfield Area Chamber of Commerce which was sponsoring the Fourth of July observance. He continued in the post for several years. Beginning weeks ahead of the Fourth, he visited business places and professional offices to obtain monetary gifts to make the fireworks display possible. One year while out seeking gifts, he was togged up as a blind man and carried a tin cup.

He purchased the fireworks, set up the mechanical part of the display, and cleaned up the grounds afterward. His last couple of years as coordinator, he hired a local rock and roll combo to entertain the crowd while everyone waited for darkness to fall. It was some rather harsh criticism of the music that caused him to be disenchanted with the project and step down from his post.

Meanwhile what was going on at his businessplace was well reflected in a feature story that appeared in a 1963 *Carletonian*, Carleton College student newspaper, included in Tiny's biographical file at the *News*. Tiny was quoted, "When I took over this place, there was $330 worth of stuff in it. The last time we took inventory, it was $18,400...."

"His income comes mostly from his many regular customers whose loyalty to Tiny's is attested by the graduation pictures that thickly cover the doors of the cabinets," the story stated.

"'They come in and bring their kids to show me what they produced. Now here,' Tiny said, turning to a group of pictures behind him, pictures in little gold frames. 'This one is his baby,' Tiny said turning to point at one of the cabinet pictures, 'and that one belongs to him.'

The story also said, "Tiny prides himself on running an orderly place. 'I had a lady ask me if her son behaved himself here. "Does he come in?" I asked, "then he behaves." I throwed out a minister's son one day for swearing.'

"Later, in the back room, we talked to one of the pinball devotees. 'It's kind of hard to put your finger on him,' he said, 'but Tiny's a pretty good guy. Tiny's keeps more people out of trouble than the cops do.'"

A story that appeared later that year in the *News* quoted Tiny's famous motto, "If we don't have it, you don't need it." Tiny groaned at the mention of year-end inventory and said, "You can't make a living selling any one thing anymore." Hence the shop had not only tobaccos, but a newsstand, thousands of sundry items ranging from tooth paste to practical jokes, a sandwich bar, and the three tables of pocket billiards.

The story mentioned the incident of a college couple stopping in one Sunday, the young woman inquiring whether Tiny had any nylons to sell. "I've got 'em, but they may not be your size and color," he said, bringing out the shop's assortment. She chose a pair and then informed Tiny that she'd won a bet. She was sure Tiny would have nylons, but her boy friend didn't think so.

The story said, "Although some parents have considered Tiny's shop beyond the pale, largely because of its masculine newsstand, many others have found Tiny a ready ally in helping a boy behave and go straight. 'We've never played billiards on Sunday morning,' Tiny said. 'I'm not going to have it said that some boy didn't go to Sunday school because he was too busy at the pool hall.'"

Tiny rented the building in which his shop was located, but when it came up for sale, he purchased as an investment the historic Scriver Building which now contains the Northfield Historical Society's museum. He did some very necessary repairs, including replacing a leaking roof. There was no historic district nor Heritage Preservation Commission in those days, but he was concerned about the integrity of the building. While it is not flat, the roof he had constructed is much closer to the original roof than the one he had removed.

When Tiny heard about a city council meeting at which it was suggested that a group of elderly men not be allowed to sit in Riverside Park — they were referred to as "characters" — Tiny carried a sign through the downtown area proclaiming, "I am a Character." He then proceeded to establish the Characters' Club in a room in the lower level of the Scriver Building. Friends helped him by providing paint, furniture, a television set and also refreshments. He made a gift of money to the park board for improvements in Riverside Park where the "Characters" liked to sit in the summer.

He also commissioned Darlene Raadt to paint a mural of Division St. and Bridge Square, including the Scriver Building, as the famed Bank Raid of 1876 took place. That was hung for a time in the Characters' Club.

In Tiny's biographical file is a picture of him costumed as Diamond Jim with a black beard and a diamond stick pin. He had won the Chamber's costume contest that was conducted on a Crazy Day.

It was at the end of 1963 that Tiny decided to sell the shop to Steve MacKay who had been employed at the shop for a year after being discharged from service. The *News* story said, "Tiny isn't going to disappear from the downtown scene, however. He plans to continue working in the shop, a sort of habit he's formed since November of 1946."

The story also said that Tiny "figures he's going to be giving Mrs. Johnson the nicest gift in years on their 35th wedding anniversary, March 1, 1964. The couple will move on that date from the second floor apartment at 318 Division (it's 26 steps up there) to the house they've owned for several months at 3 Fareway Drive (Tiny loves to call the addition 'Poverty Park')."

The Johnsons lived there for about three years, but it was Ethel who sorely missed being downtown! So the couple fixed themselves a very nice apartment on the second floor of the Scriver Building.

Of course there wasn't any place there for a flower garden — or a vegetable garden for that matter. Tiny found a plot near Dundas where he could grow the vegetables. But it was at the Don Kimber place south of town where he grew and cared for a humongous flower bed. One year it was planted to form an American flag. When the *News* featured a picture of Tiny in his flower garden, he was quoted, "The funny thing about it all is that when I was a boy, my mother had to force me to pull weeds and work in her garden."

Tiny also had flower boxes planted to petunias and lobelia on the iron railing that guarded the entrance to the Characters' Club, now the Scriver Building meeting room.

In 1970 the Johnsons, Tiny and Ethel, flew to St. Lucia island in the Caribbean where he had helped construct a flight strip during World War II. They also visited friends in the Bahamas and Florida. The next winter they visited friends in New Mexico.

In 1971, Tiny was presented with a Friend of Youth Citation given by the Rice County Youth Emergency Service (YES). In making the presentation, David Hvistendahl, general coordinator of Yes at that time, said that Tiny "had Northfield's only youth center for more than 20 years."

It was in the winter or 1973 that El Dorado, Inc., of Cannon Falls, an insurance, investment and realty company, purchased the Scriver Building from the Johnson's, but the Johnsons continued to live on the second floor.

The community had an opportunity to honor Tiny in 1975 when he was named grand marshal of the grand parade of Defeat of Jesse James Days. This must have been particularly pleasing to him as he told the *News* that he considered the parade the most important part of the celebration.

The Johnsons' 47-year obviously happy marriage came to an abrupt end on July 4, 1976 Ethel suffered a heart attack in the apartment while visiting with friends and died less than a week later at Northfield Hospital.

Her obituary noted, "Mrs. Johnson always worked with her husband, helping to keep Tiny's clean — physically and morally. She therefore had a wide acquaintance among Northfielders of various generations. It may have been her influence that encouraged Tiny to stock many 'emergency' type items — everything from nylons to candles — for the evening and Sunday hours when Tiny's would be the only place open for business in Northfield."

Tiny had been ill when Ethel died and his death followed hers by eight days, on July 12, 1976.

His obituary revealed that he was born on Oct. 25, 1905, at Morris. He grew up there and was married there.

For quite some time he was employed by the Minnesota Highway Department and at the same time worked a shift as a policeman in Morris.

During World War II he not only worked on St. Lucia but helped lay the pipeline along the Alcan Highway.

When he died, Tiny not only had the two daughters, but 12 grandchildren.

8 November, 1996

1947: City Recorder has unusual fishing problems
John Larson could add four-digit columns in his head

It was Bill Schilling who had some fun with Northfield's city recorder, John Larson, in his "Heard on the Square" column in the Aug. 7, 1947, *News*.

Bill wrote, "It was pretty tough on John Larson to have to go way up to Canada to catch the big fish and then to discover when he got there that he had left his tackle at home."

Everybody in Northfield knew that Larson was crazy about fishing, so that's really all Schilling had to say.

About his moving to Northfield from Chicago in 1918, Larson always tied that in with fishing. He would say that he was on a fishing trip when he stopped in Northfield over night — and decided to go no further.

For 12 years he was assistant treasurer and accountant for the Northfield Milk Products Co., a firm on W. Fifth St. that processed and canned evaporated milk. The firm, which was later purchased by Carnation Milk and eventually closed down, was on part of the current site of Malt-O-Meal Plant II.

When Larson was first elected to the city job in 1932, the city recorder's duties did not take full time. He also served as secretary of the Northfield Retail Merchants' credit bureau. For 16 years he was secretary to the Northfield Hospital board. He also served privately as a tax consultant.

One of the *News'* stories about Larson's re-elections, said that while he is "an inveterate fisherman, his best parlor trick is to add a column of figures in his head faster than a rival with an adding machine."

In 1948, the *News* had a story about Larson's adding ability. "The adding machine in the city recorder's office that has been in constant operation for more than 75 years flatly refuses to work on Sundays," the story started out.

"'Not unless I have to,' John Larson said, selecting one of his eight or 10 fountain pens. 'Here, write down a column of figures, four

digits to a column. All right, now draw your line at the bottom. . . . Here's your answer.'

"And it was, right on the nose.

"'I can beat an adding machine any time. How'd I learn to add so fast? I was one of several young fellows at Marshall Field's in Chicago whose job it was to check the tally books turned in by the sales girls each evening. I started work at 4:00 in the afternoon. I had to add fast if I ever wanted to get out of there. A world's fair was going on at the time. I didn't want to hang around the office all night with so many things going on.

The story continued, "'Northfield? Stopped off here on a fishing trip once. Never left the place. Except to go fishing, that is. I can usually win sandwiches and soda pop for the boys by my adding. You know, against the fellow behind the counter wherever we're stopping."

Larson, who was born in Chicago's north side, was employed as an accountant after he reached adulthood. He was married and had two sons and two daughters. (When he died, he also had nine grandchildren and 13 great-grandchildren.) None of the clippings in Larson's biographical file at the *News* reveal the fate of that first marriage, but he was not married when he arrived in Northfield.

While he was employed at Northfield Milk Products, he arrived at work one day and, beaming his brightest, said to a female co-worker, "It's somebody's birthday today." It was Feb. 5 and he meant his own birthday, but the woman exclaimed with delight, "How did you know?"

This story, which appeared in the *News* when Larson retired from his city work, commented, "Whether this bit of attentiveness on John's part did the trick is not clear, but ever since they have shared the same birthday cake."

Larson was the first recorder to occupy offices in the Community Building (now Northfield Arts Guild downtown). There was no city hall as such at the time, but the city owned the building and he found space to carry on his duties. Later, for some years,

the building was used as city hall.

Larson was 77 when he decided that he would not be a candidate for re-election. He continued the work for the hospital board for two more years.

His wife, Mildred, apparently died at about the time he was 79. His obituary said she had been dead for five years and he was nearly 84 when he died.

Until just a few months before his death, he continued private accounting. A large portion of his time was spent with the C. M. Grastvedt Plumbing and Heating Co.

In October of 1959, he underwent surgery after a period of ill health. He then made his home at the St. Olaf Nursing Home. After suffering a stroke, he was moved to Northfield Hospital where he died on Christmas Day of 1959.

The funeral was held at the Moravian Church where Larson was a member. Interment was in Northfield Cemetery.

He was a member of Masonic orders — Social Lodge No. 48, AF&AM, Corinthian Chapter No. 33, RAM, and Northfield Council No. 12, R&SM.

8 August, 1997

1947: Company headed by Carlson to be mustered out

Victor E. Carlson, businessman, active in community

"Northfield's Co. G, State Guard, to be mustered out of service," was a headline in the June 5, 1947, *Northfield News*.

The story began, "With the discharge of its officers and members on Monday, June 9, Co. G, 1st Infantry, Minnesota State Guard, will have completed the period of service to the state for which it was originally organized, a little less than 6½ years.

"Previous to actual entry of the United States into participation in World War II, Headquarters Company, 68th Infantry Brigade, was ordered into federal service early in 1941, and sent to Camp Claiborne, La., for field training.

"Co. G was activated Feb. 24, 1941, with V. E. Carlson as captain, Arthur N. Persons, 1st Lt., and Elsner M. Machacek, 2nd Lt., all three of whom have functioned continuously since the organization of the unit. The three officers had received their commissions from the state Nov. 20, 1940."

The story included some of the mechanics of the mustering out. It also stated that during the time Co. G had been in service, it had trained more than 500 men from Northfield community, practically all of whom were inducted into active service during World War II.

"With the benefit of this training," the story said, "many of the members became officers or non-commissioned officers in one of the branches of the service in which they chose to serve.

"At one time during 1943 company G had 116 men on its roster, authorized by the adjutant general's office because so many students from both colleges wished preliminary training previous to their induction into the armed forces for war service."

The story stated that during the annual inspection in 1946 by the military training office in Omaha, the unit was highly complimented. "The property of the company was first class, supply room spotless, arms and equipment excellent, and all records in good shape. The inspection showed excellent instruction and leadership. . . as evidenced in military courtesy, close-order drill, first aid, interior guard duty and riot formations."

A clipping in Carlson's biographical file at the *News* shows that in May of 1945, the company also came through inspection "with flying colors."

Carlson had been a resident of Northfield since 1920. He was born in March of 1894 at Mankato, attended the Mankato public schools and Mankato Business College. He served in the United States Army in France during World War I, attaining the commission of first lieutenant.

Although he had been in shoe business in Mankato before the war, when he got out of service he took a salesman's job with Wilson & Co., meat packers, with headquarters in Albert Lea. He felt this job would give him the opportunity to look over the territory for an ideal place to open a shoe store.

When he had decided on Northfield for a location, he rented space in the Sumner Building (now occupied by Radio Shack) and began making repairs. But P. G. Reynard, owner of the Boston Shoe Store at 17 Bridge Square (current location of Midge's Hair Salon) made him a proposition for buying that business. Carlson was able to interest his friend, Joseph Ziegler of Mankato in a partnership and the already established store was purchased. The two men officially became owners of the Boston Shoe Store in May of 1920. Gust Arneson and Helen Johnson were employed as clerks.

On the 25th anniversary of the business, Carlson told a *News* reporter that for several years business was very good. "Then a sudden change in styles from high shoes to oxford styles for both men and women created a surplus of unsalable merchandise and a corresponding financial loss. The years 1925–27 were good years, followed by the Great Depression."

In October of 1921, a year after entering business here, Carlson married Hilder Anderson, native of Illinois. She was a graduate of Mankato State and the couple met while he was in the shoe business at Mankato. Before their marriage she had taught for three years at Cottonwood.

In 1933, Carlson bought the interest of Ziegler and Mrs. Carlson became active in the business. Very well liked in Northfield, she now became known as a patient and knowledgeable shoe salesman. The name of the store was changed to Carlson's Shoes.

When the Carlsons retired in 1962, the business was taken over by their daughter and son-in-law, Allen and Margaret Berg, and was called Berg's Shoes.

Through the years Carlson was active in organizations in Northfield.

When the Rotary Club observed its 50th anniversary in 1975, Carlson was the only surviving charter member. He was honored during the anniversary dinner at the St. Olaf Center cafeteria. Five years before, he was honored as the only surviving charter member who was still a member. At that time he recalled that the organizational meeting had been held in the law office of Frank Clark who was the first president. He said that 18 members were needed to obtain the charter, but that 23 signed up.

In 1974 he received a 25-year certificate as a member of Social Lodge No. 48, AF&AM. He was also a member of other Masonic bodies, the Council Chapter, Knights Templar and Shrine.

He was long active in the American Legion. He served as commander of the local post, as Third District commander and second vice-commander of the Department of Minnesota.

An enthusiastic supporter of the Farmer Labor party (and later the DFL), he was appointed by Governor Floyd B. Olson in 1933 as one of 21 delegates to attend the historic Minnesota prohibition repeal convention. Also in 1933, he was named secretary of the education unit of the new Rice county organization of the Farmer-Labor Association.

In 1934 he ran for state senator from Rice County, emphasizing the need for tax reduction. He was not successful, however.

For many years he was marshal of the Memorial Day parades in Northfield. Always uniformed, he rode a horse at the head of the column of march.

He was a member of St. John's Lutheran Church.

Carlson suffered a heart attack in November of 1976. He received care at Northfield Hospital and the Dilley Unit until his death on Dec. 28, 1976. He was 82.

He was survived by his wife and two daughters. Mrs. Carlson, who had suffered a heart condition for more than a decade, died in June of 1980.

6 June, 1997

1947: E. B. Anderson sells Anderson Farm Hatchery
Anderson known as coach, politician, businessman

"Anderson Farm Hatchery sold" was a headline in the June 12, 1947, *Northfield News.*

The story began, "Lester and Mildred Linton of 900 Forest Ave., Northfield, formerly of Bellingham, Wash., have purchased the Anderson Farm Hatchery."

The hatchery had been owned and operated by Mr. and Mrs. Endre B. Anderson. They had started the business in 1922 at the west end of Forest Ave. near what was then their home. In 1925 the hatchery was moved to the West Side business district for three years. It was then moved to the Onstad building, now Dr. Garlie's office, on Division St.

Until 1928 the business was known as the Northfield Hatchery. A story that appeared in the *News* on May 20, 1927, stated that seven incubators with a total capacity of 112,000 chicks every three weeks were in operation. Six of the machines were operating in Northfield and one in Faribault. Five of the six incubators that were in Northfield were in the Onstad building; the other one still in the West Side building.

The story also stated that Anderson, the proprietor, was the president of the recently organized Minnesota Baby Chick Cooperative Association, a post he held for five years. He was a state director for many years and was a director of the International Baby Chick Association for six years.

In 1928 the Andersons bought what was known as the Pengilly or Ames farm, remodeled the buildings and renamed the business Anderson Farm Hatchery. These buildings were located on land that has in recent years been developed by Glenn Lubbers, behind McDonald's, Fashionette Beauty Shop, etc.

The five-bedroom house in which the Andersons lived was in 1961 bought by the Percy Johnsons and in 1974 was moved to 1016 S. Linden. The Johnsons lived in the house for 24 years then sold it in 1984.

The story at the time the Andersons sold the business said that since 1935 the capacity of the company had been 200,000 eggs and that the hatchery hatched and sold from 300,000 to 400,000 chicks each spring.

"An important addition to the hatchery business is the starting of baby chicks. Many customers prefer their chicks to be started from 10 days to four or eight weeks and the Anderson Farm Hatchery has been a leader in this field with the capacity for up to 50,000 started chicks on hand at any one time, and added facilities to carry several thousand up to eight to 12 weeks."

The story also stated that the Anderson Farm Hatchery had pioneered in the practice of chick sexing. This was the art of separating newly hatched chicks into their respective sexes, a system introduced to this continent in about 1933 by Japanese working in British Columbia and northern Washington.

In 1934, Anderson had hired Linton — who had learned the chick sexing art from the Japanese through the Cooperative Poultry Association of Washington — to conduct the first chick sexing school in the Upper Midwest. The school was held at the Anderson Farm Hatchery.

Later a number of schools had been conducted here and several expert chick sexers developed. These included the Andersons' three sons, Lende, Elliot and Einar. With the increased demand for the service, the brothers organized the Anderson Brothers Chick Sexing Service, serving more than a hundred hatcheries in Minnesota.

Following the sale of the business Anderson intended to continue managing the sexing service with an office in the hatchery and also expected to assist Linton in the operation of the hatchery. He and his wife were to move to the house they had purchased at 508 E. Third.

Endre Benoni Anderson was born in Yellow Medicine County in April of 1892. He attended the public schools of Cottonwood, then came to Northfield. He graduated from St. Olaf College in 1914 after having won fame as an Ole baseball player. He also played basketball for the college.

Keenly interested in athletics, he was a high school athletic coach at Yates Center, Kansas, from 1914 to 1916; at Rochester, Minn., from 1916 to 1918; and at River Falls Normal in Wisconsin for one year.

He came to St. Olaf as a football coach in the fall of 1919, the year St. Olaf joined the Minnesota Intercollegiate Athletic Conference. When he was elected to St. Olaf's Athletic Hall of Fame, it was stated that he had built the Oles "into a strong athletic position, his football teams during the first several years winning 33 games and losing 14." Later he also coached basketball. In 1926 he was made director of athletics and remained an active coach of only football.

He served as secretary of the Minnesota Intercollegiate Athletic Conference for 16 years.

When he decided to resign from coaching at St. Olaf in the fall of 1928, he had become a representative of an incubator manufacturer in addition to operating the hatchery.

In politics, Anderson regarded himself as a progressive and in 1938 he became the Farmer-Labor party's nominee for Congress from the First District. The *News* said editorially, "He is respected for his character, his personality, his sincere liberalism by everyone in this community who has had the pleasure of contact and acquaintanceship with him. Anderson is a high-minded man, tolerant of others' opinions, thoughtful in his approach to public questions and keenly alive to the aspirations of the common man. . . . He would be certain to represent the First District in Congress in a creditable manner."

An election pamphlet urged voters to "elect a real progressive to Congress who knows and understands the problems of the farmer, the worker and independent businessman from actual experience." But Anderson was not elected; the First District was strongly Republican. He did serve the party as Northfield, Rice County, and First District chairman.

For several years he was a member of the Northfield Rotary Club. He was a member of St. John's Lutheran Church.

In January of 1917 he had married Rebecca Lende of Cottonwood. They had attended Cottonwood High School at the same time although she was a year ahead of him. They never dated in high school, but according to family legend, he often told her that he was going to marry her. She laughed it off.

After they had graduated from different colleges, she was teaching at Albert Lea when he took the coaching position at not-too-far-away Rochester. He resumed his overtures and she finally agreed to marry him.

A tragedy of their lives was the death of their son Elliott as a bomber pilot in the South Pacific during World War II. In his memory the Andersons gave a 1100-acre farm near Pillager to St. Olaf in 1946. Income from the fund was to be used to endow a chair in the department of economics.

By that time Anderson had purchased several large tracts of land in North Dakota and Minnesota and had settled down to be a "gentleman farmer."

In about 1950, he suffered a serious illness, but he recovered what appeared to be hearty good health. Therefore his death in August of 1953, when he was only 61, was quite unexpected. While preparing to leave on a trip to the Anderson summer home near Pillager, he collapsed, dying from coronary thrombosis.

Mrs. Anderson lived until December of 1989, dying at age 98. The last 25 of her years, she lived in the state of Washington, relatively close to family members.

13 June 1997

1947: Ervin G. Farrankop celebrates 80th birthday
Farrankop successful at grain elevator operation

"Ervin G. Farrankop, who maintains he has been in the grain business most of his life by virtue of being born in a granary, celebrated his 80th birthday anniversary Nov. 17," a story began in the Nov. 20, 1947, *Northfield News*.

The story continued, "He hastens to explain that his parents, Frank and Louise (Tralle) Farrankop, were residing in a granary, the only building on their new farm, during the housing shortage of 1867, and that he has spent all but a few months of his life in a bona fide house, moving with his parents into a brand new farm house in the spring of 1868.

"He has served as manager or director of several grain elevators, garnering a reputation as one of the community's outstanding citizens."

The story tells about a family birthday party that was held in Farrankop's honor, then reveals that on Monday evening he had been the honor guest at a turkey dinner given by the board of directors of the Northfield and Dundas Farmers' Cooperative elevators at Moffett's Dining Room. The 25 present included the directors, managers, their wives and the office staffs.

During the program of music, a reading and short congratulatory talks, Farrankop in response reminisced about his 80 years and more particularly about the 10 years he served as manager of the Northfield elevator.

The story said that "included in the flood of birthday remembrances which has come to him within the past few days is a telegram from his close friend, United States Senator Edward J. Thye, congratulating him for exemplary citizenship during his 80 years."

Whoever wrote the story added, "Farrankop has been 'retired' since 1935 and during that time has traveled to the west coast four times. Though he is not supposed to be doing anything, his activity would put many younger men to shame. 'I just don't get paid for it!'" he was quoted.

When Farrankop was interviewed by the *News* in 1951, he told of his father, a native of Germany. Frank Farrankop had served in the Germany army during the Baden rebellion. As soon as his army term was completed in 1850, he immigrated to America, working at first on farms in New York state and Illinois.

Farrankop told that his father then forged further west, traveling part way by river boat and landing at Hastings. He took a stage coach to Cannon City which was then a thriving trade center, and found a job hauling goods from the Hastings port to the Cannon City general store.

He was married and had five children when he settled on a farm 1¾ miles out of Dennison. The granary was set on pegs and was as yet unsided. A couple of months later Ervin was born.

Ervin grew up on the family farm and attended the same district school as Tom Bunday and A.W. Bierman, both of whom became prominent Northfielders. The Bierman and Farrankop farms adjoined.

His teacher persuaded Ervin to complete his public school education in Northfield, so he attended school here in the year 1881–82. He attended Carleton Academy the following year.

While attending school in town, Farrankop stayed at the home of a Hunt family that operated a grocery store and butcher shop. He recalled that the family operated a butcher wagon in the rural areas in the summer, giving many farm people an opportunity to buy the only fresh meat they had between butchering seasons.

Farrankop recalled, "Mrs. Hunt wouldn't let me go out with the other young fellows at school in the evening and I resented it at first. But I soon found out that I had my lessons the next day and they didn't. So I continued to do what she told me."

In the spring of 1883, Farrankop returned to the home farm and dickered a little in farm implements. But he hankered to follow his older brothers who had taken government land at Brookings, S.D. He went out there when he was old enough to take land, but he returned to Dennison community in the fall of 1896.

According to the 1951 interview, farmers around Dennison were then agitating for the building of a farmers' elevator and they interested Farrankop — who was farming — in the venture. When the elevator was opened the group hired an elderly Northfield grain man to run the business. He planned to commute daily by horse and buggy, but after a couple of round trips, he and the board decided to call off the deal.

At that point, Farrankop, with no elevator experience whatsoever, was drafted to his first job in the grain business. He managed the Dennison elevator for 20 years.

Farrankop recalled that in those days a young man made sure he had a paying position and was able to provide a home for a wife before he considered marrying. He thought that he had probably waited too long as he was nearly 35 years old when in July of 1902 he married Ida Fish who had been a teacher in the Dennison school district. He did have a house paid for when they married.

When their only child, Helen, was old enough to attend high school, the family moved into Northfield.

They bought the northwest lots at Union and East Fourth. The house that is now in the middle of the block on Fourth, between Benson Funeral Home and the corner house, was then in the middle of the property. They had a new excavation dug and moved the house to the west. They then, in 1917, had the corner house built and Farrankop lived there the rest of his life.

Farrankop had a notion to retire, at least from the grain and elevator business, when the family moved to Northfield. But the United States was entering World War I and conditions were so unsettled that when an opportunity presented itself, he was back in the business.

He was driving across town when J. W. Alexander, manager of the Northfield Farmers Elevator stopped him and begged him to come and assist at the elevator. They worked together three years until the board of directors sold the business to a new group which organized under new cooperative laws.

At that time Sheffield Milling Co. and Commander Elevator Co. of Minneapolis contacted Farrankop concerning the mill and elevator they had just purchased at Kenyon. He managed that combination for two years.

Meanwhile the Northfield elevator suffered from poor management, Farrankop said in the 1951 interview. The board fired the manager and when the books were examined, it was found that the business was nearly broke. The directors persuaded Farrankop to take the management.

This was in 1925 and by 1928 he had wiped out the deficit. He continued as manager with a splendid record until his retirement in 1935 when he was 68. He continued to serve on the board of directors until he was 82. He then requested the nominating committee not to submit his name to the stockholders at the elevator annual business meeting.

Before Mrs. Farrankop became very ill with

Parkinson's disease and died in September of 1946, the couple made four trips to California. They made the leisurely trips by auto, exploring several western states.

Farrankop said that he took little time out for hobbies during his busy life, but that he did love to drive. In his mid-80s he still would drive across the state when the mood struck him. He frequently drove around the community to visit old friends. The 1951 story closed, "They're glad to see him coming too, for an afternoon with Erv is one of pleasant recollections and hearty laughter."

As he looked back at his more than 40 year of service to grain elevators, Farrankop recalled that managing meant more than buying and selling and keeping books. "If the machinery broke down, I had to be a mechanic too. The hours were long."

When he was 87, Farrankop suffered a stroke, lived less than a week and died Dec. 16, 1954, at Northfield Hospital. The funeral was held at the Congregational-Baptist Church in the same block as his house and burial was in Oaklawn Cemetery.

His daughter, Mrs. I. B. Johns, earned her Ph.D. in foods and nutrition and became a university teacher in the eastern states.

21 November, 1997

1947: George Campbell's dairy extensively remodeled
Campbell takes lead in resettling displaced persons

"Campbell Dairy plant enlarged" was a headline in the Aug. 28, 1947, *News*.

The story began, "Culminating a remodeling program that has extended over a period of 18 months, the improvement campaign at the Campbell Dairy Products plant, 114 E. Fourth St., is now nearing completion.

"Although new office furniture and fluorescent lights are not as yet installed, the new equipment in the work rooms and most of the area afforded by the enlarged building is already in use.

"Following a design by architects Lein & Tudor of Minneapolis, the remodeling began March 10, 1946. A second story was added to the building and the entire building was finished with white stucco."

After various construction facts, the story listed new equipment in use in the plant. Included were two 200-gallon stainless steel spray type pasteurizers, a 100-gallon stainless steel cream pasteurizer, a stainless steel bottle filler and capper (capacity 36 quarts or 55½ pints per minute), a plate type new style stainless steel milk cooler, a 20 h.p. Kewanee gas burning boiler, a 1,000 gallon stainless steel milk tank for transporting raw milk from the Twin City Milk Producers Association plant, a 200-square foot refrigerator room cooled with two new-type forced air Freon blowers. The cooler room is maintained at a 45-degree temperature."

A story that appeared in the *News* when the project began stated that the work was made necessary by increased business volume.

George Rigg Campbell came to Northfield and started the business in 1925. He was born in Hopkins, Mo., in August of 1891. He grew up on a dairy farm and attended high school at Fort Scott, Kans. He graduated from the Kansas State Agricultural College at Manhattan, Kans., taking a four-year course in dairy husbandry.

He spent seven years in the employ of the United States Department of Agriculture's

bureau of dairy industry, primarily inspecting butter plants. He and Ebba Olson Campbell, to whom he was married in June of 1920, lived in Washington, D.C.

It was Campbell's vision to establish a very modern dairy in Northfield and he built the plant that is now the home of Olson Brothers Construction, Inc. He bought the business of O. H. Shirley who had established milk routes in the city. Differing from farm dairies in the community, Shirley had purchased his milk and had hired delivery men who were not members of his family.

A 1927 story in the *News*, two years after the establishment of Campbell Dairy, reported that the company that was supplying milk, cream, butter, buttermilk and cottage cheese to the city "is now occupying a place of growing importance in the dairying business here. Through this retail plant, the products of the Northfield farmer are furnished the Northfield householder — a relationship of both economic and community necessity."

The story said that the business was one of the most up-to-date retail milk plants in the state. "It is completely equipped with the most modern sanitary equipment obtainable for handling pasteurized milk and other dairy products.... With the aid of modern equipment, it is possible to handle a large volume with the services of but four people."

A 1935 story said, "Ten years of growth and success are being commemorated this week by the Campbell Dairy Products Co. which has assumed a position of prime importance in the dairying activity of Northfield and community."

The story cited constant improvements in equipment and steady growth in distribution. Milk delivery was still by horse-drawn conveyances and the story said that "teams of the firm have jogged more than 75,000 miles since the time that the company was organized in 1925. Two teams made daily runs, one of 6½ miles and the other of 13 miles."

There were stories about those horses. They knew the routes as well as their drivers. If the driver was to serve several houses in the neighborhood, he would take a quantity of dairy products in a wire basket and the horse would proceed to the appropriate place for the driver to get aboard again.

Campbell of course saw the horse give way to the truck as well as vast changes in equipment, and finally the change from the milk bottle to the carton.

Campbell owned the dairy solely until 1929 when Carl Gulbrandson became a member of the firm. Gulbrandson operated the dairy during the years 1929–1933 when Campbell operated Old Home Creameries in the Twin Cities, specializing in the manufacture and distribution of cottage cheese. That new firm was then jointly owned by Campbell and the Twin City Milk Producers Association. When Campbell returned to Northfield, Gulbrandson went to St. Cloud

to operate the St. Cloud Dairy.

When a feature story about Campbell was written for the *News* in 1981 — when Campbell was 90 — Dorothy Anderson, a dairy employee for many years, was quoted. "He was a fine man to work for," she said. "He treated all of us like family and he was interested in our families. It was fun to get up in the morning and go to work."

She said that because of the excellent working conditions, Campbell kept his employees for many years and they became able to operate the plant effectively whether he was there or not. "For that reason he was able to devote a lot of time to civic activities," the story said. Anderson recalled, "He thanked us for it. He said he would not have been able to do it if it were not for us."

His most notable activity was with the resettling of displaced persons from Europe in the wake of World War II. Campbell worked quietly, but tirelessly to meet the immigrants at the Twin Cities train depots, to arrange for housing and furnishings, to find employment for them, to help them adjust to Northfield living over many months. There was not a day when Campbell would not be involved in visiting and helping the new residents.

In 1964 when St. John's Lutheran Church celebrated the 15th anniversary of the arrival of many of the DP's with a reunion, the *News* reported that "Campbell gave a moving appraisal of the new citizens' contribution to this community, reminding his audience of the high academic achievements in the Northfield schools and colleges of their children, of their high credit rating in the community, of their conspicuous absence from the police records, and their above-average giving in the church."

At this event, Campbell was presented with a scrapbook of letters and pictures "in gratitude for his quiet, but untiring efforts in behalf of all the new arrivals in Northfield." Also during the program a wire was read from the director of the Intergovernmental Committee for European Migration in Geneva, Switzerland. It said in part, "Please transmit to your congregation and particularly to George R. Campbell my sincere appreciation of the magnificent work accomplished during the past 15 years in the resettlement of more than 250 European refugees. The achievements of St. John's Lutheran Church are a challenge to other groups throughout the world...."

A story in Campbell's biographical file at the *News* refers to a letter written by Charlotte Lobitz about the arrival of her family in St. Paul during a snow storm. She said, "There finally is the man we are waiting to meet. A tall, white-haired gentleman said, 'Hello, my name is George Campbell and welcome to America.' I wonder if he speaks German. No, he doesn't, but there is something about him that makes us feel at home and for the first time secure and we are not any more afraid."

Campbell was active in the Lions Club, working with many of its projects and continuing his membership until he was 89. He was a lay representative on the Evangelical Lutheran Church council, Southern Minnesota district, until the 1960 synodical merger.

He served on the Northfield Board of Education. He once ran for mayor, losing by only 19 votes to Andrew Meldahl. In 1936 he headed the Northfield Association, a forerunner of the Chamber of Commerce. He was for many years a director of the bank that is now Community National Bank.

Campbell retired, selling his dairy to Meyer Brothers of Wayzata in February of 1964.

The Campbells, who were parents to two sons and two daughters, celebrated their golden wedding anniversary in June of 1970.

Campbell had excellent health until he was in his very late 80s. He received care at the Minnesota Odd Fellows Home (now Three Links) in his last years. He died there on Nov. 8, 1983, at the age of 92. Ebba Campbell died at Three Links Care Center in September of 1990 at the age of 96.

A couple of other clippings in the Campbell file are of special interest. One includes a picture of Campbell buying the license plate for his private automobile. It seems that in the days when there was a new license plate for each year, Campbell was traditionally the first in line, buying the first plate sold in Northfield.

The other clipping is about a trip Campbell made to Europe in the spring of 1948. He sailed to Europe on the Holland-American Noordam at a time when Americans were frightened of the forthcoming elections in Italy. Only 42 including Campbell made the voyage. After driving 5,000 miles through central and southern Europe (he was in Italy the day of the elections when nothing went wrong), he returned to America on the *Queen Mary* among 2,000 passengers. He had spent five weeks with a son-in-law and daughter while the son-in-law was stationed in Germany.

That story ended with a paragraph, "High spot of the trip for Campbell was Venice with its historic canals and bridges. There he found the most friendly people and the most interesting shops. 'And here I'd always pictured it as a town full of beggars!' he said."

29 August, 1997

1947: W. T. Nelson elected Junior Chamber president
Nelson serves Northfield community in many ways

"Junior Chamber elects officers" was a headline on the front page of the April 24, 1947, *Northfield News*.

"It looks like a busy year ahead for Willard 'Red' Nelson," the story began. Elected alderman from the first ward at the city election held March 11, he was chosen president of the Northfield Junior Chamber of Commerce for the coming year at the annual meeting held April 16."

The Junior Chamber, then in its second year, according to the story, has since changed its name to Jaycees.

Nelson unexpectedly got rid of one complication in his life. At the end of summer, he purchased a house in the second ward and he and his family moved out of the first ward on Sept. 24. He therefore resigned from his three-year post on the city council.

He had stated before the election that he was interested in seeking the office because he felt it was time that some of the younger men in the community took part in policy making in the city.

He said he felt that the rehabilitation, orientation and solution of other problems of World War II veterans would be an important community function. As a veteran himself, he felt he could serve with understanding.

He also pledged to examine carefully all possibilities for income for the city, for social and economic betterment.

He also expressed fears that the city was inadequately protected from fire and pledged his support in replacing the antiquated fire fighting equipment then possessed by the Northfield Fire Department.

At the beginning of 1948, Nelson was awarded the Junior Chamber of Commerce Gold Key at a presentation dinner. Mayor H. B. Kump made the presentations, citing among other things the accomplishments of Nelson while he did serve on the council. He spoke of Nelson's work on the gas franchise project, his aid with the successful registration of more than 2,200 voters in the city, his work concerning the installation of parking meters. He also called attention to Nelson's "fruitful activities as president of the Junior Chamber of Commerce."

That year Nelson also became a member of the $150,000 honor volume club of Bankers Life Co. as a result of his production record during 1947.

In 1952 he was elected worshipful master of a Masonic order, Social Lodge No. 48, AF&AM. In 1955, he was chosen president of the Rice County Realtors Association. He was elected president of the Northfield Lions Club in the spring of 1956. In 1958 he was elected commander of Eugene H. Truax Post No. 4393, VFW. That same year he was elected to the board of directors of the Minnesota Association of Mutual Insurance Agents for a three-year term. He represented one of six Minnesota regions on the board.

In the spring of 1960, Nelson filed for election as mayor of Northfield. He stated that in serving on the city planning commission (three terms) he had come to feel that the commission should have more authority. He also said that it appeared that the city health officer did not have adequate authority to clear up some kinds of problems. Nelson expressed support for a proposed charter amendment that would give the Northfield Hospital board more autonomy.

He also stated, "It is my understanding that the mayor should express his views and opinions and guide the council on its actions. However, I will definitely state right now that if I am elected mayor and should the council make a decision which is contrary to my thinking, I will accept its judgment and no grudge or ill feeling will be carried out of the council rooms by me. I sincerely hope that I can persuade the members of the council to act the same way. I may be wrong sometimes, and the majority rules."

Nelson won the office in 1960, but in 1961 he had to run again as a new city charter had been adopted and all officials were required to participate in the city's first fall election.

In the meanwhile he was elected president of the Minnesota Association of Mutual Agents. He and his wife Margaret attended the convention of the national association which was held in Washington, D.C. Nelson was not only a delegate to the convention but was also a member of a national committee.

In the fall of 1963, he was one of the Minnesota mayors who were given an Operation Understanding tour. The United States Army Air Defense Command sought to acquaint key citizens of the Midwest with the nation's defense installations in Texas, New Mexico and Colorado.

When Nelson retired from office, the *News* editorially saluted him for a job well done. "We think he has been an excellent mayor," the editorial stated and continued, "Perhaps the thing that will be remembered longest about Mayor Nelson in connection with his official position, which is but one of the many civic contributions he has made, is the courtesy and consideration he has shown. There

are many irksome aspects to the mayor's job as well as its time-consuming demands, but he has met all of the responsibilities with a kindliness of manner and a respect for other citizens that everyone appreciates."

During the first council meeting of the new year, outgoing Mayor Nelson was presented with the Northfield Area Chamber of Commerce Award of Merit in recognition of outstanding service to the city.

Mr. and Mrs. Nelson participated in an outing of the Minnesota Professional Insurance Agents Association at Mazatlan, Mexico, in the late winter of 1978. The *News* pictured Nelson with the 149-pound striped marlin that he caught. The couple also traveled to California at least twice during that decade.

But in November of 1979, Mrs. Nelson, 68, died at Northfield Hospital.

The next fall, Nelson and a former Northfielder, Millie Linton of Phoenix, Ariz., were married in Phoenix. The couple came to Northfield after the wedding. A block party reception was given in their honor and they remained here for several weeks.

A short time after they returned to Phoenix, Nelson underwent surgery for an aneurism. He was able to return to his home on Christmas Eve.

In the spring of 1983, Nelson, long-time owner of W. T. Nelson Realty in Northfield, sold his business and the building at 414 Division to Christine Hager who had been a member of the agency

After Millie Nelson's death, he moved in the summer of 1994 to Dallas, Texas, where one son and other relatives lived. He had been hospitalized in Phoenix for several months before the move.

He was hospitalized again in Dallas and was expecting to undergo surgery when he died at age 77 on Dec. 17, 1994. The ashes were brought to Northfield the following summer and a memorial service was held at the First United Church of Christ (Congregational) where Nelson had been a member. Interment was at Northfield Cemetery.

Nelson was born near Dennison, but

moved with his parents, the Thomas J. Nelsons, to a farm just east of Northfield when he was ready to attend the first grade. He attended Washington School and graduated from Northfield High School in 1934. He attended Augsburg College, Minneapolis Business College, and later completed four courses concerning insurance given by the Bankers Life Co.

He worked at the Gamble Store in the late 1930s, then went into insurance work in 1940. He served in the U.S. Army for 20 months during World War II, 13 of the months in the European theater.

He was already married, having wed Margaret E. Moore, daughter of Dr. T.J. and Eva Moore of Rochester, on Nov. 6, 1938. The couple had one son and three daughters.

In addition to activities already mentioned, Nelson's obituary stated that he had been a state vice president of the Jaycees; a director of the Northfield Area Chamber of Commerce; president of Northfield Golf Club; president of the Northfield Baseball Association; president of the Cannon Valley Shrine Club. He was a member of the American Legion and of the Odd Fellows Lodge. He served as chairman of the board of trustees of his church and served on the church's Boy Scout committee.

25 April, 1997

1948: Henry B. Kump is re-elected Northfield's mayor

Kump enthusiastically participates in civic activities

Henry B. "Hank" Kump was re-elected mayor of Northfield in March of 1948, it was reported in the March 11 *Northfield News*.

Kump was more experienced than you might think at being mayor by that time. He had become acting mayor of Northfield on three different occasions upon the resignation of a mayor. This was the first time he had stood for election and he was unopposed.

When O. S. Jackson was called into active military duty during World War II, N. M. Jacobson was vice president of the city council and became acting mayor. However in February of 1942, Jacobson decided to run for mayor and resigned from the council. Kump, who had then been vice president of the council, became acting mayor.

Later when Mayor George Zanmiller (Kump's brother-in-law) left for World War II service, Kump once again found himself acting mayor.

In the municipal election of 1944, Andrew Meldahl was elected mayor. A story about the reorganization meeting of the city council that appeared in the *News* stated, "Kump, vice president of the council who has been acting mayor during the absence of Mayor George Zanmiller, escorted the mayor-elect to the chair and presented Meldahl to the council as their official head for the next two years. In making his presentation, Kump expressed his appreciation in having been able to serve the city as its nominal head for several months, despite the fact that at times he found some aspects of the position far from pleasant."

Meldahl was re-elected mayor in March of 1946, but in early April he accepted a posi-

tion as training officer for the Veterans Administration. His headquarters were in Minneapolis and he and his wife continued to live in Northfield for a couple of years. However he soon resigned his position as mayor and Kump once again was acting mayor.

The *News* commented, "His experience on several of the important council committees over a period of years has given him a keen insight into the city's affairs."

This time, after serving two years as acting mayor, he was elected and served two more.

Henry Bernard Kump was born in Northfield Oct. 12, 1896, the son of Michael and Dorothea (Wiederholt) Kump. He attended public schools here, then served in the transportation corps during World War I. Part of his service was overseas.

On Aug. 30, 1921, he married Elizabeth Zanmiller. They lived in Northfield — 202 N. Spring — throughout their married life.

Kump worked for W. E. Johnson at the Ole Store and when Johnson bought the D. D. Springsted department store in the West Side business district, Kump had a financial interest. He was named manager of the store, located in a substantial brick building that was many years later razed for the relocation of TH 218 (now 3).

Eventually Kump bought the downtown business. For many years he operated a grocery store located on Water St. in part of the building now occupied by the Eagles Lodge.

It was a friendly store with loyal patrons. As an example of family-style business procedures there was a dog who lived a couple of blocks from the store, who arrived at the store every forenoon at just about the same time. Kump would wrap something a dog would like in butcher paper and tape it shut.

The dog would carry it home and eat it there. This went on every day excepting Sunday when the dog had somehow learned the store would not be open. Perhaps he connected Sunday with a different sort of activity at home. Also the dog did not know about daylight-saving time and arrived an hour late all summer.

Kump was long active in Northfield Post No. 84, American Legion. When he was elected commander in 1930, the *News* commented, "Kump is one of Northfield's younger business men, and an aggressive and energetic leader in community affairs. There is no project for the betterment of Northfield that fails to interest Hank or to enlist his enthusiastic support. Northfield Post is assured of a helpful and progressive administration under his leadership." When he was reelected in 1931, the story began, "Proud of a fine record of service and achievement during the past year, Northfield Post No. 84, American Legion, at its annual meeting Tuesday evening reelected Henry B. Kump as commander." With Kump's picture, the cutline read, "In recognition of his energetic leadership, Kump has been reelected commander of the Northfield post."

In 1940, Kump was named president of Northfield's Willkie-for-President club. Through the years he served as president of the Northfield Businessmen's organization, a forerunner of the Northfield Area Chamber of Commerce. He served as president of the Northfield Rotary Club. He was vice-president of the South Central Minnesota Area, Boy Scouts of America. He belonged to the Northfield Council, Knights of Columbus.

He died on July 26, 1959, after an illness of more than a year. He was at his summer home at Lake Mazaska when he was taken seriously ill and brought to Northfield Hospital where he died soon after. He was 62.

Mrs. Kump lived to be 82, dying in 1975. The couple brought up a son and a daughter.

Mr. and Mrs. Kump are buried in the National Cemetery at Fort Snelling.

13 March, 1998

1948: History of Solomon Stewart, first mayor, read

Stewart takes leadership roles in new settlement

A paper on Solomon P. Stewart, first mayor of Northfield village and second mayor of the incorporated city, was read at the spring meeting of the Rice County Historical Society in 1948.

It had been written by his son, Carl L. Stewart of Los Angeles and was appropriately read by Elizabeth Kelsey of the St. Olaf College faculty. The Kelsey family long lived in half of the house that Stewart had built on what was to be E. Second Street, on the portion known as Skinner Hill.

The paper began, "In the late 1830s two young men, Solomon P. Stewart and Jerome I. Case, left their homes in Massachusetts and went together to seek their fortunes in the West. They stopped at Racine, Wis., where they got work helping to run one of the first threshing machines ever made.

"The Lake Michigan winds did not agree with Stewart, so he decided to go farther west into the then wild forests of Minnesota where he became an expert ax wielder, felling trees and chopping logs.

"J. I. Case remained in Racine and eventually became a millionaire manufacturer of farm machinery.

"Stewart's work and life in the forest built him up into an unusually strong and husky man. He was six feet tall and weighed 200 pounds. After a few years of this work in the Indian-inhabited forest, he decided to use his savings to start a general store. He selected the little village of Northfield and his store was on the ground floor of a two-story frame building on the west side of the Cannon River, known as the Mansion House."

The paper revealed that Stewart married Mary Allen and they had two children, Granville and Belle. (Both of the children died relatively young, leaving no offspring.)

After the death of Mary, Stewart married Emily Tuttle who had come to Rice County with her parents from Connecticut and had settled at Faribault. Stewart's new family

lived over the store in the Mansion House. There twins were born to them — Carl Linden and Earl Burton. The latter died when he was only nine months old. Stewart's only surviving son was likely in his mid 80s when he wrote the history of his father.

The paper continued, "In those days there was no railroad to Northfield and goods had to be shipped by boat to Hastings, then hauled overland. Later when it became known that a railroad was coming, Stewart decided to go into the lumber business. The first freight to Northfield over this railroad was three cars of lumber to start the new lumber yard which was located just south of the new railroad depot.

"Stewart was doing well in business and decided to build a home in the residential section of town. He bought nearly half a block running south of Second St. and west of Union St. There was a large lawn, flower garden and croquet grounds. He built a fine residence which was later enlarged to 12 rooms. There were a large vegetable garden and a big barn west of the house, along with many shade and fruit trees. It became one of the finest homes in Northfield." The house was known to have the first bathtub in Northfield.

Two daughters were born in the house, Carrie Eveline in 1871 and Mary Blanche in 1873.

The son included in the paper a couple of stories that had come down through the years. He began, "Stewart was a man of few words and with a quiet and kindly disposition. He never used tobacco or drank liquor of any kind or used profane language and would not permit such language in his presence. One day a man, an ex-prize fighter who ran a saloon near the depot, was in Stewart's office and started swearing. Stewart told him to stop, whereupon he used more bad language. Stewart grabbed him and threw him out onto the dirt road in front of the office. The ex-ring man picked himself up, looked at Stewart with amazement and said, 'No one ever did anything like that to me before.' Stewart answered that he would get it done to him again if he swore in Stewart's office. The ex-pugilist walked slowly away and from then on was one of Stewart's most loyal adherents."

The other story began, "One summer the country was infested with tramps. They were so numerous and dangerous that housewives were advised to keep their doors locked and not to open them unless they knew who was calling. One evening at about 6:00, Stewart was in the barn when three big, tough-looking tramps knocked at the side door of the house. Not getting any reply, they went around to the rear and saw Stewart coming up from the barn. They approached him in an insulting manner and demanded food. Stewart took out his watch and said, 'I will give you three minutes to get off my property or I will throw you off.' They looked at Stewart and at his square shoulders and heavy build and turned and walked away."

The son's paper continued, "S. P Stewart and J. I. Case were great horse lovers and good judges of blooded stock. Stewart had a large, powerful horse shipped up from Kentucky that traveled so fast that one had to hold onto the seat. He also had a team of beautiful bay mares from Kentucky that were so much alike they could not be told apart. Stewart sold this team to Governor Pillsbury for $500, a lot of money in those days. J. I. Case had his stables in Racine filled with the finest horses obtainable. He was the owner of the fastest trotting horse in the world, named Jay Eye Cee after himself.

"One summer Case and his family were visiting the Stewarts in Northfield. The country east of Northfield was a rolling prairie covered with wild grass in which lived a species of grouse called wild prairie chickens. Stewart and Case were fond of hunting and went out one day to get some chickens as they were very nice eating.

"Shotguns then were all muzzle loaders. The powder had to be poured in and paper wads rammed down with a ramrod. Then the shot was put in and also wadded down.

"The pointer dog going ahead of the men suddenly discovered chickens in the tall grass and pointed. Case discovered he was out of wads, so reached quickly into his pocket and pulled out some paper money which he used for wadding. The pointer dog charged, the chickens flew up and Case got his grouse, although it was a pretty expensive one."

The son then wrote of Solomon Stewart's relationship to Northfield's famous bank raid. "In September of 1876, eight gangsters from Missouri, two James brothers, three Younger brothers with three others, came to Northfield and attempted to rob the First National Bank. Joseph Lee Heywood, the cashier who had been a clerk in Stewart's office several years before joining the bank, refused to open the vault and was killed. In the meantime two robbers who were riding on horses up and down the street in front of the bank were shot and killed by Northfield citizens. The bandits came out of the bank, jumped onto their horses and rode away.

"Stewart was mayor of Northfield at this

time and he got together the posse that followed after the surviving bandits until they were surrounded near Madelia."

The paper then revealed that Stewart became a member of the state legislature "where he did lots of good work for his county and the state." Stewart was also president of the Citizens State Bank of Northfield up to the time of his death in 1883. Stewart was for many years owner of Northfield's leading hotel, then called the Archer House. He also owned half interest in a building on Division Street occupied by a furniture company. (This was probably at 415–417 Division.)

"Mr. and Mrs. Stewart were members of the Congregational Church, active in church work, and they were also greatly interested in and helpful in many ways to Carleton College. Mrs. Stewart was highly respected by all and loved by those who knew her well."

Stewart died Feb. 22, 1883, at the age of 60.

His wife Emily died July 14, 1894, also at the age of 60. They are buried in Northfield Cemetery along with their baby son Earl. A tall granite monument with an urn-shaped top marks their resting place.

When the imposing Stewart house — with shutters, ornamental brackets under the eaves and a widow's walk on the roof — was divided, part stayed at the original site at 208 E. Second, and part was moved to 206 E. Second.

When the Stewarts lived there, no roadway had been built up the hill. There was instead an elevated walkway with railings on both sides. Stewart and the owners of the properties on the other corners of Second and Union joined in drilling a 60-foot well on the west edge of Union and in the middle of what became Second Street, obtaining their drinking water there for many years.

12 June, 1998

1948: Ralph Fjelstad joins faculty at Carleton College
Fjelstad serves fellow citizens in various public positions

Dr. Ralph S. Fjelstad, who with his wife Margaret now lives in the Northfield Retirement Center complex, has been a Northfielder for 50 years. The *Northfield News* of Aug. 12, 1948 announced that he would be joining the Carleton College faculty as assistant professor of government on the Edward B.C. Congdon Foundation.

He remained on the faculty until his retirement in the spring of 1981. Through the years, he has served the Northfield community in several significant ways and has also held important posts in the Republican party.

Dr. Fjelstad, who was born at Emmons, spent his childhood at Stoughton, Wis., and graduated from high school at Thief River Falls. He received his A.B. summa cum laude from Concordia College in Moorhead. He did his graduate work at the University of Minnesota and Northwestern University as a Norman Wait Harris Fellow. He received his Ph.D. in political science from Northwestern in 1948.

During World War II, he had served as director of personnel for the war department at the Illinois Ordnance Plant at Carbondale, Ill., and then had served in India with the Army Air Forces as a classification specialist.

In the spring of 1952, it was announced that Fjelstad had been awarded a Ford Fund Fellowship for the academic year of 1952–53, one of three offered in Minnesota and of 246 given throughout the nation. The Ford Foundation would pay the full salary for each fellow plus expenses incurred in the study undertaken. Dr. Fjelstad studied the functioning of Minnesota's state legislature. Among the specific research problems he studied was the efficiency and workability of Minnesota's non-partisan setup of that time. Minnesota was then the only state in which members of the legislature were elected without party designation.

Among the early assignments in service to the community that he undertook was chairing the Community Chest in the spring of 1956. He also served on the Northfield advisory committee of education and as secretary of the Northfield Charter Commission. He served on the board of deacons at St. John's Lutheran Church.

In November of 1957 Fjelstad, by then full professor, was appointed temporary consultant to the United States Small Business Administration. He was to make a comprehensive study of local development foundations in Minnesota. The announcement, released by U.S. Senator Edward J. Thye, stated that Minnesota was a leading state in the adoption of development foundations at the town and city levels. There were in Minnesota more than 200 such foundations promoting and encouraging industrial and commercial growth.

Fjelstad frequently presented lectures on political matters to organizations in Northfield and the Twin Cities. In 1960, he gave a 10-week series of discussions of governmental matters for the political action study group of the Northfield Area Chamber of Commerce.

On leave from his teaching duties during the late winter and spring of 1961, Fjelstad was awarded a Louis W. and Maude Hill Family Foundation travel grant. Accompanied by his wife and three children, he spent four months in Oslo, Norway, studying the unique Norwegian parliamentary system.

A story in the *News* explained that although it is referred to by the British term of parliament, the governmental system for Norway was set up much like the federal government of the United States except that all members are elected to the lower house and then selected by their co-members for service in the upper house. Fjelstad said that he was interested in determining how the arrangement would affect parliamentary and general government leadership.

The family sailed to Europe on the Stavangerfjord and the children attended school in Norway.

The family made a camping trip on the continent before returning to Northfield in time for the opening of school in the fall.

That fall Fjelstad was one of 10 Minnesotans appointed to the Governor's Tax Study Committee asked to make a study of the tax problems of the state and report in advance of the next legislative session. Serving with the 10 persons were four ex officio members and the majority and minority leaders of the house and the senate.

The following February, Fjelstad was named chairman of a commission to study state constitutional revision. The membership of the committee represented a cross-section of the state's citizens and both political parties were represented.

It was in the spring of 1963 that Fjelstad filed for election to the Northfield Board of Education. He told the *News* that he had been interested in education at all levels for a long time and that he was then especially interested in the public schools since he had three children attending them. "I want to be useful for education in my community," he said. The children were then in second, sixth and eighth grades.

Fjelstad was elected, there having been five candidates for two posts.

Fjelstad was re-elected in 1966. He did not seek re-election in 1969.

It was in his role as a member of the school board that your writer, then an editor of the *News*, particularly enjoyed observing Fjelstad. She recalls that he would sit quietly, listening to the expression of opinion — sometimes quite spirited — by the other board members. Finally he would speak, very ably summarizing what had been said, and then making his recommendation. So clearly did he analyze the various situations, that his opinion was more often than not adopted.

At the state Republican convention in the summer of 1963, Fjelstad was elected third vice-chairman with the assignment of stimulating and motivating interest and action for the Republican party within the academic community.

That fall he addressed the Young Republican Workshop at Lake Independence on party image, charging that the party was being hurt by its image. "What people think we're like and what they think we'll do is the basis on which they decide whether they will or won't support us," he explained.

As reported in the *News*, he said that the Republican image, as seen by Democrats, had come to be the party of the few and the well-to-do, with no broad views, no warm hearts — the party of memory. He suggested that to improve the image, the Republicans "had better make it clear that we are interested in human needs first. We should say that we are concerned about the freedom of the individual and that if something has to be done, we're not going to say 'no' to it.

"The feeling that if something needs doing, the Republican party won't do it if it means increased government is a real problem," he said. "This is the kind of image that doesn't win elections."

In January of 1964, Fjelstad was the subject of a feature story in the *Minneapolis Tribune*, one of a series of profiles of outstanding teachers at Upper Midwest colleges and universities written by Richard P. Kleeman of the *Tribune* staff. It was headed, "Carleton's Fjelstad fans political fires." Kleeman cited "Fjelstad's untiring efforts to bring the real world of public affairs into the classroom, and thereby kindle students' interest in political participation."

Kleeman quoted a former student of Fjelstad, "Instead of making politics seem like something dirty, he teaches the fun, the intrigue and the importance of it. He has a feeling and spirit many other teachers fail to capture."

Noting Fjelstad's various ventures into public life, Kleeman said that he was "about as far from the ivory-towered theoretician as an academic type can get."

But noting Fjelstad's GOP activities, Kleeman had asked whether classroom objectivity might be lost by open partisanship. Fjelstad had replied, "I feel it's imperiled but not lost. In fact, at times I find myself a bit more severe on the Republicans than the Democrats."

Kleeman reported that Fjelstad, with Ford Foundation support, had given a course on the legislative process while the Minnesota legislature had met in the spring of 1963. "His class of 15 students made the state capitol their laboratory at least one day a week. 'Station wagon discussions' as they traveled with Fjelstad to and from St. Paul were as much a part of the course as the final oral and written reports" the students gave.

In the fall of 1964, Fjelstad resigned from his state GOP post. He had already indicated that he could not support Goldwater in his GOP candidacy for United States president.

In the spring of 1970, Fjelstad, then professor of government and chairman of the department of government and international relations at Carleton was elected to a four-year term as a member of the commission on institutions of higher education of the North Central Association of Colleges and Universities. That commission's principal responsibility is to determine standards of accreditation and evaluation for colleges and universities in the states which compose its voluntary membership.

In the aforementioned Kleeman story, Fjelstad was quoted, "The wonderful thing about teaching is how often you can start over!"

14 August, 1998

1950: Frank DeMann sells his interest in DeMann Motors
DeMann was one of the earliest Chevrolet dealers in area

"Frank DeMann sells interest in DeMann Motors" was a headline in the Dec. 28, 1950, *News*.

The story began, "Frank DeMann, actively engaged in the garage business in Northfield since 1919, sold his interest in DeMann Motors, Inc., to his son-in-law, Russell Enfield, the past week. He will continue residing in Northfield although his future plans are indefinite."

The story continued, "DeMann first became a Chevrolet dealer in this area in 1915 and is now one of the oldest Chevrolet dealers — in point of years of service — in the Great Lakes region."

Enfield, the husband of the former Dorothy DeMann, had been employed in the business for several years. He had at first been employed in the mechanical department, but Frank encouraged him to try sales, something he learned to like intensely. (The DeManns also had a daughter Frances who as an adult lived on the west coast.)

Frank DeMann was born May 6, 1889, in Rice County, the son of Charles and Margaret (Meehl) DeMann. He graduated from the school of agriculture of the University of Minnesota in 1908. He then operated the family farm on Circle Lake in Forest Township from 1908 until 1913. On June 27, 1911, DeMann married Ruby Herkenratt at her parental home in Dundas.

The DeManns moved from the farm into Dundas in 1913 when he became employed as an engineer in the flour mill there.

In 1914 he became a partner with his father in the business DeMann & Sons for farm machinery sales at Dundas. Soon they decided to sell automobiles also and in 1915 the DeManns established one of the first Chevrolet dealerships in the Great Lakes region. Later Frank's brother Jake joined the firm. While Frank sold cars, Jake was service manager.

While he was living in Dundas, Frank De-

Mann served as village clerk and for several years, as a member of the Dundas board of education.

In 1919, Frank established a garage business and Chevrolet dealership in Northfield while Jake continued the business at Dundas. The first location of Frank's Northfield branch was in the north end of what is now the Perman Building — into which the Art Store recently expanded. He later recalled that he had to take the moldings off the doors of that building to get a car inside. "Even though the cars were mighty narrow in those days," he said.

He moved three more times — including to a site where the post office is now located — before putting up his own building at 618 Division (current location of Lansing Hardware) in 1929. A large addition to that building was under construction in 1950 when

DeMann retired.

DeMann served for a time on the Northfield City Council. He was a member at the time that there were strong feelings in the community in the late 1930s as to whether a municipal light plant should be built here. (Two elections were held regarding this matter and the plant proposal was defeated.)

He also served as a director of the Northfield Iron Co., long a leading industry here. He was a director of the Northfield National Bank, now the Community National Bank. He was a member of the Lions Club, elected president in 1933. He was a member of the First Baptist congregation, part of the Congregational-Baptist Church, now the First United Church of Christ.

He loved to hunt and fish and also collected Indian relics.

Eventually the DeManns established a winter home at Englewood, Fla., on the Gulf of Mexico. Directly after he sold his interest in DeMann Motors, Mr. and Mrs. DeMann took off for Englewood, but they normally returned to Northfield in the spring, residing at 107 W. Fremont during summer.

Twelve years later, the DeManns did show up in the spring although Frank had been seriously ill in Florida for some time. However he died in Northfield Hospital on July 2, 1962.

Interment was in Oaklawn Cemetery.

Mrs. DeMann survived her husband by nine years, dying on March 31, 1971, in the Dilley Unit of Northfield Hospital.

30 December, 2000

1950: George Christian presides as water pump is installed

Christian kept water running with little financial support

George Christian, for 27 years superintendent of the city water department in Northfield, periodically warned the city council of the possibility of problems with the city water supply. But the council constantly transferred water tax money to support other departments of the city, such as street maintenance, and no reserve was ever allowed to accumulate. Hence it was never possible to follow one of Christian's recommendations — there was never any money to do so.

A story about the use of the water tax that appeared in the *News* years ago joked that Northfield is constantly supported by some kind of liquid. It used to be water, but at that time the municipal liquor store had assumed the burden.

At any rate, one of Christian's dire predictions came true in 1950 when the water pump broke down. Strangely the city had finally acted on the recommendation to establish a second well for the growing city, but it was nowhere near completion. The page one headline on Jan. 26, 1950, stated, "City council acts promptly to relieve water shortage emergency — buys new pump."

The story began, "An emergency meeting of the city council was held Wednesday noon at the water pumping station on Water St. and the council unanimously passed a motion to purchase a band new water pump for $4,452.50.

"The pump was in possession of the McCarthy Well Co. of St. Paul and its journey to Northfield was begun immediately, with the promise that it would be in operation Thursday morning.

"Crews of the water department who have been on duty since the old pump failed Monday evening, will work continuously until the new pump is in operation.

"George Christian, superintendent of the water works department, told the *News* that he heard a loud grinding noise at 7:00 PM

Monday. Simultaneously, water pressure fell to zero."

After a rather technical description of the cause of the breakdown, the story continued, "The pump had been in operation only since 1945. Leonard Hager, chairman of the water committee, blamed the breakdown on faulty material obtained during the war years.

"The new pump, manufactured by Fairbanks-Morse, contains all of the features that would have been ordered in the normal course of events for the new well now being sunk by the McCarthy Co. at the Fremont and College pumping station.

"The new pump, fortunately, was in St. Paul awaiting delivery to another locality, but on urgent pleas from city officials, the manufacturer released it for emergency installation here.

"Since Monday, Northfield's water supply has come from the two colleges and the Northfield Milk Products plant." (The milk plant was on W. Fifth St. in the current location of Malt-O-Meal Plant No. 2.)

The story continued, "The only source of water for the city hospital has been in 10-gallon cans carried in by college employees. Toilets and sterilizers there were inoperative Wednesday.

"Armstrong's Locker plant (at the Ole Store) was able to operate only during the night when private consumption fell off. The plant's compressors are water-cooled. Customers were denied entrance to the locker Wednesday in order that air inside would not be warmed by the constant opening of the door.

"A water main in the Northfield Milk Products plant burst Wednesday morning when a steam-operated pump built up a pressure in excess of the pipe's capacity. Workmen replaced the main Wednesday night."

George Christian was born Jan. 15, 1879, at Dodge Center. He came to Northfield community with his parents when he was a young boy. As a young man, he learned the plumbing trade. He also at one time engaged in ice business, cutting ice on the Cannon River and delivering it with horse-drawn vehicles.

In 1912 he married Annie Lillemoe and they resided in Northfield all of their married life.

Christian remained in the plumbing business here until 1928 when he was appointed to the city post.

When, more then four years after Christian's death, the city was finally planning modernization of the city water system and doubling the city water rates to support the changes, Christian's son Clayton of Waterford recalled that his father had recommended these improvements 30 years before.

A story in the *News* on Jan. 2, 1961, stated that Clayton Christian said, however, that it was a tribute to the planning of the city fathers of the late 1800s and early 1900s that the system had worked as well as it did for so many years.

The story continued, "Northfielders who have resided here for as long as 30 years can remember that George Christian soundly warned the council that the water fund reserve should be built for replacement of equipment. He told city officials repeatedly that the mains would need to be enlarged and the reservoir was becoming inadequate. Long before his retirement, there were problems with low pressure in the summertime when lawns were being watered extensively. "Christian devoted untiring efforts to keeping the department running smoothly."

When Christian first took over the water department job, he handled all phases of the work including figuring the customer bills, filling out and addressing the statements by hand. Finally, after several years, the council told him he didn't need to do all that work himself. The department grew from serving 750 customers when he undertook the duties to 1,500 in 1955 when he retired.

Christian carried his gardening interests into the pumping station. There were always green plants inside the station. Outside the old station in the 100 block of N. Water he built a handsome cobblestone and concrete pool in which he grew water lilies and kept ornamental fish.

He also established an elaborate rock garden in the back yard at his home, corner of College and Fremont. Finally he and his sons covered the entire exterior of their frame house with van-colored field stones. His obituary said, "Christian always had one project in process and another in view."

The *News* of Aug. 8, 1955, reported that Christian had submitted his resignation to the City Council. "In accepting his resignation, the council unanimously adopted a resolution commending Christian for his many years of faithful service to the city"

Christian died a year later, on Sept. 8, 1956, after being seriously ill for six months. He was 77. He was survived by his wife and three sons. Interment was in Northfield Cemetery.

The aforementioned 1961 story noted that "the pumping station and water well were at the Water St. location when Christian began the superintendency in 1928. About 20 years ago, while he was still active, the old well was severely criticized by the state department of health and a new well was dug at the location of the present pumping station (at College and Fremont). Several years later, a second well was added."

The story noted that the currently recommended improvements (in 1961) included the erection of a two-million-gallon reservoir tank on Manitou Heights, replacing the 66-year-old entirely inadequate tank with a capacity of 240,000 gallons (which sat among buildings on the St. Olaf campus). An enlarged system of mains from the pump house at College and Fremont, across the town to the new tank, was also planned. "Northfield will again have adequate water pressure and a large enough supply of water in times of dry weather or serious fires," the story said.

28 January, 2000

1950: Mader retires from school board after 18 years

Harvey H. Mader is in business in Northfield for 33 years

H. H. Mader, retiring member of the Northfield School Board, was introduced at the 1950 Northfield High School commencement by P. B. Hinds, board chairman.

Hinds noted that Mader "had served faithfully for 18 years, missing only two regular board meetings during that time. For the past eight years he has been treasurer of the school district."

"I served all those years because you elected me, and because I like young people," Mader said. He added that he was retiring because younger people should now participate in the work of the board.

Mader was born on the family farm in Dodge County near Oakfield, Wis., on Sept. 1, 1887.

He graduated from the Oakfield High School and received his B.A. degree from Ripon College in 1910. He taught for nine years in high schools in Upper Michigan and in North and South Dakota before deciding to go into business for himself.

He decided that the tire business looked like a field that would really develop with more and more automobiles being made. He bought the tire shop at the corner of W Second and Water from A. J. Plaisance. (This site, now vacant, was most recently a bike and ski shop.)

The first winter he was here, heavy snowfalls tied up traffic completely. He recalled in an interview on his retirement that "no wheels were rolling so I closed up from early December until March 9. Horse manure was piled two feet high downtown by the time

spring came."

He remembered that in 1920 the first pavement in these parts was laid part way from Northfield to Faribault. With the advent of pavement, trucks converted from hard rubber tires to pneumatic tires. He recalled selling his first pneumatic truck tire to the Adams Lumber Co. here. For the one tire and tube he received his year's coal supply and $125 in cash.

For a new Dodge in 1920, the cost of equipping it with five of the new cord tires was $230. These tires were manufactured completely by hand. The best that one worker could produce in a day was eight tires.

Mader remembered that a typical Sunday's business included the fixing of 25 flat tires. That was in the day of fabric tires. He also remembered when a Sunday trip from St. Paul to Northfield on the dirt road would result in a motorist being covered by an eighth of an inch of dust.

When more cars were being used, Mader expanded his tire shop into a gas station. Through the years, he expanded his building twice, the second time after a fire did some damage.

The retirement story stated, "Surrounded by youngsters wanting him to fix their bicycles is the way one of Mader's friends pictures him in complete contentment. His patience and ability in repairing bicycles during the past 33 years while he has been in the tire and oil station business has won for Mader a place in the hearts of many youngsters. And since 1919, many of those youngsters have grown from kids with broken bicycles to faithful customers."

Another newspaper story about Mader stated that he seemed to "belong" almost from the day he arrived in Northfield.

During his 33 years in business here, he was very active in community affairs. Besides his service on the school board, he served as president of the Lions Club, served as master of Social Lodge No. 48, AF&AM, as a trustee of the Congregational Church (now First United Church of Christ), and on Boy Scout committees.

He was forced to slow his pace in December of 1950 when he suffered a heart attack. He sold his business in the fall of 1952.

Mader said on retirement that his hobby was driving a car. "I like to get out and see the country." He said that he and his wife had taken their first long trip in 1951, driving East through the New England states.

Shortly before he retired, Mader sold the car he had been using to your writer's father. It was in beautiful shape. Dad learned from the shop employees that every time Mader returned from a drive, he washed the car and covered it with tarp.

On retirement, Mader said that he also needed to look after his farm in Wisconsin. He and his wife were visiting that farm — which had been in the family for 102 years — and with his sister in nearby Oshkosh when he suffered a heart attack in May of 1957. He received care for two days in an Oshkosh hospital, then died on May 5. He was nearly 70.

Surviving him were his wife, the former Eunice Hughes who had lived in Oshkosh; two sons, Harvey, Jr., and Richard. His burial was in Oaklawn Cemetery.

A tribute that was part of his obituary noted that the years had brought revolutionary developments in the industry of which Mader was a part, "but Harve Mader was the kind of man who grew with them. He kept young as a patient friend of countless boys and girls who came to his shop to have their bicycle tires fixed. There was always the same pleasant smile for them, the same good service, that their elders received at Mader's. There was genuine regret throughout the whole community when Harve Mader, following a heart attack, found it necessary ... to retire from active business, and many warm expressions of appreciation of his services and his citizenship."

9 June, 2000

1950: Norm Olsen inspired by Minneapolis meeting

Olsen helped boost every kind of civic project

Norman "Norm" Olsen, secretary of the Northfield Chamber of Commerce (Area hadn't yet been inserted in the name), had just returned from a meeting of the Minnesota Commercial Secretaries in Minneapolis when he was quoted in the Feb. 23, 1950, *News*.

"I did not realize what a serious business session this would turn out to be," he reported. "I received a wealth of ideas that I hope can be used locally."

Each of the secretaries attending the meeting was asked for a promotional statement regarding his or her town. Olsen's, which was quoted in the *Minneapolis Tribune*, was: "As a community of Cows, Colleges and Contentment, Northfield has much that makes for pleasant living. Of the town's 7,500 population, 3,000 are students at Carleton and St. Olaf colleges."

There is no way of knowing what ideas Olsen gleaned or whether he was able to use them. But anyone who remembers Northfield a half century ago knows that Olsen worked diligently with every kind of project that was dreamed up for the city.

He was not a Northfield native. He was born in Bird Island on June 17, 1910. He came to Northfield with his family in 1919 and graduated from Northfield High School in 1928. He received a bachelor of science degree from the University of Illinois in 1933.

He planned a career as a civil engineer and sought work on the West Coast. But that was the time of the Great Depression and strikes had also resulted in the lay off of many employees. When there wasn't an engineering job to be found in California, Olsen went to Oregon, only to find the same conditions.

He just missed getting a surveying job that would have taken him far into the mountains for several months. He ran out of cash and took a job as a dish washer.

After a few months he was compelled to leave the area because the damp climate was proving to be hard on his health. Many years later he told a *News* reporter that had the climate agreed with him, he might have toughed it out and remained in the West. Instead he returned to Northfield in 1935.

Soon he was working as an engineer and foreman for a road construction company in Iowa. A year later he became an engineer and surveyor for the Minnesota Highway Department.

He lived part of the time in Northfield and decided to buy the Art Floral Shop in a 22-foot-square space of the Scriver Building in 1937. He did not assume management until he stopped working for the highway department in 1942.

During World War II, for 3½ years, he was a member of the faculty of the Navy Pre-Flight school conducted on the campus of St. Olaf College.

When he took over the Art Floral business, the shop sold flowers, gifts, cameras and greeting cards and also provided photo finishing.

Taking snapshots was very popular at the time. A "sleeper" was the greeting card. While people had sent birthday cards for years, suddenly the cards were much more attractive and were becoming cards for all occasions.

Olsen soon decided to discontinue gift items and instead stocked phonograph records. Either he had a good sense of what was soon to develop, or he was just plain lucky, because records became very popular.

In the spring of 1948, KDHL — Faribault radio station — started planning a remote studio in Northfield. This was many years before KYMN was established and the city was served only by non-commercial WCAL.

In June of 1948, the remote studio began operating in his store so that Olsen could put on his own programs for advertising purposes. A little more than a year later the studio began broadcasting programs for other Northfield advertisers. Soon a daily program, "Breakfast in Northfield," was aired. A Saturday afternoon show featured Johnny Western, Northfield youth who later blossomed in the entertainment world nationally. A Friday evening program was "Session for Mouldy Figs," featuring Dixieland jazz.

In 1949, Olsen began the manufacture of Joco Records cut by Doc Evans and his Dixieland band. Evans, who worked successfully with both classical music and jazz, was for a time a member of the Carleton College faculty. The commercial pressing of the records was done in Hollywood. Distributors were located all over the United States and also in Switzerland, England, France and Sweden.

Olsen knew many accomplished Dixieland musicians. Once the director of folk artist music for Columbia Records was guest on his "Mouldy Figs" program.

Finally it became impossible to operate in the cramped space and Olsen moved across the street to 411 Division (current location of Present Perfect), opening on Sept. 1, 1952.

In later years, Olsen was known to say that the original tiny location had one distinct advantage. From his window he could look across the street into the Montgomery Ward order office where Borghild Dale was employed. A courtship followed and the couple was married on Jan. 15, 1944, in Minneapolis.

In 1947, Olsen was awarded the Junior Chamber of Commerce (now Jaycee) Gold Key as the man younger than 36 who had done the most for the city of Northfield during the past year.

A story in the *News* stated that the award was based on service to the Junior Chamber as secretary in which "Norm Olsen has been the spark in bringing to a successful fruition several civic projects sponsored the past year by the Junior Chamber such as the 1946 Fall Festival, cooperation with 4-H clubs and other projects. Another secretaryship held by Olsen is that of the Northfield Golf Club which acquired a new club house last year and a substantial increase in membership."

Olsen helped establish Northfield's annual festival marking the anniversary of the Northfield Bank Raid. He served on the public library board and was a member of a city charter commission. He was a member of St. John's Lutheran Church.

His obituary stated that he was at the time of his death at Rochester, a member of the Masonic Lodge, Sons of Norway, the Minnesota Association of Professional Engineers.

The couple brought up three daughters and Olsen said in a 1952 interview that he considered Northfield an excellent place in which to raise a family. "Everything considered, he is very thankful for the chance factors that led to his settling in his home town."

However in 1962 he accepted a position as instructor of engineering subjects at the North Dakota State school of Science at Wahpeton, N.D. He sold his shop here and the family moved to Wahpeton.

In 1969 he took a similar teaching position at the Rochester Area Vocational-Technical School.

He had known of a heart condition for several years, but at the time of his death, he had spent a normal day of teaching and an evening of relaxation at home. He died from heart failure while sleeping on Feb. 19, 1974. He is buried in Northfield's Oaklawn Cemetery.

25 February, 2000

1951: Arneson has been rural mail carrier since 1919
Fred Arneson concludes 38-year postal career

A story about Fred B. Arneson appeared in the Nov. 22, 1951, *News* as part of a series about local mail carriers. The story was as follows:

"Rural Route 2 carrier, F. B. Arneson, entered the employ of Northfield post office in 'the wet spring of 1919 — the year we couldn't drive automobiles until mid-May. We used horses all winter.'

"Beginning as a regular carrier, Arneson first served Rural Route 1 for nearly 21 years. He transferred to Route 2 eleven years ago.

"Leaving the post office at 9:30AM daily, he first drives about four miles west on TH 19, then loops through country roads and returns to Northfield. His second loop takes him  to Waterford and back. A third portion of his day's journey takes him about six miles east on the Wall Street Road. A famous customer on that loop is Senator Edward J. Thye. Arneson's return to Northfield is on TH 19.

"'There have been a lot of improvements in the country roads since 1919,' he said. 'I'm fairly lucky with some paving on my route. Of course there are some dirt roads too.' Arneson is back at the post office at 2:00PM.

"Through the years Arneson has owned 17 or 18 different cars. The first three were Model T Fords. He also had three models of the now extinct Star. The rest have been a mixture.

"At present Arneson uses nylon seat covers for good sliding to that right-hand window where the mail goes out.

"Outside of his job, Arneson admits that his principal interests are his home. And through the years he's had quite a bit to be interested in." The story then listed his 10 children.

One of those children, Ruth Coates of Northfield, just died in Nov. 2, 2001, at age 85. Two sons have also died by now, but only one of them preceded their father in death.

A son Ralph has returned to Northfield to live in recent years.

Fred Arneson was born in Norway on April 29, 1887, the son of Arnold and Susannah Arneson. The family came to America in 1890, settling in the area of Castle Rock, Minn. Arneson attended the Castle Rock schools.

On May 10, 1916, in Solor Lutheran Church, Webster, he married Lillian Henrietta Knutson. She was born in New Market Township but grew up in South Dakota.

The newlywed couple lived for a couple of years at Webster where Arneson operated a store and the Webster post office.

They moved to Northfield in 1918, a few months before his being appointed a rural mail carrier. The Arnesons for many years — until their deaths — lived at 809 E. Third.

Arneson concluded his postal service on Tuesday, April 39, 1957. He was honored that evening at a steak dinner at the Riverside Cafe, the event given by his fellow employees.

A citation of commendation from the United States Postmaster General was presented to Arneson by the Northfield postmaster, C.C. Heibel. Arneson's co-workers gave him a leather billfold which contained a gift of money. It is likely that the billfold was made by Heibel who was an expert at leathercraft.

Congratulatory remarks were made by men representing the various departments of the local post office — Rolf Solum for rural carriers; Walter Dean for city carriers, Joseph Wang, clerks; Charles Hatfield, custodial service; M. F. Meyers, supervisors. Frank Gallagher spoke in behalf of retired employees.

In 1966 the Arnesons celebrated their golden wedding anniversary with an open house at Christiania Lutheran Church.

All of the family, except for Harold who had died, was present. The *News* story about the event reported that "music was presented by a family choir, most appropriate the Arnesons reveal, since the family members especially like to sing together during any kind of reunion."

Ralph Arneson who then lived in DeKalb, Ill., expressed the welcome as the program began. A meditation was given by another son, the Rev. Frederick Arneson who survived his parents but died in 990.

Mrs. Arneson died at age 78 on June 27, 1970. She had fallen and had broken her hip earlier that month.

Arneson lived another six years, his death rather appropriately discovered by a mail carrier. When the carrier on E. Third St. realized in early April of 1976 that no one had picked up Arneson's mail for a couple of days, he called in at the door and got no answer. He then phoned the post office from which the message was forwarded to the police department. Police entered the house and found that Arneson had died. He was 88.

Burial of the couple was at Highview Christiania Cemetery near where Arneson had lived for many years.

He was a member of the Letter Carriers Association. He was also a member of St. John's Lutheran Church in Northfield.

24 November, 2001

1954: Charlie Nichols, farmer and columnist, dies

Nichols leads a busy and colorful life for nearly 88 years

"Charlie Nichols, pioneer resident, dies at 87 following hip fracture" was a headline in the July 8, 1954, *News*.

Few obituaries start with such a statement as, "A man who brought joy and good humor to his friends because he knew how to enjoy to the full the simple things of life, Charlie (C.O.) Nichols died early Wednesday morning, July 7, in Northfield Hospital. He was nearly 88."

The story continued, "Working in his vegetable and flower garden, which had given him great pleasure after his retirement from farming, Nichols fell July 1 and fractured his hip. Although he had lost his hearing and a series of slight strokes had impaired his eyesight and his ability to hold a pencil, Nichols was in fair health and very good spirits until this serious accident brought his death. He never fully regained consciousness after surgery on his leg.

"Until he was unable to write, Nichols shared his pithy opinions on farm problems and things in general with Northfielders through his 'Heard on the Square' column in the *News*."

A granddaughter, Marianne Fox of Minneapolis, a nurse, was here to take care of Nichols during his hospitalization.

Nichols was born Oct. 18, 1866, in an apartment in the 500 block of Division St., the son of Joseph and Ellen (Sherpy) Nichols. His father was engaged in shoemaking at the time.

Two years later the family moved to a farm east of Northfield where Nichols grew to manhood. He attended the District 78 rural school and Carleton Academy.

While he was still single, he took a trip to England and France with J. L. DeLancy, local horse merchant who brought Percherons from Europe.

On Oct. 15, 1871, Nichols married Mary E. Spink; the Rev. F. B. Cowgill, pastor of the Northfield Methodist Church, officiating.

The young couple at first lived on a farm near Cannon City. But a year later they moved to Nichols' home farm where he had grown up and they farmed there until their retirement in 1938. They then moved to the house at 710 Washington in Northfield.

In retirement, Nichols raised bees and sold honey.

Nichols served as president of the Northfield Seed Co. for several years early in the 20th century. In 1911 he was appointed by Minnesota's Governor Eberhart as delegate to the national corn show in Columbus, Ohio.

That same year, Professor C. P. Bull of the agriculture department of the Minnesota Experimental Station spent several days at the Nichols farm, selecting corn to be used in trial plots.

The story in the *News* stated that the Nichols farm had been chosen to be turned into a trial station, the purpose of which was to try out new types of seed corn, to breed better and earlier types of corn and to attain a type especially adopted to this locality.

The story stated, "Bull spoke highly of the cooperation he is receiving from the Northfield Seed Co. in this work."

Nichols served as president of the Pioneer Farmers Club in the late 1920s. He was active in other farm clubs and he served as president of the Dennison creamery. For many years he served on the Northfield Township board of supervisors. He was town clerk for 10 years. He also was a member of the District 78 school board.

The couple celebrated their 50th wedding anniversary in 1941 and celebrated again on the 55th wedding anniversary. They were able to celebrate the 60th anniversary in 1951.

Nichols was survived by his wife who died the following year; also by three daughters, Ruth Bickel (Mrs. William F.), Jessie Fox (Mrs. M. D.) and Hazel Wright (Mrs. Frank).

One son had died in infancy.

Nichols' 'Heard on the Square' column appeared irregularly, usually about once a month. In 1949, he wrote an ode to the pancake.

He wrote, "I was reading the other day about a scientist who while exploring a cave in which cave dwellers had lived thousands of years ago, found proof that these people who lived in the stone age baked pancakes on stone griddles. He also found thin stone paddles, supposed to be pancake turners. So that puts the humble pancake way back in ancient history.

"Then came the iron age and Mr. Pancake found himself baking on an iron griddle over coals in the fireplace.

"In most all the countries in the north temperate zone, the pancake is counted as a popular dish. In some countries pancakes are eaten at noontime, in others in the evening. But in the good old U.S., we eat them for breakfast.

"Do you old timers remember how we hurried the morning chores to get to those buckwheat cakes? How, when we opened the kitchen door, there was a thin blue haze in the air? Mother was already at her morning task.

"The appetizing smell of coffee and frying sausage and the faint aroma from the buckwheat cakes was something I have not words to describe.

"I don't know how it was possible for a small boy to pack away so many buckwheat cakes. Remember when you came in for breakfast, Rover slipped in with you and sat patiently by your chair, waiting until the edge of your appetite was worn down a little and you would sneak a bit of pancake to him?

"Poor mother had the worst end of the deal. It was quite a job to bake cakes for even an average family. One good thing about the pancake, it is a winter fruit and mother has a pancake vacation in the summer."

10 July, 2004

1964: Death saddens Revier's community
Revier enters business while at NHS

A headline on page one of the April 23, 1964, *News* read, "Bill Revier, Beloved Northfield Man, Dies." Revier had not lived in Northfield for a while, but he was still very much loved and highly regarded here, as your writer can remember.

Revier had had three careers, two of them in Northfield, the other one benefiting people all over the state of Minnesota. He had conducted a camera and gift shop in Northfield for many years, he had been engaged in management and public relations work for Northern States Power Co., and he had served as state commissioner of veterans affairs under four Minnesota governors.

The story of Revier's death began, "William E. Revier, native Northfielder who never forgot his hometown and the old friends, died Saturday morning, Apr. 18, 1964, at the Veterans Hospital in Minneapolis.... An active force in the business, civic and social life of Northfield for half a century, Bill Revier's passing brought a sense of loss to scores in this community. 'He was in a class all by himself; there'll never be another like him,' was the warm tribute on many lips."

The story revealed that Revier was born in Northfield in 1896 and grew up in the town where his father, W. H. Revier, was postmaster. Bill graduated from Northfield High School in 1915, went into service during World War I. While he was still a junior in high school he opened a store, Bill's Kodakery.

Another story that appeared in the *News* at the time of Revier's retirement stated

that he could recall giving a camera to O. E. Rolvaag with which the St. Olaf professor "took pictures used in preparation of his famous novel, 'Giants in the Earth.'"

The business was conducted in several different buildings through the years. In 1931 he was named chairman of the year-old Northfield Retail Merchants organization. The *News* stated, "Bill's middle name ought to be 'Booster,' for there is no man in Northfield who for a period of years has more steadily and consistently boosted every project of civic betterment and development than Bill.... He brings to his new place of leadership not only a fine spirit and enthusiasm, but an understanding of the problems to be solved and needed enterprises to be undertaken by the businessmen of Northfield."

In 1933 Revier accepted a position in the Northfield office of NSP, then located in the 400 block of Division St. He was to assist R. H. Moses, superintendent, who was in ill health and unable to perform all of his duties. Revier continued operation of his shop, then called Bill's Art & Gift, for a time. (Some people never stopped calling the shot by its catchy initial name, Bill's Kodakery.)

After being active in Chautauqua here as a very young man, Revier became a charter member and spirited songleader of the Northfield Lions Club. His ability as songleader and master of ceremonies caused him to be in demand for a variety of events not only in Northfield but in neighboring communities, eventually much further afield. He served as a song leader at the Lions International convention in Toronto in 1931.

He was a commander and service officer of the local post of the American Legion. Later for several years he was a member of the rehabilitation committee of the Minnesota department of the American Legion. He was a member of the VFW and of Masonic orders here.

He was an early member of Northfield Golf Club and returned in 1961 to speak at the dedication ceremony and dinner dance at the newly enlarged clubhouse. He described fun and problems of the early days, recalling that the first golf course was near the Cannon River at the southwest edge of Northfield. The present course was built, he revealed, in the mid-twenties when 70 interested Northfield men each contributed $100 to purchase the 40 acres of land upon which the first nine holes were built.

Known for his relief work for war veterans, Revier was appointed first Minnesota director of veterans' affairs. The post had been created during the 1943 session of the state legislature, the new law having consolidated the various state veterans' agencies. His four-year appointment was made by Governor Harold Stassen just before the latter's resignation and it became effective July 1, 1943.

Revier continued to serve under Governors Edward J. Thye (a fellow Northfielder), Luther W. Youngdahl, C. Elmer Anderson and Orville L. Freeman. When Freeman was elected, he asked Revier to resign although there were two years remaining of his term. Freeman said that he wanted to built up his own administrative family. But Revier continued to serve out his term, completing his state service in 1957. A story in the *News* at the time of his retirement said that the state post had included "heavy responsibilities and great activity during the periods after the close of World War II and the Korean Conflict."

During the period he served the state, Revier was on leave of absence from NSP and he worked from 1957 until 1961 in public relations for the power company with headquarters in Minneapolis.

Before his death, he had been in ill health since November. He had undergone surgery in March.

Concluding the story of Revier's death was the following paragraph: "For Northfield an era seems to have ended with Bill Revier's death. One of his old friends has said of him: 'Bill was one of those wonderful beings whose loyalty, high spirit and generous goodwill helped everyone who ever knew him to meet both "triumph and disaster" and added courage and the feeling that all's well. His sense of humor and jolly spirit brought light and warmth wherever he was, and behind them was a continuous outgiving to others. It is hard to believe that this cheering light is gone — but really it is still here and always will be as long as memory lasts. I know I shall never forget him for among all the friends of a lifetime, there is not another Bill Revier.'"

The obituary was written by the late Carl Weicht, long editor of the *News*. He was a bit younger than Revier, but the two were close friends. One wonders whether Weicht himself was the "old friend" quoted at such length.

Revier had a long and happy marriage to Esther Lee, born in Northfield a half year later than Revier. She graduated from Northfield High School and in 1920 from Carleton College. The couple was wed in the summer of 1922. They had one daughter, Suzanne. Mrs. Revier died about a year ago on March 27, 1988. Husband and wife are buried in Oaklawn Cemetery, Northfield.

13 April, 1989

1965: Death ends 60-year Carl connection

L.A. Headley active in community

"Headley Dies, Funeral Set for Friday," was a page one headline in the May 27, 1965. *News.*

It was Leal Aubrey Headley, prominent Northfielder and professor emeritus of psychology and education at Carleton College, who had died May 22, 1965, after a short illness.

"Born Jan. 2, 1884, at Winnebago, Dr. Headley devoted his life to education, church and community," the story said. His father having been a merchant, Headley lived in several Minnesota towns before coming to the Carleton College campus as a student in the class of 1907. The *News* story stated, "Graduated in 1907 from Carleton, he headed a line of family members who have attended the college — his son and daughter, his sister and one brother, nieces and nephews

The story stated that "before joining the Carleton faculty in 1911, he taught and was superintendent of schools in two Minnesota towns. He taught at Carleton for 41 years."

It was at the time Headley graduated from Carleton that the college trustees moved to "enlarge the scope of courses in education and to establish distinct department . . . to give the professional training most needed by a high school teacher." According to the book *Carleton: The First Century*, this action was practical and timely, "for Minnesota and neighboring states were enacting legislation that would require of college graduates some 18 credit hours in education for certification as high school teachers — and Carleton seniors in significant numbers were preparing themselves for careers in this very field."

After Headley had taught philosophy and education for dozen years, courses were regrouped to make a separate department out of philosophy and to combine the work in psychology and education. According to *Carleton: The First Century*, Professor Headley "was confronted with a difficult choice. With doctoral work in metaphysics, post-doctoral study in education, and teaching experience in both areas, he was well suited to head either department. He chose the field which, in 1926, was formally designated as the department of psychology and education and he served as chairman until 1952."

The book further states, "Professor Headley, one of Carleton's most devoted and highly respected teachers, moved easily from the status of undergraduate and alumnus to the position of professor and departmental administrator."

Harvard (from which university he had received his master's degree) awarded him the Ph.D. in 1916 and Carleton honored him at commencement in 1964 with the degree of Doctor of Humane Letters. A dozen years earlier, at the time of his retirement in 1952, he had received an Alumni Achievement Award.

"During his years at Carleton," the reference continues, "he wrote two widely used books, *How to Study* (1926) and *Making the Most of Books* (1932).

"In all, he had intimate connection with the college for just over 60 years. Dr. and Mrs. Headley have been generous benefactors of the college in many areas — notably in the maintenance of the Headley Faculty

Travel Fund — and their home has been regularly the center of student and alumni gatherings."

At the time of his death, Dr. Headley was engaged in writing the comprehensive history of Carleton College which was to be published during Carleton's Centennial the following year. He had made copious notes for the book during his retirement. Completing the task was M. E. Jarchow who wrote in the book, "Any expression of my appreciation and indebtedness must begin, of course, with a bow to the late Dr. Leal A. Headley. Without his major contribution — his years of meticulous research, his typed and cross-referenced note cards, his intimate acquaintance with and his affection for his subject, his outline for the presentation of the Carleton story — this book probably would not have appeared at all, let alone been published in time for the college's centennial celebration."

Jarchow's hand is visible early in the book where he comments on the aforementioned travel grants. "Although the senior author of this volume with his usual modesty might have omitted it, the fact should be mentioned that among the financial benefits deriving to Carleton faculty members are travel grants to attend meetings. These grants are made available by the Headley Travel Fund, amounting to $50,000, established by Professor and Mrs. Leal A. Headley in 1933."

The book mentions other ways in which Headley served the college. "The first serious attempts of the college to organize liaison between students and prospective employers came in 1916 with the establishment of a bureau of appointments. To its direction, a fourth of the time of Dr. Headley . . . was allotted.

Headley also chaired a faculty standing committee created in 1936 to cope with "individualized programs of study." According to the book, "this committee was to arrange and approve such special programs for certain students, upon their requests, as would 'enable them to use the facilities of the college most advantageously for their intellectual development.'"

There is mention too that Dr. Headley and his brother, Louis, both members of the class of 1907, were on the Carleton College debate team that set an outstanding record their senior year.

But Northfielders will be more interested in Headley's community involvement. He served as chairman of the Northfield Hospital board for 25 years and took a particular interest in the landscaping of what was then a new building. He was honored with a dinner when he resigned in 1956. Toasts were offered, expressing appreciation for the "tremendous amount of time and effort that Dr. Headley has expended in behalf of the city in this post."

His obituary mentioned that he had long served in office in the Northfield Improvement Association, a group through which he contributed greatly to the beautification of Northfield parks and boulevards.

In 1930 he was elected president of the Northfield Rotary Club; in 1932, he was named Rotary governor for the ninth district which embraced the states of Minnesota and North Dakota and the city of Superior, Wis. In 1943 when the 88th annual meeting of the Congregational Conference of Minnesota was held in Northfield, Dr. Headley was elected moderator of the conference for the coming year. He had previously served as moderator of the local church, now the First United Church of Christ.

The citation that accompanied the Alumni Achievement Award spoke of Headley's varied activities. "Since 1911, Leal Headley has been a member of the Carleton College faculty. For most of that period of over 40 years, Professor Headley has been chairman of the department of psychology and education.

"He holds the degree of Doctor of Philosophy from Harvard University and is nationally known as a scholar in his field and an author of successful books. He has lectured widely in the Upper Midwest and has given many commencement addresses in this area.

Two generations of Carleton students know him well as a stimulating chapel and vesper speaker.

"In Northfield, Dr. Headley has been an indefatigable worker in all worthy civic movements. He has served in a wider area as a district governor of Rotary International and as moderator of the Minnesota Conference of Congregational Churches. He has been active throughout the years in numberless committees of both the college faculty and the Carleton Alumni Association."

When he received the L.H.D. at the 1964 Carleton commencement, the citation stated in part: "At various times, and usually in his spare time, Professor Headley was Carleton's admissions department, its appointment and admissions bureau and a few other public relations offices in one, although his major effort was toward improvement of teacher education in Minnesota and development of the intellectual, educational and physical environment of the Northfield community."

The memorial service for Dr. Headley was held at the Congregational Church with its pastor of the time, the Rev. Mark Follansbee, and the college chaplain, Dr. David Maitland, officiating. The story of the service said that "flowers in the church were lilacs from Dr. Headley's garden and from the Carleton campus. Dr. Headley had been an enthusiastic gardener."

Although one quoted passage from *Carleton: The First Century* hints at it, none of the references enlarge on Dr. Headley's modesty or report on his quiet, but delightful sense of humor, both recalled by your writer.

Dr. Headley's widow, Harriet Marston Headley, has in recent years resided in the city of her childhood, San Diego, Calif. Like her husband, she was active in local and state organizations and in her church while she lived in Northfield. Now at 101, she is still alert and enjoys going out. Her daughter Margaret resides with her.

During the past several years, Northfielders have enjoyed the presence of the L.A. Headleys' son and daughter-in-law, Marston and Dorothy Headley who have continued the parental pattern of community service.

24 May, 1990

1965: Marie Piesinger named top senior citizen
Local woman pharmacist long influential

"Miss Piesinger given award as state's out-standing senior citizen" was a major headline on page one of the March 4, 1965, *Northfield News*. A picture accompanying the story showed Marie Piesinger receiving a bouquet of roses from O. H. Ause, then president of the Northfield Area Chamber of Commerce.

"They must have had a difficult time," Miss Piesinger was quoted in the story lead regarding the judges who had chosen her the Outstanding Senior Citizen of Minnesota. "I met several of the other candidates, wonderfully qualified men and women. How they ever chose me, I'll never understand!"

These words had been spoken at a "welcome home" reception at the Community Building (now Northfield Arts Guild) "hastily arranged by the Northfield Area Chamber of Commerce when it was learned at what time the well-known Northfielder would be returning."

The story continued, "Assured by her fellow townspeople that they had always been confident she would bring home the honor, Miss Piesinger added, 'The honor would be utterly worthless if my friends didn't feel that I deserve it. It would be just a heartache then.'"

The award had been presented at the opening session of the fifth biennial Governor's Conference on Aging in the Pick-Nicollet Hotel in Minneapolis. Governor Karl F. Rolvaag had made the presentation. After reading the words on the plaque, "In recognition of a lifetime of service to community, state and nation," Rolvaag had paused to say, "I've known this lady since I was 'that high.' You know Northfield is my home town."

Rolvaag then read the citation regarding Miss Piesinger's activities through her active business years and retirement, based on papers submitted to the state awards committee after Miss Piesinger was given the Rice County award in January. But the awards committee had, probably in deference of Minnesota's DFL governor, eliminated any mention of Miss Piesinger's enthusiastic work in behalf of the Republican party.

The *News* story reported, "At the conclusion of the citation the Governor said, 'This paper doesn't mention that she's a Republican!' Then he traced her active work in politics, summarizing, 'And that's as it should be in our two-party system.'"

The story revealed that Miss Piesinger and her sister Barbara — long her business partner and her housemate — were brought back to Northfield by Dr. Roy A. Waggener who was chairman of the Rice County Committee on Aging. As he approached Waterford, the *News* story said, "he told Miss Piesinger that some Northfielders would probably be there to meet them. She chuckled, thinking it entirely unlikely, and wondered, when she saw the Northfield police car at the side of the road, what could have happened there. But the police car and a caravan of business people in autos lining Waterford roads escorted the Waggener car into Northfield and to the Community Building."

The text of the complete entry considered by the judges was very familiar to your writer because she wrote it at the request of Miss Piesinger. It is much too long to use in full here, but a summary is in order since Northfielders should not forget this woman who played an important role in city life from her arrival here in 1925 until her unexpected death in October of 1965, just seven months after the senior citizen award.

One of a family of 10 children, she was born and grew up at New Prague. She decided she wanted to become a pharmacist, an almost unheard of aim for a girl in that day. She graduated from the Minnesota Institute of Pharmacy, Minneapolis, in 1901. Unable to obtain employment in the male-dominated profession, she enrolled in nurse's training at St. Peter State Hospital. However she left in her senior year to accept a position as relief pharmacist in a drug store at New Prague. She was subsequently employed in several drug stores, then purchased a drug store in Northfield in 1925.

Adding distinctive lines of tableware, gifts and cosmetics to her pharmacy, she continued the prescription department until 1949; the other lines until the very successful business was sold in 1957. (The business was conducted in a Central Block space that is now empty, Donna Mathre Gifts having moved from there several months ago. The Piesingers sold the business to the late Donald MacKenzie and Marian MacKenzie who is now the wife of former Governor Rolvaag.)

In tracing the entry information, the story in the *News* said at this point, "This much of Marie Piesinger's story would be enough to satisfy many a person, but it reflects only a fraction of the activities of this sturdy woman who even today is active in 16 organizations and boards. 'As long as I'm well, I should do what I can,' is her philosophy as a senior citizen."

Professionally, Miss Piesinger had attracted enough attention by 1919 to be elected to the state board of pharmacy. In 1925 she be-

came president of the board, the only woman to have served as president of a state board of pharmacy in the United States to the time this story was written in 1965. She again served as president of the board in 1930. In 1929 she was elected a life member of the Minnesota Pharmaceutical Association. In retirement, she was a member of the Veteran Druggists Association.

That same year she headed the Northfield Community Chest (now United Way) and in 1957, after her retirement, she chaired the fund drive which went over the top for one of the few times in that decade.

She was a charter member and first secretary of the Commercial Club, a forerunner of the Northfield Area Chamber of Commerce. In 1937 she was president of the Northfield Association, another forerunner. She continued her Chamber membership and committee work into retirement.

In 1941 she brought the state conference of the Minnesota Council of Catholic Women to Northfield. She was elected president of the state group in 1943 and again in 1945 and 1947. She once again brought the conference to Northfield in 1955.

In 1941 she headed the Northfield Improvement Assn. which worked at beautification of Northfield's parks and was a board member of the Northfield chapter of American Red Cross and for seven years advisor to the Junior Red Cross. She served as president of the Northfield United Nations committee which brought speakers here. She was active in the Northfield Business and Professional Women's Club.

After her retirement she became president of the Garden Club and helped establish the flower beds in the heart of downtown. Years earlier she had been particularly influential in establishing the nativity scene on Bridge Square at Christmastime.

At the Church of St. Dominic, she had for many years been active on countless committees. At the time of the award she was either holding office or very active in six Catholic organizations at local or state levels. She was especially interested in overseas mission work and her knitting needles were constantly clicking as she made warm garments for children in desolate areas of the world.

In retirement she twice chaired a citywide interdenominational church census.

She was elected to the city council from the Second Ward in 1944 and was re-elected twice. She was then named to the city planning commission, serving as secretary for a time and then as chairman. She was a member of the charter commission that drew up the charter adopted in 1961. In retirement she was very active in getting out the vote for that election.

Also after her retirement, in 1958 she was appointed to the Northfield City Hospital Board and helped plan a large addition to the hospital. She furnished a private room in that wing. She also helped plan the Dilley Unit, one of the first of its kind in the state. Active in the Northfield Hospital Auxiliary, she was named its first life member.

She had served twice as secretary to the Rice County Republican Committee in recent years and was the first chairman of the Federated Women's Republican Club of Rice County which had been organized after her retirement. She was a member of the Northfield Women's Republican Club.

In 1951 she was given the Northfield Citizenship award by the Junior Chamber of Commerce (now Jaycees) for having "labored untiringly and unselfishly in the interests of the Northfield Community." In 1960 she was given the Archbishop William O. Brady Achievement Award for distinguished service to her church and to the city of Northfield.

She was a member of the Northfield Memorial Foundation that raised funds for such improvements as the swimming pool. She was active on the Northfield Senior Citizens Committee.

She had made many trips to Mexico, Europe and the Holy Land.

The information supplied the judges concluded: "Although Miss Piesinger retired in 1957 there has been very little difference in the amount of energy she has expended. What once went into her business has now been added to what she expends for community, church and party.

"She is well known for her brisk step and the firmness with which she takes hold of a project for which she has been given responsibility. Her interests are broad and her activities still reflect the wide range of matters with which she has worked all her life."

Several years later, in 1976, Marjorie Neuhaus paid tribute to Miss Piesinger in a BPW Club program. She concluded, "Marie, who proved to a skeptic world that women make good pharmacists, laid the groundwork for the women who followed in her field. Today, almost half of the students of the pharmacy school at the University of Minnesota are women."

Your writer has many delightful memories of Marie Piesinger, but to give you an idea of her business principles, I asked her one day the price of a beautiful tray that was displayed on a high shelf in her drug and gift shop.

"It's $xx," she said — the price is no longer remembered, but it was substantial. After thinking a bit, I decided I could hack it and told her I'd buy the tray.

She climbed up a stepladder and said as she lifted the large metal tray, "Ho! this is bargain week." As she came down the ladder with the tray, she announced that the price tag said — about $8 or $10 more than the price she had quoted.

I recoiled and said, "Oh dear, I guess I can't afford it."

"I said it was $xx and it is $xx," she announced as she wrapped up the tray. Atop a luggage rack, the tray still serves as my bedside table.

1 March, 1990

1965: W. W. Pye, well-known attorney, dies at age 94

Pye, self-educated, pursued many interests

"W. W. Pye, attorney for 65 years, dies" was a major headline on page one of the Oct. 21, 1965, *Northfield News*. Pye had long been a civic leader in Northfield.

"In his 94th year — after being retired only four years from the practice of law — W. W. Pye died Friday, Oct. 15, 1965, at his home," the story began. "He had retired because of ill health and had been confined to his home since that time." The Pye home on Fourth St. is now the property of Ruth and Dannie Gustafson.

Pye's obituary stated that "William Watts Pye was born on Christmas Day in 1870 in a log cabin in Northfield township, Rice County, the son of Charles William and Lucy Amelia (Cooke) Pye."

In an autobiographical story that Pye had written for *Northfield News* supplements in 1962 and 1963, he stated that he could trace his family back to Norwich, Norfolkshire,

England, and spoke of the many attorneys among his forebears. "So far as I know, my own purpose to be a lawyer must have come from that ancestry," he commented.

In 1872 the Pye family moved from Northfield township into the city of Northfield, residing at first on Woodley St., probably at 206 E. Woodley. In about 1876, Pye's father built a new house on the corner of Woodley and Division — 917 Division. There W. W. Pye spent his boyhood.

His father continued to teach for several years in Northfield township schools, according to the obituary, returning home only on weekends. He later became a justice of the peace in Northfield and was classed as a lawyer although at that time there were

no law schools. Pye had commented in his own story that in that era "both lawyers and doctors had grown up more by practice than education."

Pye wrote about his boyhood jobs in his reminiscences. "My first job was to take a cow a mile to pasture and bring her back each night. For this I received 50 cents a week. My next job was to get a basket and, in the spring, peddle apples. The apples all came from the East in barrels and some lasted until spring. I sold these apples at houses and even went over to the railroad station where I sold them through the windows to the passengers. I then got a job with a gardener. We started work at 5AM, picking peas and vegetables to be sold around town, starting at 8AM after we had breakfast. This was a 12-hour day for which we were paid a few cents an hour.

"Later, when I was 11 years old, I went to work on a farm riding a lead horse and driving another, as part of a five-horse team, operating what was called a self binder. I became so homesick that I ran, barefoot, five miles home one night and back the next morning. I was paid for this work 50 cents a day, a day lasting 12 hours. When I was 13 I did the same work on the same farm. This farm work gave me a knowledge of agriculture and horses which was later very valuable. I was reading the whole history of the horse, including the various breeds and their diseases, at the time. Later, when I traded horses, I used this knowledge to advantage.

"About this time, as was the custom, my father said I wasn't old enough to handle money and took charge of my earnings. I had used my money (until that time) to buy all of the historical novels I could get hold of. I also bought skates made of cast iron, which sold at 50 cents a pair. During the winter we skated on ponds and the Cannon River. We also built ski runs and made our own skis from barrel staves. Also during this period I learned to swim. We had swimming holes in the river at various places where we went regularly without any guard or any instructor. We looked after each other and, to my knowledge, no one was drowned."

Both his own story and his obituary emphasized that Pye read avidly during his childhood. "From the time I could read, I had read everything that I could get," Pye wrote. "The early settlers had constructed a building known as the Lyceum where all public meetings were held (the present-day dental office of Dr. Alvin Heiberg). They had acquired a small public library to which books had been donated. . . . I read most of them" including works of Dickens, Washington Irving, Mark Twain, English history, English novels, French novels, and all of the Roman history he could obtain.

Pye wrote that while he was in the public school, he always expected to attend Carleton College. But when he enrolled in Carleton Academy, he found he had already read everything that was being studied. "For that reason I left the academy and did not enter the college later. . . . My extensive reading has covered everything that I needed in my future life. I have not touched on science or mathematics for the reason that, except for the usual knowledge, I've had no use for them in my life work.

"During my growing years, I helped my father so that I gained in knowledge of the court practice in justice court which covered the bulk of the legal action at that time. Long before I was of age, I could carry on a case in justice court where one did not need to be a lawyer. . . .

"My first lawsuit involved a lady at Nerstrand who was engaged to marry the local constable. She started a lawsuit against her father to replevin some cattle. This is, and was, an intricate procedure in justice court. I was sent to Nerstrand to defend the suit. The time was winter and there was a large gathering as was usual. I proceeded to show the local judge that his proceedings were entirely wrong so that when I was through and he was compelled to dismiss the suit, he announced that, 'We would be all right if the lawyers would leave us alone.' The victory was celebrated by a dinner, attended by about 20 people."

Pye said that by the time he married Ruth Violet Goodman of Cannon City in 1892, he had decided he would be a lawyer. In the couple's first home he completed his self-education. He read all the phases of common law, studied the rules of practice and reviewed the many legislative laws of Minnesota. As he was completing three years of study, the state law was passed requiring a written examination for admission to the bar, an examination that took three days. In September of 1894 he was admitted to the bar and was sworn in as attorney by Judge Buckham at Faribault. Pye was always proud that the notes he had made during his study were subsequently used by several young men in preparation for the bar examination.

Early on, Pye won the office of Rice County attorney. He angered the Faribault people by carrying out the duties in his Northfield office.

For many years Pye's office was on the second floor of the Central Block, his windows overlooking Bridge Square.

In 1905, Mr. and Mrs. Pye bought three lots on E. Fourth and erected the English Tudor home in which they resided the rest of their lives.

Pye served as city attorney on several occasions. He served on the school board and was its president. His obituary stated, "He served as an officer in bar associations and was active in civic organizations. In the Northfield Improvement Assn., he arranged for the planting of many trees — along the Wall

Street Road on the way to Oaklawn cemetery (those elms are now all killed by Dutch elm disease), at Northfield Golf course, in Riverside park, on residential boulevards. He was instrumental in obtaining river walls. Still civic minded, during the past spring he accepted the honorary chairmanship of the fund drive for the Lutheran Home of the Cannon Valley. . . .

"He was one of the founders of the State Bank of Northfield (which grew into Norwest Bank) and at times owned rural banks including the ones at Webster, Stanton and Morristown. At one time he was influential in obtaining passage, in the state legislature, of a law that in some degree eliminated fee systems. On his retirement, his extensive law library was presented to the University of Minnesota."

Because of his intense interest in reading, the Pye family furnished a room in the old public library which housed local historical information. The area in the new library which contains this information is still named for him. The family also commissioned four bronze reliefs to be used in that space, the work of the late Paul Houston. Titled for the four seasons, they depict particular interests of Pye in those seasons. The spring bronze depicted tree planting and Pye family members noted a strong resemblance between the tree planter and the late Mr. Pye.

When the bronzes were dedicated, Pye's son Robert recalled that as Northfield Golf Club was started, Pye "provided the finances for purchase of the Pruett farm and all of the members turned out to make it into a golf course. The Pye family was soon there planting trees. The younger children have memories of going out to the golf course before school in the morning and watering these trees from milk cans filled with water."

The summer panel depicts a circus in a small town and Robert Pye remembered that at least one circus would come to Northfield each summer, usually setting up on Pye's Highland Park addition which then had two or three blocks without houses on them. "He had a broad acquaintance among these circus people and his sons who usually accompanied him were much made of by the managers, clowns, lion tamers, acrobats and other members of the entourage."

An older couple picnicking is depicted on the fall sculpture and Robert Pye said, "Through spring, summer and fall months, almost any Sunday would find Will Pye picnicking in some woodland spot in the area. . . . Even in the cold winter months, he would find a spot along the river where a sandstone cliff would shield the picnickers from the north wind and reflect the heat from the blazing campfire. On rare occasions he and Mrs. Pye would picnic by themselves, but usually he was accompanied by his children and their friends, his friends, and later his grandchildren." Pye said his father continued to picnic into old age.

Because of Pye's love of skating, it is skating on the river for people of all ages that is depicted on the winter bronze relief. Robert Pye said, "Will Pye skated from childhood until he was 60. He often took his skates to his office and went to the rink on the mill pond for an hour of skating before dinner. . . .

"Throughout most of the year, when skating wasn't possible, he walked or hiked. Nearly every day of his life until he was in his 80s, he walked. . . . He loved the outdoors any time of year and never lost his enthusiasm for outdoor activities."

Pye's funeral was held at All Saints Episcopal Church where he had been an active member. Both he and Mrs. Pye, who had died in 1956, are buried at Oaklawn.

26 October, 1990

1966: Former mayor dies after active life
Zanmiller eager to serve fellow man

"Former 3-term mayor dies" was a headline on page one of the July 14, 1966, *News*.

The story began, "After a long illness borne with high courage and spirit, George J. Zanmiller, native son of Northfield and three times elected its mayor, died Thursday, July 7, at 8:20PM, at Northfield City Hospital.

"Although he has known for months that he was suffering from cancer and could not recover," the story continued, "Zanmiller carried on his work as a funeral director until within a few weeks of his final illness, and active plans for his family and his dedicated interest in the community he loved occupied every waking moment until the last summons came. Despite the pain and suffering, he never really lost his smile. He filled the counted days with an inspiring expression of his faith."

The story was written by Carl L. Weicht, then editor emeritus of the *News* who had known Zanmiller most of his life. He continued, "He was finally stricken while on a fishing trip to Crane Lake, reminiscent of similar outings with friends and relatives which had brought pleasure throughout his life, for he was an ardent outdoorsman.

"After being brought back to Northfield, he was cared for at his home by his devoted family, but was hospitalized ten days before his death at the city hospital."

In reporting that the funeral was held at the Church of St. Dominic where Zanmiller had been a lifelong member and that local posts of the American Legion and Veterans of Foreign Wars had participated in military rites at Calvary Cemetery, the story revealed, "During World War II, Zanmiller served with the Seabees and his son, George, was in the Navy also. They were the only father-son team from this community to be in service at the same time."

The story then traced Zanmiller's history, "George Jordan Zanmiller was born July 13, 1903, in Northfield, the son of Jordan and Katherine (Beck) Zanmiller. He attended the Northfield public schools, graduated from Northfield High School in 1922, and also attended Carleton College. He was employed by the late W. E. Revier at Bill's Art and Floral Shop for 11 years while attending school and after his graduation from high school."

It would be interesting to know how much that first job influenced Zanmiller because he had a lifelong interest in flowers and in artistic endeavor.

The story continued, "Zanmiller graduated from the School of Mortuary Science at the University of Minnesota in 1934 and established the Zanmiller Funeral Home, which for many years now has been located at 917 Division St.

"His marriage to Esther Rachel Davis of Wibauz, Mont., was solemnized at the Church of St. Dominic June 3, 1926." He had met her while she attended Carleton College. Born to them were son and a daughter, George Davis, who is now deceased and Rachel who is now Mrs. Gerald Fisher.

The story continued, "George Zanmiller had a strong sense of the obligation of citizenship and a passion for community service. The former found expression in his dedicated interest in city affairs, to which he brought in three terms as mayor of Northfield an intense desire not only to serve well in the administrative duties of office but to improve city government and to arouse in fellow citizens a similar feeling of obligation. His intensity sometimes led him into controversy but no one ever doubted his sincerity or the value of his point of view, which was always expressed in the public interest. He wanted to improve the form as well as the function of city government and tried to convey to others his own conviction that participation in local government is the basis of the best American citizenship and that integrity is the heart of public service.

"His sense of duty as a citizen was further expressed in his service during World War II when he served for 2 months in the Naval Construction Battalion, the majority of this period being spent in the Pacific Theater of Operations." (Bear in mind that he was 40 years old when he enlisted. Seabees — named for the initials C. B. — constructed and defended outpost bases. They constructed floating dry docks, storage tanks, various other buildings, did the work of stevedores, installed camouflage, etc. Zanmiller, coming from a family of highly skilled sheet metal workers, could do well with various building trades.)

"Zanmiller was elected mayor of Northfield three times, first in 1942 for a term which he was unable to complete because of his war service in the Seabees beginning in October of 1943. He was again elected mayor in 1956 and re-elected in 1958."

In 1960 when Zanmiller decided not to seek re-election, he announced to the *News* at least two months before the election that he would not file and "urged interested Northfielders to take their turn in serving the city."

The obituary continued, "Zanmiller's interest in the community found expression in various ways. He was the first president of the Junior Chamber of Commerce (now Jaycees), served in the Northfield Improvement Association and the Northfield Safety Council, as well as other groups. He was interested in the youngsters of the town and he personally helped see to it that they had a good skating rink in the winter. As his grandchildren grew up he devoted a lot of effort to their interest.

"An avid sportsman himself he worked on many local committees and was responsible for introducing pheasants, quail, Hungarian and chucker partridge to our rural community. As a boy he loved to go fishing with his father in the Cannon River and fishing became an avocation, matched though it was by real effort in the field of conservation. Thus he was able to say that his most pleasing accomplishment when he was mayor was to turn the switch that started the municipal sewage disposal plant into operation for this meant restoration of the Cannon River as a place where Northfield boys of the future could go fishing again. Some of them, he was confident, would aim later to serve their home town as he had done all his life."

It is interesting to note the these insightful words were written by a man who headed up the organization to establish an outdoor swimming pool for the kids of Northfield while Zanmiller fought the project, at least city ownership of a pool, with all his might!

Especially during the early years that he was active in Northfield politics, Zanmiller was very supportive of a municipal power plant. He believed such a project would earn good money for the community and he was very suspicious of the motives of commercial power companies.

There are many kinds of clippings in Zanmiller's biographical file at the *News* office, but one from 1957 showing his off-beat sense a humor pictures him competing in a milking contest at the Rice County Fair. Mayors of the cities in Rice County participated.

The cutline says, "Mayor George Zanmiller of Northfield was the winner of the mayors' milking contest at the Rice County Fair Friday, but was disqualified by the judges. It seems Mayor Zanmiller's pail, which weighed 24 pounds, contained canned Northfield Milk furnished by the Northfield Milk Products Co. Mayor Zanmiller distributed his prize-winning milk to bystanders." Northfield Milk was then one of the city's major products, canned in the original part of the present-day Malt-O-Meal No. 2 plant.

19 July, 1991

1967: Death takes prominent hog breeder
Cap Peterson named to Hall of Fame

"Death takes prominent breeder" was a headline in the May 18, 1967, *Northfield News*. Under the head was the obituary of Casper "Cap" Peterson, nationally-known breeder of Poland China hogs.

His death had occurred May 11 at Northfield Hospital when he was 77 years old.

The story said, "After many years of successful hog breeding, Peterson received his greatest recognition in 1960 when he and his sons showed the national grand champion barrow at the National Barrow Show at Austin, and in 1961 when he was named to the Livestock Hall of Fame, his picture being hung in the Livestock Hall of Fame at Peters Hall, University of Minnesota Institute of Agriculture, St. Paul.

"He was made a life member of the Minnesota Swine Producers Association in 1960. He was a past president of the National Records Association of Poland China Breeders.

"Peterson was born on April 8, 1890, on a farm near Randolph, the son of Mr. and Mrs. Torkel Peterson who had come to the United States from Denmark. When he was seven years old, he moved with his family to a farm in the Union Lake community."

There the Petersons were neighbors of Mr. and Mrs. Ole Lockrem who had come to the United States from Norway by sailboat. He was to marry their daughter Julia on March 18, 1914. She had in the meanwhile been employed at the Odd Fellows Home in Northfield.

For the first year of their marriage the newlyweds farmed in the Union Lake commu-

nity. They then moved to the Jim Alexander farm northeast of Northfield. In 1918 they purchased 80 acres of what was to become 600 acres of farmland on TH 19 East.

The obituary stated, "Peterson founded his purebred Poland China operation in 1924. The operation grew into one of the most highly regarded of the Poland China herds in the central western states. The farm also had a high-class dairy herd. General crops were raised through the years and beef cattle were fed after the discontinuance of the dairy herd (in about 1961).

"Realizing the value of advertising, Peterson showed his hogs at many fairs and hog shows, winning more than 1,000 trophies, plaques and ribbons. His colorful sales of breeding stock at his farm attracted breeders from a wide area. Several years ago a delegation of Russian agricultural experts observed the methods used on the Peterson farm.

"Although ill health (an asthmatic condition) made it impossible for Peterson to actually participate in the farming in recent years, he remained very interested in the operation that is being carried on by his sons (Donald and the late LeRoy "Bud").

"As a younger man, Peterson served as a director of the Tri-County Cooperative Oil Co. of Northfield (which later merged with Cannon Valley Co-op) for 25 years and was president of the company for several years. He was a long-time member of his local rural school board."

The citation devoted to Peterson when he was, as a complete surprise, named to the

Livestock Hall of Fame included some of this same information, but also such statements as:

"In the Northfield, Minnesota, community, long known for its upright, substantial citizens, Casper Peterson has been for about 40 years one of the most progressive of rural leaders. His cheerful, helpful attitude has made 'Cap' a friend of hundreds of Minnesotans and of hog breeders from half of the states of the Union.

"Like all industrious Danes, 'Cap' had a busy boyhood going to country school and working at home, as well as picking corn and cutting wood for neighbors.

"'Cap' founded his herd of purebred hogs with the purchase of two sows from the Hunter Brothers who were his neighbors at that time.

"A remarkable accomplishment has been the steady, year after year high quality of the pigs bred and sold. Through periods of extreme changes in the type of many contemporaneous herds and the fluctuations from boom to bust in the pig business, hundreds of breeders appreciated the sound, profitable breeding stock available from the Peterson herd.

"'Cap' started showing pigs at the county fair in 1926 and at the Minnesota State Fair in 1927, where he has never missed a show since. He has won top premiums consistently wherever he exhibited his herd including the Illinois and Iowa State Fairs and the National Barrow Show.

"At the age of 71, 'Cap' is still setting a strong pace for his children and grandchildren. He runs the combine and the corn picker and when repairs are needed on some of the good machinery he owns, he does the work himself.

"The Minnesota Livestock Breeders' Association honors Casper Peterson primarily for his work in greatly improving livestock and also because of his aid and encouragement of many other breeders and farmers, ambitious to improve their herds. He has been a good citizen, friendly neighbor and a convincing example that hard work, ambition and intelligent management are the keys to achieving a real success as farmer and livestock breeder. He continues to set an outstanding example of the merits of good judgment, integrity and interest in one's fellow man for those who aspire to be successful in the purebred livestock business. May he continue for many more years to enjoy good health and the happiness with which his chosen profession has rewarded him and his family."

In Peterson's envelope in the *News* biographical file is a story of a Poland China sale held at the Peterson farm in the fall of 1960. Pictures show breeders seated around the auction ring. Seventy-one head were sold in about three hours with Elmer Franks of Green Valley, Ill., serving as auctioneer. He was a professional Poland China auctioneer. About 200 buyers attended from several states including Indiana, Illinois, Iowa, Oklahoma, South Dakota, Wisconsin and Minnesota.

At that sale, the Minnesota State Fair junior champion boar went for $2,420, the highest price the Petersons had ever received for a single animal and the highest price paid for any Poland China animal that year. An Illinois breeder was the successful bidder.

Headlines on various stories in the same envelope include: "Peterson hogs winners again," "Peterson prize winners again show superiority," "Peterson entry grand champ," "Petersons win most important barrow award," "Peterson Poland China hogs take show honors," "Win prizes in hog carcass contest at South St. Paul," "Win trophy at meat type hog show," "Peterson hogs win awards," "Northfielders take high honors at State Fair," "Peterson sow takes honors at New Ulm Show."

Mrs. Peterson lived on until she was 96, surviving her husband by 20 years. She continued to live on the home farm, aiding her sons wherever possible. Ill health forced her to leave the beloved farm and reside at the Odd Fellows Home the last three years of her life.

22 May, 1992

1967: Grastvedt, colorful businessman, dies
Medal given for service to Norway

Issues of the *Northfield News* in November of 1967 carried news about the unexpected death and funeral of a Northfield business-man. Christian M. Grastvedt, who had in-stalled plumbing and heating in Northfield for many years, had suffered heart failure at his home at 616 E. Fifth on Nov. 1. He was 75.

A friendly person, he was all the more col-orful because of his memories of childhood and youth in Norway and his deep inter-est in the history of the American frontier. When he came to Northfield in the early years of this century, he not only knew all about Jesse James, but he knew about Indian attacks, about the military forts in the Upper Midwest, and he was deeply disappointed to find that the average Northfielder could not add to his knowledge or even equal it!

Part of his charm was a lifelong mix of Norse and English (British) accent. He had been exposed to the latter as a youth work-ing on the North Sea.

Grastvedt was born in December of 1891 at Egersund, Norway, the member of a fam-ily that had been seafaring for many genera-tions. His father had already been to Ameri-ca, had sailed the Great Lakes and knew Lake Superior. These places he'd described to the boy Chris when the latter was old enough to help him on his boats in Norway. Grastvedt's grandfather, licensed by the king of Norway to serve as a pilot along the coast of Norway, had built a small farm on a high knob called Grastvedt (translates Grass Hill) so that he could see the topmasts of approaching ships before his rivals who lived along the low shore.

Grastvedt elected to use the place name for his family name when he arrived in this country. He later said he was sorry to have done that because his name was frequently and severely mispronounced. He'd recall that one customer addressed him as "Grasstoad."

When Grastvedt arrived in the United

States in 1910, he headed directly for Duluth where he obtained a job on the S.S. America. However he came to Northfield that same year, probably when winter brought an end to Great Lakes shipping, taking a job with a prominent plumber, R. Leivestad. He estab-lished his own plumbing and heating busi-ness in 1928.

Although he wound down his business in the '60s when he suffered from a heart ail-ment, he remained active at plumbing and was downtown as usual in the days before his death. His business was in the building where the Mandarin Garden Restaurant is now located.

Grastvedt was known locally as an avid gar-dener. He was long active in the Northfield Improvement Association and served as its president in the late '40s. That group, one of the oldest organizations in Northfield, worked with beautification of the city.

A picture in Grastvedt's biographical file at the *News* office shows him with a bird of paradise plant in flower at his home green-house. He had started the plant three years before from a root about as big as his index finger, the plant was now a yard tall.

A World War I veteran, Grastvedt was a member of the American Legion. He was also a member of the Masonic Lodge and the Eastern Star.

During World War II, he was active in gathering funds and clothing for Norway Relief over a period of four years following the Nazi invasion of his native land. Clothing packed and shipped by Grastvedt during that period totaled more than 35,000 pounds. In the fall of 1947, he was awarded the Liberty Medal by His Majesty, King Haakon of Norway, for outstanding services to Norway's cause during World War II.

Grastvedt celebrated his 70th birthday in Norway, spending 2½ months with relatives and friends. At that time he presented precious possessions to Norwegian relatives (he and his wife, the former Fay Williams, did not have children).

One of these objects was a watch that had once been the property of Sweden's King Oscar II. The silver pocket watch, just over three inches in diameter, had been made in France with 19 rubies as jewels. On the back of the watch was engraved the likeness of King Oscar and the dates 1872 when Oscar became king and 1897 when his 25th anniversary as king was celebrated and he was given the watch.

Grastvedt revealed that when the late Swan J. Turnblad of Minneapolis, publisher of *Svenska Amerikanska Posten*, then the largest Swedish-language newspaper in the world, visited the king, he was unexpectedly given the large watch for his exceptional service to Sweden.

When Turnblad was building the huge gray stone house that is now the American Swedish Institute in Minneapolis, he employed a skilled carpenter, Walter Beers. The man was doing excellent work with the building's beautiful staircases when he tired of the job and gave notice. Turnblad urged him to stay, Grastvedt had learned, and promised that he would make him a fine gift if he would continue the work.

"There is only one thing you have that I want," said Beers, "your watch." Turnblad, according to Grastvedt, was taken aback, but promised Beers that if he would stay until the building was completed, he would receive the watch. This period of time proved to be three years.

Beers eventually came to Northfield to live with his mother. Grastvedt helped Beers install plumbing in their old-fashioned home to provide some comfort for the elderly woman. Several years later when Beers had an accident with an emery wheel and suffered a severe facial cut, Grastvedt was present. He quickly gave Beers first aid and took him to a doctor. While the man lay ill at home, Grastvedt took him malted milks that would be easy to sip through his wounded lips, and otherwise cared for him on a daily basis.

A short time before Beers died, he told Grastvedt that he had done far more for him than could ever be expected of a friend and he gave Grastvedt his most precious possession — the watch.

For many years thereafter the watch, which had never been repaired and still kept perfect time, was on display at the American Swedish Institute, but Grastvedt requested its return before his trip to Norway. At that time he gave the watch to a relative who had been an English-trained commando who parachuted into Norway and constantly radioed information to British and Norwegian navies during Norway's occupation. To that man's brother, he gave the King Haakon medal. Another relative, a young man who had become a ship pilot in the home area, he gave a key-winding watch that had belonged to Grastvedt's grandfather who was the ship pilot.

Grastvedt's wife survived him, dying in 1970. Among the three brothers who survived him were two in Norway and one in Northfield, Karsten Grastvedt who had worked with Chris for many years and who died in 1985.

20 November, 1992

1967: Sid Freeman honored by Carleton
Clothing chain founder active here

"Alumni awards to be granted" was a headline in the June 1, 1967, *Northfield News*. A picture of the late Sid Freeman, then a Northfield businessman, appeared with the story as he was one of ten alumni of Carleton College who were to receive an Alumni Achievement Award.

The ceremony was to take place Friday, June 10, in Skinner Memorial Chapel. It would be an event of Carleton's alumni centennial reunion weekend.

Freeman was listed as owner of the men's clothing store, The Hub, in Northfield and board chairman and president of Skeffington's, a chain of men's formal wear.

According to the story, "Freeman, '27, will be cited for 'outstanding service to Carleton College and its Alumni Association, significant accomplishments in business and community service.'

"Freeman served as national chairman of the college's annual alumni fund drive for two years (1965–1966). Long active in civic affairs, he is also a strong supporter of not only local athletic events but also the Minnesota Gophers, the Vikings and the Twins." What the story didn't mention was that the two years Freeman headed the drive for Carleton funds were record-breaking years from the viewpoints of money given and number of contributors.

Freeman, who died in 1986, was born at Cannon Falls in 1905 and grew up there. The Hub in Northfield was originally purchased as a bankrupt business in the mid '20s by his father, Henry Freeman, and his uncle, Sam H. Fink, both of whom were in business in Cannon Falls. The uncle was active here for about six months, then sold his interest to Sid who dropped out of college to operate the store. Later Sid's brother Dan, now deceased, was in partnership here for seven or eight years. Eventually, in 1963, Sid's son Dan became a partner after working in the store since grade school.

In the late '30s the Hub operation spread to three other cities — Rochester, Winona and Owatonna — with Arthur and Randall Forselius in partnership. But Freeman sold off the stores because he found it too difficult to control quality.

Then in 1948, Freeman and a former employee, Jack Skeffington, organized Skeffington's Men's Formal Wear shops, making use of an idea Freeman had developed during the Great Depression. He had noted that college students who bought tuxedos for the prom wanted to sell them back cheap, perhaps for as little as $5. He bought and stored the slightly worn suits and hit upon the idea of renting them. He bought a few dozen more tuxedos from market to carry out that program in the '30s.

When the first Skeffington store was set up in Minneapolis more than 15 years later, it was thought to be one of the first such ventures in the country. Freeman bought out Skeffington in 1952 and continued to expand the business. During the '50s the chain had 23 stores in nine states — in such cities as Cincinnati, New Orleans and Dallas. Freeman sold off all but five nearby stores during 1977–78 when he wanted to slow down a bit. He had retired from the Northfield store in 1975.

At the time of that retirement, Freeman told your writer how he happened to meet his wife, the former Lydia Bennett of Owatonna. While she was attending Carleton, she dropped in at The Hub, hoping to find an orange polo shirt. Freeman didn't have one, but promised to obtain one for her. Forty-five years later he admitted he hadn't tried very hard to get the shirt because he found her so attractive, he wanted to keep her coming back. A romance developed and the couple married in 1934. Mrs. Freeman never did get her orange polo shirt until 1974 when Freeman saw one in Acapulco, Mexico, and bought it for her.

The couple traveled widely and spent considerable time in Mexico where Mrs. Freeman now resides in Manzanillo.

The Hub was always a hangout for college kids and also became known to athletes on major teams and to friends Mr. and Mrs. Freeman made in Hollywood.

One of their contacts with known entertainment personalities was with the late Jack Carson. Carson had attended Carleton and left Northfield owing money at The Hub. One night when Freeman was attending a movie at the Grand Theater, Carson appeared on the screen. "That guy owes me a bill!" said Freeman and made it his business to contact the actor. They became close friends and several years later Freeman was one of Carson's pallbearers!

George Gobel, renowned comedian, met the Freemans through a priest who served the Church of St. Dominic for a time. He bought his suits here and in 1983, as a favor to Freeman, participated in Northfield's Defeat of Jesse James Days. Dennis Day and Morey Amsterdam were a couple of other entertainers who visited the Freemans here and saw them in California.

Through the years, many Northfielders appealed to Freeman for help in getting tickets to athletic events. His efforts helped bring some of the professional teams to Northfield.

The Hub also served as a headquarters for downtown practical jokes for many years. Freeman said that the best jokes were back in the Depression years. "Nobody had any money and there was nothing doing," he explained. "We had to make our own fun."

Also during the Depression, several members of the families of both Mr. and Mrs Freeman experienced difficult times and lived with the couple for a time. Among them was Mrs. Freeman's niece, Sylvia Chase, now a nationally known television commentator. The Freemans had three sons and one daughter of their own.

In 1966, Freeman was named Outstanding Boss during the Jaycee Distinguished Service Award banquet. The citation mentioned that Freeman had been an all-state quarterback in 1922 while playing football at Cannon Falls High School.

The citation also stated that "over the years this man has been one of Northfield's most active citizens, donating time and energy to projects ranging from street signs for our city to rebuilding and improving Northfield Golf Club. He has supported professional and amateur athletics, sponsored teams in softball, peewee baseball, bowling and basketball." The citation saluted Freeman for his spirit of cooperation with the Defeat of Jesse James Days celebration, allowing his son to devote many hours to that celebration as well as other civic projects.

It continued, "Countless men have been trained in his store through the years, men who have gone on to be successful in many fields, all receiving the benefit of his zestful approach to life and business. He has made friends all over the world and has a knack of meeting important and average people in the same easy manner, making them feel comfortable immediately. Counted among his friends are statesmen, entertainers and big league athletic stars. But more importantly, he has never forgotten his friends at home — here in Northfield."

Freeman himself was Defeat of Jesse James Days parade grand marshal in 1976. At that time he was still commuting to Minneapolis daily to manage Skeffington's. That year about 200 friends, relatives and employees of Freeman gathered at the Sheraton Motor Inn in Minneapolis for a testimonial dinner marking his 50th year of business success and many years of benevolence.

Freeman's health began to decline in 1983. Slowed down by Alzheimer's disease, he eventually received care in San Diego, Calif., where he died in his sleep on May 16, 1986.

His obituary in the *News* on May 22 began, "No matter where you go in the United States, it has been said, you will find someone who knows that Jesse James raided a Northfield bank and you will find someone who knows Sid Freeman."

The story mentioned that in 1946–47 Freeman was president of the Northfield Association, a forerunner of the Northfield Area Chamber of Commerce. He was also active in the Northfield Lions Club and Masonic orders. He served as a director of the Northfield National Bank, now Community National Bank, elected in 1966. He was active in the Minneapolis Minute Men, helping bring professional sports teams to Minnesota.

The obituary also revealed that as a youth, Freeman was an accomplished violinist, being a member of a group that accompanied silent films in the movie theaters of Northfield and Cannon Falls. He also played in dance bands.

The obituary closed with a tribute written by Tom Hart who had been business manager at Skeffington's for many years: "Sid was kind of humble in a way, yet he was very helpful to many, many people. I used to hear a lot of students coming from Carleton who said he helped them get their clothes. Many of the people he let have credit whether or not they had a credit rating. He was really a person to trust people. He had a confidence in people that if you did something for them, you didn't have to worry about being paid back because it would come back around to you."

5 June, 1992

1968: Prominent merchant dies unexpectedly
Jacobsen cited for civic contribution

"Businessman dies unexpectedly" was a headline in the *Northfield News*: "After a very short illness, Ralph A. Jacobsen — Northfield businessman since the fall of 1947 — died at Northfield Hospital Saturday forenoon, Dec. 30, 1967.

"He had worked at the store (Jacobsen's) as usual on Tuesday and Wednesday, but complained of being tired. On Thursday he stayed home to rest and on Friday consulted his physician. The doctor recommended immediate hospitalization.

Suffering from a heart ailment, Jacobsen had been given a year to live 19 years ago. He had also had emphysema for several years. Although his extreme fatigue last week was probably caused from these ailments, his death seemed due to pneumonia."

The story said that Jacobsen had been born on a ranch at Leigh, Neb., on Nov. 5, 1899. The family moved to Iowa when he was six months old, living first at Cherokee and later in Larrabee where the family conducted a general store.

"Jacobsen grew up in the store, but because he also loved being outside, he frequently worked for friends on farms. As a young man he went to Texas for construction work. On returning home in the fall of 1918, he expected to enter World War I service, but the Armistice was signed and no more enlistments were accepted. He then enrolled in Buena Vista College at Storm Lake, Iowa."

There he met Aura Clough whom he later married. But before his marriage, Jacobsen worked in a hardware store, later was a traveling salesman for Wallace Farmer, and then worked in a clothing store at Cherokee. That store was the Leuthold-St. Clair, related to the Leuthold's store that was once located on Bridge Square in Northfield.

The story continued, "Entering the employ of the J.C. Penney Co., Jacobsen was made assistant manager of the store at Mitchell, S.D. In 1935 he was named manager of the

Penney store at Waseca and later managed Penney stores at Blue Earth and International Falls."

After he had been employed by Penneys for 19 years, Jacobsen came from International Falls to Northfield to buy the Federated Store which he later renamed Jacobsen's V-Store. Mrs. Jacobsen actively assisted her husband in the Northfield store from the time of their arrival here until her illness and death in 1966.

A few months after her death, Jacobsen sold the home they had built at 514 Union and bought another at 1115 Maple. His son Richard and family moved here from Hopkins, sharing that house with him.

The obituary stated, "A very active citizen, Jacobsen received in the spring of 1950 a Northfield Jaycee scroll as the adult contributing the most to the city's well being during the past year. He was through his years here active in the Northfield Chamber of Commerce, serving on many committees, as a board member and as president. He was a member of the Northfield city charter commission and had headed the United Fund. He was very active on the board of the Northfield Industrial Corporation.

"He was active in Scouting (he had served at Indianhead Council level as well as locally) and had received the coveted Silver Beaver Scout award. He sponsored a series of Wacouta District Boy Scout awards.

"He was president of the Rice County Agricultural Society, sponsor of the county fair, besides serving for several years on the society's executive committee. He was a member of Masonic orders and the Northfield Lions Club. A member of the Congregational Church, he served as trustee at various times.

"In 1964, after 17 years in business in Northfield, he was singled out for special recognition by the V-Store organization on its 25th anniversary. He had at that time served for six years as a director of that 14-state organization and had been chairman of the board in 1963. Named V-Store's Man of the Year, he was given a plaque."

A story that appeared in the *News* at the time of the V-Store award stated that "ordinarily board members and chairmen are not re-elected under a rotation system, but Jacobsen was persuaded to serve for another year on the board by appointment."

A special citation accompanying the V-Store award said that the honor was for "special contribution toward the improvement of the V-Stores program and the benefit of all V-Stores. A special citation accompanying the award said he had provided a very special brand of leadership that had advanced the V-Stores as one of the premier merchandising forces in the Northwest. . . .

"Mrs. Jacobsen who had accompanied him to the convention at Clara City, said she could not suppress a tear, she was that proud of her 'colleague' in business in Northfield. 'I know how he responds beyond the call of duty,' she said, 'and it just overwhelmed me to see this appreciation.'"

The family recalls that the master of ceremonies said he was pleased that Aura Jacobsen was there with her husband. He emphasized that they worked as a team and added that he had never seen them walk across the street together without holding hands.

An enthusiastic horseman, Jacobsen kept a horse at a local rural home and he was one of the founders of the Rainbow Saddle Club. He was a member of the Northfield Farm Bureau and was a director of the Rice County Health Association.

The story that appeared in the *News* when the Jacobsens arrived in Northfield tells that he had been president of the Chamber of Commerce in International Falls and that he had been active in civic and community organizations and in Boy Scouting wherever he had lived.

The story said, "Jacobsen states that he is very much impressed with Northfield as his future place of business and home. The friendliness of the people with whom he had come in contact, the modern, up-to-date business establishments, the many churches with services well attended, the well-staffed schools, and the apparent prosperity of the citizens convinced Jacobsen of the business possibilities in Northfield. Before purchasing the local Federated store, Mr. and Mrs. Jacobsen investigated business openings in several other cities in Minnesota and Iowa and their final choice was the Northfield location."

Jacobsen was survived by two sons and it was his son Robert "Bob," then living in Arlington, Va., who moved to Northfield and for many years guided Jacobsen's Store, assisted by his wife Elaine. They are still active, but now one of Ralph Jacobsen's grandsons, Bob and Elaine's son Roland "Rollie," heads the firm and his wife Shar is active in the business.

15 January, 1993

1969: 'Army' heads Industrial Corporation
Armstrong slows down very little

"Industrial group chooses officers" was a headline on page one of the April 10, 1969, *Northfield News*. The story began, "A. E. Armstrong was re-elected president of the Northfield Industrial Corporation during its reorganization meeting."

Other officers chosen, according to the story, were Burnett Voss, a new member of the board, vice president; Hilbert Reese, re-elected treasurer; Robert Jacobsen, secretary.

The story continued, "The board indicated that it plans to work very closely during the coming year with the Northfield Area Chamber of Commerce, in efforts to attract industry to Northfield.

Jacobsen made a plea for anyone with a new idea about "attracting industry, about what kind of industry is needed here, about anything pertaining to the Northfield Industrial Association's work," to contact one of the officers.

Armstrong worked tirelessly for the N.I.C. over a span of several years. Eventually the industrial park for which he expended much energy was named for him and a road within the park is named Armstrong.

Several years earlier he had worked with the Northfield Area Chamber of Commerce at high pitch and he was devoted to the Rotary Club, editing its newsletter for some time.

A man comparatively small in stature, but with the nickname "Army," he seemed tireless, even at 92. But he died in that year — April 9, 1976 — after only two days of illness following a stroke. He had been especially active in his last few weeks, attending meetings and being honored at the annual meeting of the N.I.C. — that's when he was presented with an "Armstrong Road" sign.

A feature story that appeared in the *News* at that time said that after Armstrong retired, he was still "very much about the town, always popping in on store owners, pointing to this and that strategy, making a change here and there, and even selling merchandise if the

store was busy! 'You have to keep going, there are things to be done,' said Army."

Armstrong's roots were in Michigan and he could lay claim to having been born in a log farm house. He was born March 28, 1884, in Hillsdale County, Michigan and grew up on that farm. His father had come from Ireland and his mother from England.

Armstrong attended a country district school and later the high school in the town of Frontier. He lived at the home of a sister while attending Hillsdale College. During the school year he worked in a men's clothing factory. In summers he traveled throughout the state of Michigan selling Underwood & Underwood stereo views to homes and libraries.

At their time of graduation, several of his classmates were selected as YMCA candidates to teach in schools in China and Japan and Armstrong's appetite for travel developed. He arranged to represent Underwood & Underwood in China.

A revolution developed in China after he had been there six months and the stereo view business collapsed. Armstrong decided that the Chinese would be more interested in machinery than pictures and he went to work for the Singer Sewing Machine Co. He bought a 35-foot launch in Shanghai and lived on board while traveling the provinces of Hupeh, Hunan, Honan and Kiangsi — an area of 200,000 square miles. He promoted sales, set up agencies and established sewing schools since few Chinese know how to operate a sewing machine. It wasn't always possible to travel by boat — Armstrong also got places by mule cart, pony, sedan chair, even wheelbarrows propelled by coolies, and sometimes afoot.

He also had his hands full trying to protect Singer interests in Hankow where the revolution was particularly intense. The Chinese were revolting against the Manchus and subsequently set up the Chinese republic. The city was almost entirely burned. Armstrong was later honored by the Sun Yat Sen government for rescuing children from a school for the blind while it was under Manchu fire.

It was in Hankow that Armstrong met Elsa Felland, native of Northfield and graduate of St. Olaf College. She had arrived in China to teach in a Lutheran mission school, but the American official who was to meet her boat was taken ill. Armstrong was asked to go down to the dock to do the honors. "You might say my ship came in," he told a *News* reporter back in 1952. The young people were married in Hankow in 1914 and remained there for another three years.

The Armstrongs returned to the United States in 1917, settling in Bronson, Mich. He bought a large general store and converted it into a department store. He served as mayor of Bronson for a time and was a deacon in his church.

In 1941 Mrs. Armstrong received word that no one was going to be living in her beloved family home at 1212 St. Olaf Avenue in Northfield. So the family moved to Northfield.

Armstrong and his sister-in-law, Valborg

Felland, bought the Ole Store, a business that had been established in the 19th century. The business included a grocery store and meat market, Ole Lunch and a freezer plant, established at a time when there were comparatively few home freezers. He continued to own and be active in the store until he was 75.

In addition to the aforementioned activities in Northfield, he served on the Rice County Nursing Board, served on boards and taught Sunday school at St. John's Lutheran Church, helped raise funds for various causes including the building of the Northfield Retirement Center where he and his wife went to live in 1972.

In 1962 when he was 78, Armstrong had a special thrill. He had longed to return to the Orient, but had not considered it possible. However that year he accompanied one of his sons, the late Philip Armstrong, on an inspection trip of the facilities of the Far Eastern Gospel Crusade of which the latter was executive secretary. They spent nearly three months in Japan, the Philippines, Cambodia, Hong Kong and Okinawa. After returning to Northfield, Armstrong delighted in showing slides taken on that trip.

When the Armstrongs celebrated their golden wedding anniversary in 1965, two people were at the open house who had attended the wedding in a little stone chapel in the mountains, an area cool in summer where missionaries to China often spent the hot months. They were the Rev. Edward A. Sovik, Sr., and Gertrude Sovik. The latter was among the school children who had gathered flowers on the mountainside to be used at the wedding.

The Armstrongs celebrated their 60th wedding anniversary after moving to the Center.

15 April, 1994

1970: Gill named to Rice County planning post

Much effort given in behalf of fellow citizens

William R. Gill — still very much alive and active — was named Rice County planning and zoning administrator by the Rice county board of commissioners, according to a page-one story in the *Northfield News* of Jan. 1, 1970. Gill was to succeed Lee Fullerton who had resigned after serving in the post since its inception.

The story said, "Gill is considered well qualified by the board which cited his service on the county board of parks and recreation since its formation in 1966.

"Gill is a former member of the Northfield city council. Much of his adult life, he has been engaged in insurance work and real estate sales. He also operated a hardware store for a time. He is a native of Northfield."

Gill grew up on a farm near the west edge of Northfield and graduated from Northfield High School in 1936. He attended Carleton College and served in World War II. On his return from service he became an agent for Prudential Life Insurance Co.

His first important venture into public life was his election to the Northfield city council from the first ward in the spring of 1956.

He also served on the board of directors of the Oaklawn Cemetery Association in those years.

In 1958 he purchased the Schrader Hardware Store on Bridge Square (present location of Centerfield Music) which had belonged to his uncle, Delmer Schrader, who had recently died. Gill had worked in the store while in high school.

The following spring he successfully ran for reelection to the council. Although his interests were broad, he had especially redesigned the city's insurance program. As a result, coverage was complete, payments were equalized and the city's various insurance agents were being treated alike, a *News* story stated. It was possible for city officials to be in constant touch with the insurance program.

Because of a city charter change, Gill ran

for office successfully again in November of 1961, this time as councilman-at-large. But the following fall brought a big change in his life. He closed out the hardware stock and resigned from the council because he was moving to Germany. He had accepted a position with Capital Life Insurance Co. of Denver to sell insurance to members of the United States armed forces stationed in Germany and their dependents.

After he returned to Northfield in late 1964, Gill became associated with W. E. Thompson who had been in real estate business in Northfield for 10 years. With the two men's association, their firm was able to offer insurance as well. During the succeeding months, Gill worked at obtaining a real estate broker's license.

In May of 1966, he opened his own real estate and insurance office at 103 E. Fourth. During those years he was active in CoDeP, Northfield's community development program. He served as chair of the community facilities committee, trying to determine the community's needs for auditorium, theater, library, city hall, fire station, police station, civil defense facilities, meeting rooms, health and medical care facilities, tourist and conference promotion. Also for two years he managed Northfield Golf Club.

In 1968 he was named a representative of North American Life and Casualty and established his office in his home at 118 College.

During the 1970s the Gills did some further traveling. In 1975 they returned to Germany and several nearby countries. In 1977 they visited England, Scotland, Ireland and the Isle of Mann. In the latter area, Gill visited the church and cemetery in the village of his ancestors, able to trace his family back to 1730.

As county planning and zoning commissioner, Gill put his various backgrounds —farm, real estate, city government — to good use. With many new problems cropping up, he was innovative. When in 1981 he was given the Award of Excellence from the Minnesota Planning Association, the only planner honored at the MPA conference, the letter of commendation said in part:

"Bill Gill has made a number of very significant contributions to planning in Minnesota. . . . During the past 11 years, he has served as zoning administrator for Rice County and was partly responsible for developing the density control system pioneered in the county. The density control system used in Rice County has been adopted by many counties in other states including Iowa, Wyoming, Nebraska and others. The Rice County density control system was also used as a case study of protection of agricultural land by the State Planning Agency in its recently completed growth management study and by the United States Department of Agriculture in its national agricultural lands study."

The citation also included a list of committees on which Gill had served:

— Chairman of the Region 10 Land Use Committee to develop the Region 10 growth and development plan.

— Minnesota Pollution Control Agency committee to develop Minnesota on-site sewer system regulations.

— Minnesota Planning Association, long range planning committee.

— Environmental Task Force for the Association of Minnesota Counties.

— Legislative committee for the Minnesota Association of County Planning and Zoning Administrators.

— President of Minnesota Association of County Planning and Zoning Administrators. (He was elected first president in 1973.)

Goals of the new group included uniform county zoning, promotion of beneficial state legislation affecting planning, encouragement of improved technical quality of county planning, interchange of administrative thought, and more efficiency in the field of planning.

The citation concluded, "In short, during his career, Bill Gill has made a significant and long lasting contribution to the field of planning in Minnesota."

During this period of his life, Gill served as secretary to the Rice County board of adjustment.

While administrator, he attended the University of Wisconsin Institute on developing land use regulations and the Pepperdine University Land Use School.

At the end of 1981, Gill retired from the position. A period followed during which he served as a consultant in behalf of a national firm, Wehrman Consulting Associates, Inc., with main office in Golden Valley.

But in the fall of 1982 he decided to run for mayor of Northfield and was elected. Reelected for a second term, he headed the city for six years.

While mayor, he served at times on the League of Minnesota Cities committee for land use, energy, environment and transportation; on a council-school district-city hospital committee to study working together to save taxpayers money; as chair of the

Coalition of Outstate Cities; as president of Hiawathaland, tourism group that promotes southern Minnesota. (One of the special features of his terms as mayor was encouragement of tourism in Northfield.) He also, on a temporary basis, returned to his county post while a new administrator was sought.

In September of 1988, Mayor Gill joined an entourage of state leaders and business leaders on a trip to the then Soviet Union to learn about Russian life and to tell about Midwestern American life.

As retiring mayor in 1988, he explained his life, "I feel to make the city you live in a good place to live in, you should take part in community affairs." At his final council meeting as mayor, the 1988 Comprehensive Plan for Northfield was adopted, a plan he had worked hard to develop.

Honors came in 1989 — the Northfield Rotary Club's Service Above Self award (he had been president of the Rotary Club in 1975-76); the Charlie Pitts Award for promotion of James-Younger Gang activities in connection with Defeat of Jesse James Days.

In 1982 he was named recipient of Community National Bank's Hometown Spirit Award.

He was slowed down only a bit by an eye problem (1984) and triple bypass surgery (1989).

Gill and his wife Elaine were first to move into a group of condominiums in the 400 block of Woodley St. in 1984, selling a house on Lia Drive. The couple has four adult children and a group of grandchildren.

Have we omitted anything? Probably. For instance, there is a clipping in the Bill Gill biographical file at the *News* that shows Gill in the role of Dr. William Emmett in the three-act comedy, "The Curious Savage," early dramatic effort of the Northfield Arts Guild in 1961!

6 January, 1995

1970: Voss named president of Rotary

Postmaster had many activities

"Burnett Voss was installed as the 45th president of the Northfield Rotary Club at the club's meeting last Thursday," announced the *Northfield News* of July 23, 1970.

But serving Rotary was just a fraction of his activities in Northfield through the years.

He operated a transfer line and served as Northfield's postmaster but he also served on the board of education and the city council, and held office in a number of organizations. As a senior citizen he became known in Minnesota for his work on issues of the aging.

Voss, who was best known by his nickname, Buntz, wasn't born in Northfield. He was born in December of 1913 in Owatonna. But his family moved to Northfield when he was less than 2 years old. He graduated from Northfield High School in 1931 and attended St. Olaf College. He owned and operated Voss Transfer most of the time from 1935 until 1961. He worked in shipyards at Savage for a few months during World War II.

It was in May of 1961 that he sold the long distance and local moving company to the Britton Brothers who operated it for many more years. Voss was at that time beginning his duties as acting postmaster, having been installed at the close of business on March 31.

He was one of three most highly rated persons who participated in a civil service examination in the spring of 1962 and in August of 1962 was nominated for the position of postmaster by President Kennedy. He received word on Sept. 11 that his appointment as postmaster had been confirmed by the United States Senate.

While serving as postmaster, Voss was elected to office in the seventh district of the Minnesota Chapter of the National Association of Postmasters of the United States. He and his wife Beulah attended a convention of the National Association of Postmasters of the United States that was held in Hawaii in 1963.

The Vosses always loved to travel and visited many states. When he retired in December of 1975, at age 62, he told a *News* reporter that he had decided to retire quite a few years before the required retirement age of 70 because he would like to be able to do considerable traveling. The couple at that time moved to an apartment where "we can just turn the key when we want to go somewhere."

Voss served on the Northfield Board of Education from 1950 to 1955. When he was seeking that office, his biographical sketch in the *News* stated that he was serving as chairman of the board of trustees of the Congregational Church, now First United Church of Christ (later he served as deacon), had been president of the Northfield Baseball Association, was president of the Northfield DFL Club, was treasurer of the Northfield Volunteer Fire Department, and was a member of all local branches of the Masonic Lodge.

Voss was elected to the city council from the second ward in the spring of 1956. He was reelected in 1959, but in 1961 when an amended city charter made necessary an election for all city officials, Voss chose not to run. He said that he had already given considerable time and energy to the public and preferred to concentrate on his new duties as acting postmaster.

During the period he served on the council, he was a member of the finance committee for four years, chair of the utility commission for six years. The sewage disposal plant was built during that time and the city's water improvement project was awarded the North Central Water Association Award.

Voss served as chairman of both the Northfield DFL Club and the Rice County DFL organization, but resigned from those activities when he was named postmaster. A special experience resulted from his county chairmanship, however. He and Beulah were invited to attend the inauguration of President Kennedy. In Washington, they were house guests of a dear friend, a former Northfielder, and they were able to do some unusual sightseeing.

The Jan. 26, 1961, *News* recorded possibly the most outstanding experience of the trip: "Thursday morning, Voss had the hunch that getting down to the center of the city early might bring him in contact with Ex-President Harry Truman who most surely would be out for his famed morning walk. Sure enough, he not only saw Truman, but talked with him, an experience Buntz regards as one of his very best in Washington."

Voss was a member of the United Fund board for three years in the early 1960s. He headed the fund drive for two years and served as president of the board for the year 1963.

In 1962 Voss headed the Defeat of Jesse James Days celebration.

After 20 years of service to the Northfield Volunteer Fire Department, he received his honorable discharge in 1963. But that was not a sign he was slowing down. He was still serving on the city planning commission and he became chairman of the committee on upgrading the business district for CoDeP, a community development project. In 1969 he was elected a director of the Northfield Industrial Corporation and was chosen president in 1970. He chaired the Chamber of Commerce governmental affairs committee for six years.

He served on the Northfield Retirement Center board (Lutheran Home of the Cannon Valley board is the official name) for six years. During that period, he chaired the building committee and was president of the board for one year.

During his many years in the Rotary Club, he was especially interested in the student exchange program. A letter to the editor at the time of Voss's retirement from the position of postmaster said: "In addition to all the fine achievements the *News* credited to Buntz Voss, there is one more that deserves mention. His support of international understanding through student exchange programs has put Northfield on the map for people all over the world. Through the Rotary Club he worked hard to bring students here to Northfield from many parts of the world and to send Northfield students abroad. I don't suppose we can ever know how far-reaching the effects of these programs have been."

The Vosses did more than support such programs, they served as host parents to Rotary exchange students from Brazil, Australia and Thailand.

In 1974, while on one of their rambling tours, the Vosses stopped in Chicago to celebrate their 40th wedding anniversary. They repeated their vows in the church in which they were married four decades before.

A story in the *News* in the summer of 1976 regarding the upgrading of TH 19 from Northfield to Interstate 35 to a nine-ton status, noted Voss's share. "Burnett Voss, retired postmaster, has been chairman of the Chamber committee in the effort and has devoted uncounted hours to the cause."

During the last decade before his untimely death from cancer, Voss dedicated many,

many hours to problems of the aging. He served as a member of the Advisory Council on Aging of the Region 10 development committee, chaired the board of the Southeastern Minnesota Area Agency on Aging for three years, was a member of the Southeastern Health System Agency board for three years, was a member of the Minnesota Board on Aging for eight years after being appointed by Governor Perpich, chairing its legislative committee for six years, was a member of the Rice County Long Term Care Task Force in 1985-86, and served on the Senior Consumer Advisory Panel for US West from 1989 to 1992. In the late 1980s, he was active in the successful fight to enact a living will law in Minnesota.

Meanwhile Beulah, who was born in Minneapolis and grew up at Lakeville, was involved in a number of local projects. The two were honored in 1982, chosen as representative senior citizens to receive mention during Heritage Day on the Fourth of July.

At that time Voss was asked why he hadn't retired to a warm weather state. He replied, "Believe me, I never want to leave Northfield." He said that he felt an obligation to give back some of the good things he had received from the community.

His death occurred on April 16, 1992, even though he had worked diligently at early detection and in fighting the cancer.

Beulah, who still resides here, and Buntz brought up four daughters, all of whom received excellent advanced education. There are also a number of grandchildren and great-grandchildren.

28 July, 1995

1972: Everett L. Dilley, long theater owner, dies at 89
Dilley known for operating unusually fine theater

"Former theater owner dies," was a headline in the March 16, 1972, *Northfield News*.

The story stated, "Everett L. Dilley, 89, died Monday evening March 13, at Northfield Hospital. Dilley, who had been living at Waterford since his retirement, was for many years the owner of Northfield's theaters. . . .

"Dilley sold the Grand and West theaters (the latter having been subsequently razed in the path of TH 3 on the West Side) in 1947 after more than 30 years of theater ownership here.

"As a young man following his graduation from Northfield High School, he had gone on the road as an actor with a theater company. Motion pictures were just capturing the interest of the public when he returned to Northfield and he soon was running a projector in one of the early theaters that sprouted here.

"He was still pioneering and was operating on a shoestring when he and other stockholders established the Grand Theater in the Ware Auditorium building in 1917. He took over complete ownership in 1921. The Grand came to be known as one of the finest moving picture theaters in southern Minnesota. A number of times the Grand featured the Northwest premiere of a movie. The West was erected in 1937."

Dilley was interviewed by the *News* in 1971 when he was 88. He recalled the excitement and competitive furor caused by the earliest films even though they were black and white and until 1928, lacked sound.

"I had gone on the road as an actor with a theater company after I graduated from high school," he recalled, "and when we played in the bigger towns like Fargo I saw my first motion pictures. A couple of rows of chairs would be set up in a store front and they would play half-hour comedies and illustrated songs with a piano playing along.

"About half of the people at the time were sure that movies would never last, never catch on. But there were a lot of people who were convinced enough to try the business and I was one of them."

Dilley said he returned to Northfield in 1907 and engaged in painting (buildings) while waiting for an opportunity to establish his own theater.

"Once it became clear that moving pictures were becoming popular, practically every town had several theaters that tried to get started," Dilley said. "One of the first in Northfield was located upstairs above Bierman's on Division. I remember that one because the owner, Andy Wyant, hired me to paint his sign for him. He had a gasoline engine in the basement of the building that ran his own generator that powered the projector."

Dilley said that between 1910 and 1915 there were at least three theaters downtown. Most of them were in existence only a couple of months. He said that stiff competition, frequent projector breakdowns and difficulty of obtaining a variety of films at a low enough price forced them, one by one, out of business.

He recalled, "I was the projectionist at the theater at 13 Bridge Square (now Turtle Hill Bead Shop) for the two or three months it was running. We paid $15 for a movie with Norma Talmadge, a big star at the time, and advertised it all over town. We even got pine boughs to decorate the lamps in the room, made a big fuss. But instead of the Talmadge film, the distributor sent 'Custer's Last Stand.' I got really mad about that and told the owner I quit, so they closed the theater down."

One theater, the Star, started on the West Side in about 1912 in what is now the Hvistendahl & Moersch law office, 311 S. Water, and flourished for some time. Fred Boll bought it and moved it across the street into part of the Eagles building, changing its name to the Gem. Because many Northfielders were concerned about the propriety of movies, the Gem established its own restrictive codes, Dilley remembered.

"No St. Olaf students and no Carleton

women were allowed to go there, although sometimes you could see 60 young women lined up at the side door waiting to sneak in," Dilley said. He recalled that it was not until 1930 that movies could be shown in Northfield on Sunday, voters having approved the change.

In pre-World War I days a couple of people tried the movie business in the vacant Ware Auditorium, but they lost customers because they couldn't manage to heat the building.

With an operating capital of $200 each from local businessmen, Dick Shorrocks, Bill Revier, Talford McGuire, Henry King and Dilley himself, Dilley's theater opened in the auditorium on Feb. 19, 1917. With a clever projectionist who had a revolutionary idea, the Grand Theater was the only theater around that could show a movie non-stop from beginning to end. Dilley solved the heating problem by closing off some of the massive space. Dilley also purchased the Gem and he arranged for a five-piece orchestra to accompany the silent films.

Dilley remembered that during the war, the theater faced financial difficulty and all of the original shareholders excepting himself and Shorrocks sold out. By 1921 the business was flourishing, however, and Dilley became the sole owner. He installed a console organ in 1925 to replace the orchestra.

Talking pictures came on the local scene in 1927. Owners of the Minnesota Amusement Co. which owned 60 to 70 theaters meant to capitalize on their new sound equipment, Dilley remembered, and they announced the intention of erecting a 1,000 seat theater on the vacant lot where part of the Perman building is located.

Dilley said, "I decided that instead of facing that competition, it was time for me to sell out." The Amusement Co. took over the Grand and retained Dilley as their local manager.

After a couple of years, the Amusement Co. sold the theater to the Publix organization, part of Paramount Pictures.

In citing Dilley for community service in 1929, the *News* said, "A dozen years ago when Everett L. Dilley leased the Ware Auditorium and opened the Grand Theater, there were those who felt that he had set his standards too high and that 'the theater with ideals' could not be made to pay — even in Northfield. But the manager of The Grand felt that Northfield would support just such a theater as he proposed to operate, and events have demonstrated that Dilley, and not the scoffers, were right."

In 1933, Dilley bought back the business and also bought the building. At that time he began planning the West Theater to keep out the competition and to have a place to show the "C" movies that were of trade necessity purchased along with the better ones. Dilley took great care and pride in the program that he was able to present at the Grand. He was usually ahead of theaters in much larger Minnesota cities.

Through the years he constantly improved the equipment, even concentrating on good sound equipment though the building was rated as having the best acoustics in several states.

Through the years, his wife Jess, to whom he was married in 1907, had been active in the business. He was also at times assisted by his son-in-law and daughter, Erling and Eileen Larsen.

The Dilleys spent their winters in retirement in an apartment at the Larsen farm at Waterford. They spent summers at a cabin on the North Shore of Lake Superior. Mrs. Dilley died unexpectedly of a coronary occlusion in January of 1958.

Though he devoted considerable effort to his business, Dilley was active in other facets of the community. He was a charter member of the Northfield Lions Club, was chairmen of various Lions committees, served in the club's offices including president, elected in 1932. With the theater program, he joined into a number of public efforts.

14 March, 1997

1972: Pioneer family member, spouse observe anniversary

Clarence Albers serves 14 years on Rice County board

Clarence and Ellen Albers celebrated their 50th wedding anniversary with a reception held at Albers park at Union Lake on Sunday afternoon, Sept. 3, according to a story that appeared in the Sept. 14, 1972, *News*.

The story said that several of the attendants at the wedding a half century before were present for the celebration. They included Albers' sister, Frances Neary, who had been maid of honor; another sister, Harriet Furgason who had been the musician; Clarence Gustafson, brother of Mrs. Albers, who had been best man. Katherine Friberg Fry, who had been flower girl, had died several years before the celebration.

During the anniversary celebration, the couple's son, Howard, welcomed some 400 relatives and friends attending. The Rev. Lorenz Adam, pastor of the Northfield Moravian Church where the family had long worshipped, spoke briefly. Joyce Gill read the account of the wedding from a 1922 *Northfield News*. She also read several headlines from the same paper, giving an idea of what was going on in the community at the time.

Marilyn Sellars, long-time friend of the honored couple, sang. Also included in music offered on the occasion were guitar solos by Bob Gustafson. R.F. "Bud" Gustafson, master of ceremonies, entertained with original humorous poems, one written especially for the Albers.

The story stated that Clarence H. Albers and Ellen Amelia Gustafson had married Sept. 2, 1922, in Minneapolis. They had farmed for many years on the place where Albers had been born — the former H. F. C. Albers farm, three miles west of Dundas on Rice County No. 1. They had moved into Northfield — at 212 W. Woodley — in 1957, but Albers had always remained active in farming, working along with Howard.

The write-up concluded, "Until 1970, Albers served for 14 years as a Rice County commissioner. Before that he was on the Bridgewater Township board and served the community in many other capacities. He was for a time president of the Rice County Fair board."

The couple lived to celebrate their 60th wedding anniversary in 1982, that time at a quiet family party at the Double Tree restaurant. By then they were spending summers in Northfield and winters in Mesa, Ariz.

Ellen Albers died in 1986 and Clarence in 1988 at age 91.

Before he served on the county board, Albers served on the board of the Rice County Agricultural Society — sponsor of the Rice County Fair — in the 1940s. He became vice president in 1947 and in 1948 was named president. He was re-elected president in 1950.

Albers was appointed to the Rice County Board of Commissioners late in 1956 following the accidental death of Ernest E. Schrader. He was reelected to a four-year term in 1958. He resigned in 1971 when he felt that his hearing was interfering with his work. He told a *News* reporter, "It was my hearing. You know sometimes you get a fellow that's a little shy and you can't hear what he's trying to say. A commissioner's got to be sharp."

Albers took his turn through the years at serving as chairman of the board. He also at times headed the Rice County welfare board. He also served on the board of the South Central Mental Heath Center in which he was particularly interested. He served on the highways committee of the State Association of County Commissioners.

Albers expressed a strong belief to the aforementioned *News* reporter that county government has to be strong and efficient to serve the community. It was his belief that local government is best suited to serve the people directly.

"In our case," he said, "we (the county commissioners) know the people. We know what they are doing and what they need while the fellow from Washington has a problem.

"The biggest hurdle for local government seems to be overcoming the policies sent down by state and federal governments. They set the policies, they are ready-made and we are supposed to carry them out — and we can't change them." He cited example after example of the difficulty for a county board — who knows its people — to implement a plan made in Washington.

He also spoke about the necessity of working things out with other members of the board. "You won't live long enough to have everything turn out your way," he said.

Back in 1948, Bill Schilling devoted a major part of a "Heard on the Square" column to Albers, some of it very much tongue-in-cheek. He wrote in part, "Clarence Albers asked me to come out to his farm the other morning to help him extract the excrement from the rear of two rows of beautiful cows. I went and it was the very first time that I had visited the farm on which his father, Henry F. C. Albers had settled. . . . On this farm, Clarence and the seven other members of the Albers family were raised. As is so often the case, almost all the children left

the farm to take on more aristocratic professions. Clarence was selected by old Henry to take over the home farm as he had grown to gigantic proportions tramping about in the rich Bridgewater soil until special sized shoes had to be provided for him to hold together his 260 pounds of avoirdupois."

Schilling said that as a young man, Albers frequented dances at Union Lake and "there he met the Gustafson brothers who taught him his first real bad habit, that of chewing snoose. For this unkind teaching, Clarence labored for many moons to get even with the Swedes and finally did so by marrying their sister."

Schilling claimed that Albers for a time served as bouncer at the Union Lake dance resort. But because of his size and strength, he was too efficient. Young men complained to the proprietors that their bouncer played too rough and "the big boy lost his job."

Schilling wrote, "When the turkey craze hit the sticks, Clarence took to raising this great Thanksgiving delicacy and at one time had 5,000 birds. . . . Everybody began raising turkeys and then he quit, rather than flood and glut the market. . . .

"But with cows, black and white ones, is where he shines and his finest great big ones would be hard to beat. . . .

"I went out to help clean the cow barn and so Clarence took me in and had me stand in the alley between the long rows of big-uddered cows (he has ordered brassieres for them). As I stood there, he pressed a button and on both gutters the fertilizer began to literally walk out of the barn and in five minutes it was all over with. The hired man, with a big tractor and a spreader hitch, was off in a jiffy with the load to the field."

It was especially appropriate that the golden wedding celebration was conducted in Albers Park because the tract was closely associated with Clarence Albers. The story of the park dedication which appeared in the *News* on Sept. 24, 1970, stated that the principal speaker was Robert Warn of Northfield, then a director of the Rice County Historical Society who was particularly interested in the history of this immediate area.

"He revealed an interesting fact dug up by the Albers family during the week before the dedication," the story said. "Although the particular tract on the shore of Union Lake that is now known as Albers Park was owned by the Albers family for many years, it was actually homesteaded by Harry H. Humphrey, great-grandfather of Hubert H. Humphrey, Minnesotan who was vice president of the United States. It was acquired from the United States government in 1856 and was owned by the Humphrey family for about 20 years.

"There were other owners before it was purchased by the Henry Albers family in 1883. In 1888 it became a YMCA camp, named Camp Dean in honor of Edwin B. Dean, minister of the Congregational Church in Northfield who was an enthusiastic outdoorsman. After a few years, the tract was reacquired by the Albers family and remained in their ownership until the mid 1920s.

"When Rice County acquired the land for park purposes, part was obtained for tax forfeiture (not on the part of any Albers family) and the other portion was purchased from the Camp family estate. County funds only were involved in the purchase; there were no federal or state funds as in some of the other county parks recently developed.

"The park was named for the Albers family not only because the land had once belonged to them, but because that family is one of the oldest in Rice County and has contributed heavily to the development of Rice County through the decades.

"Warn traced the history of the Albers family from the arrival of Adelaide Albers, a widow 61 years old. She was accompanied by two sons, Friedrich (with his family) and — 17 years younger — Henry. The family is now in the sixth generation in Rice County and Adelaide has more than 450 descendants (in 1970).

"The family's original home was a log cabin on the present Henry Ludwig farm on the Dutch Road about six miles west of Northfield. They staked out a 16 acre claim, but at one time in his life, Friedrich was to own as many as 1,300 acres.

"There was a Chippewa Indian settlement in the neighborhood of the new park, Warn revealed, and the Indians and the Albers had a beneficial swap agreement. The Indians traded fresh pickerel caught in Heath Creek for fresh white bread made by the Albers women. The white families gladly participated for the sake of friendly relations."

Clarence Albers died Dec. 11, 1988, at the Odd Fellows Home.

His obituary said that he was born June 24, 1897, to Henry and Louise (Zimmerman) Albers in the family farm home. He attended Burlington grade school and Dundas High School.

The obituary also said that after their marriage, the Albers stayed on the family farm where he was a dairy farmer and raised hog and turkeys. "He retired from dairying in 1960 but continued with crop farming until 1973. The family farm is now owned by his nephew, Gene Albers."

The obituary said that Clarence Albers had held many church council positions at the Moravian Church. He had been a member of the Odd Fellows lodge since 1927. He was a board member of the Tri-County Co-op which eventually was merged into the Cannon Valley Co-op. His hobbies were baseball, fishing and deer hunting.

12 September, 1997

1973: Lee Dahl shepherds move to much larger building
With family, Dahl also establishes chain of stores

"Open for business Monday after a weekend move across the street was the Dahl House. The store, with a completely new front and interior, is in the location of the former Alex Marshall store." This story appeared in the Nov. 8, 1973, *Northfield News*.

The story explained that the new front incorporated the arch that was often seen in early brick and stone buildings in Northfield and which architects had been reviving in the 1970s. "The interior of the store, emphasizing blues, reds, orange and greens, was designed by Lee Dahl, president of the Dahl House.

"The move is being made in the seventh year of business for the Northfield Dahl House, first of the group." The story explained that there were also Dahl Houses by that time at Mankato and Rochester.

Although she was always president of the firm, Lee insisted when interviewed for a "Women at Work" supplement to the *News* in 1984, that, "I was the most visible. But Fred (her husband) has always been involved. I would have gone broke if he hadn't been."

Dahl said that she and her husband had long shared a dream of owning a ready-to-wear store. They moved to Northfield because they thought it would be a good place to bring up their children. But they also thought it would be a great place to open a store.

Fred Dahl was a traveling salesman for a ready-to-wear wholesaler and Lee Dahl was a salesperson at Perman's store when the couple decided, in 1967, that the time was ripe to start their own store. Fred continued to travel until 1970 when the couple opened their second store — in the Madison East Mall at Mankato.

Their very first store was on the east side of Division — at 311 Division, the store space recently vacated by Blue Marble. For awhile Lee was the only full-time employee. She specialized in junior sizes there and it was a wish to try selling "missy" sizes that caused the Dahls to open a second store across the street at 306 Division. Their lease at 311 still had quite a ways to run when the 1973 move was made.

Business remained brisk at both sites, but Lee recalled in her interview that "staff members were eternally running back and forth across the street to match up a blouse with a suit" or something of the kind. Meanwhile the two kinds of sizes were being combined in the stores that were opened in other cities.

Eventually a son and his wife decided they would like to use the 311 Division space for a children's clothing shop and all of the adult clothing was combined at 306 Division.

When the store at Mankato was opened, Fred commuted from Northfield, but often stayed overnight at Mankato because the couple felt they could not afford to hire a manager for the new store. However, the next year they opened the store at Rochester and began to enlarge their staff.

The store in the Cedar Mall at Owatonna followed in 1974; in the Mississippi Plaza at Winona in 1976; in the St. James Hotel at Red Wing in 1979.

The Dahls had no idea of owning a store outside of Minnesota, but the developer with whom they had worked at Owatonna began the Cedar Mall at Spencer, Iowa. He wooed the Dahls insistently and they opened a store that proved to be an outstanding success. The ice broken, they opened other stores in both Iowa and Wisconsin.

But one of their important stores was in Duluth in a new development in the old

Fitzger's Brewery. Another unusual location was Bandana Square, the shopping area in Energy Park, St. Paul. Eventually there were 22 stores with more than 400 employees,

The couple had another corporation, F&L Partners, which constructed a warehouse and office building on the west end of Northfield in 1980. That corporation also bought the downtown building after a decade of renting.

In the aforementioned interview, the Dahls were asked about the good and bad features of spending 24 hours together and even taking vacations together.

"I haven't found the bad," said Fred. "Fred is my best friend," Lee said. "That might sound like baloney," Fred added. "But our friends and employees have noticed that we get on unusually well. I think it's important that we don't overlap each others' areas."

While Fred was primarily interested in the business end, Lee was especially interested in the buying. By 1984, the time of the interview, buying was done three times a year in California, once a month in New York and as often as possible in Minneapolis.

"Fashions change so quickly," Lee said, and there is no longer a lag between the East Coast and the Midwest. "You look at Midwesterners walking along the street and they are current and well dressed." She said that she could see trends developing by reading trade newspapers and fashion magazines as well as by observing at market.

"It's always a good idea to remember why you opened a store," she said. "You had a unique idea that you wanted to present to the public. The public is what is important and you had better never forget that."

The couple emphasized that they had always looked for enthusiastic and outgoing personnel. They said that their fine employees had everything to do with the success of their business.

Busy as she was, Lee had time for some other activities. In 1977 she was appointed to Northfield's human rights commission.

Lee was actually a nickname. Leona Mae was born, one of identical twins, to Edwin and Esther Stratmoen, dairy farmers at Dawson. (Noel Stratmoen of Northfield is a brother.) Lee graduated from Dawson High School in 1945 and from the Minnesota School of Business in 1947. She met her husband the following year. The couple had four sons.

Lee was visiting at her parental home at Dawson in July of 1988 when she complained of a severe headache. She was rushed by ambulance to the hospital at Willmar where she died the next day of a cerebral hemorrhage.

Her obituary noted that her unique personality had been summed up by a brother-in-law, "After God made Lee Dahl, He threw away the mold." The obituary also noted that "her keen fashion sense and warmth in dealing with people were key elements in the success of The Dahl House."

The funeral service was at St. John's Lutheran Church and interment was in Oaklawn Cemetery.

When Lee mentioned in the 1984 interview that she and Fred not only worked together, but vacationed together, she perhaps had in mind that in the works were plans for a trip to the Scandinavian countries in the late summer.

Her obituary was to mention that she and her twin sister, Mae Matthews of South St. Paul, were extremely close, sharing a special love. The story about the European trip that appeared in the *News* noted that Fred had had the unusual experience of traveling for four weeks with identical twins because Mae went along with Fred and Lee. Mae's husband was unable to make the trip, the story said.

The story continued, "The trio walked a great deal and Fred said it was fun for him to drop back a bit and watch people's reactions to the two women who looked just alike. Naturally they do not dress alike anymore, but their looks, their actions, their gestures reflect each other."

It seems not at all strange that Fred, left a widower, and Mae, who became a widow, eventually decided to share their lives and were married.

6 November, 1998

1974: 'Johnny' Fremouw, former city councilman, dies
'Johnny' Fremouw in business in area for many years

"A life of public service and creativity ended Thursday, July 11, 1974, at Northfield Hospital when John Edward Fremouw died at about 3:30PM," the obituary for an outstanding Northfielder began.

The story continued, "A former Northfield businessman, he had also served on the Northfield city council for 10 years and had sought the office of mayor. Toward the end of his business career, he became highly skilled at ornamental ironwork, contracting over a rather wide area. In retirement he built grandfather clocks."

Fremouw was born Oct. 2, 1901, in Northfield. He attended the public schools here, graduating from Northfield High School in 1920. He attended St. Olaf College for two years.

His father, Edward John Fremouw, and his uncle, Frank C. Fremouw, had bought into the local ice business (refrigeration ice cut from Cannon River winter ice) in 1909 and had taken over the business entirely in 1912. John, popularly known all his life as Johnny, as a youth worked with the family enterprise. When his father died in 1925, he and his brother, Fred, took over the ice operation.

In the years before mechanical refrigeration became possible and then popular, almost every household depended upon an ice refrigerator. Cutting and year-round storing of the ice were major operations and the Fremouws established a house-to-house delivery system.

At about the time the Fremouw brothers took over the business, sanitary ice — ice artificially made from purified water — was beginning to be favored. Soon the Fremouws offered a choice between natural and sanitary ice.

Even after many homes, the colleges, the Odd Fellows Home and milk plants went to electrical refrigeration, the company did well delivering ice to markets and homes at Dundas, Dennison and Nerstrand as well as in Northfield. Also, in the spirit of "if you can't beat them, join them," the Fremouws for a while had a refrigerator sales store downtown in the current location of Dufour's Cleaners.

In 1942, John Fremouw sold his share of the ice business to his brother and went to work as a welder at a shipyards in Duluth. He had learned welding during his years in the ice business when he did his own repair work. He had even installed some highway bridges for the Northfield Iron Co., then one of Northfield's principal industries.

While John was in Duluth, his brother surrendered to the inevitable, dissolved the company and became employed in a World War II defense factory on the West Coast. He never moved back to Northfield.

John and his wife did return to Northfield, but he signed up for a welding job on the pipeline that was being laid in the Yukon territory. For five months he was at White Horse and for nine months at an oil field on the McKenzie River just south of the Arctic Circle.

Back home for a while, he commuted to

Savage for work at the Cargill shipyards. Nine months of work with the Army Engineers at Watson Lake in the Yukon followed. He ran a shop truck along the Alcan Highway, being the only welder for 300 miles in each direction. By the end of the war, he held first class welder certificates from the U.S. Maritime Commission, the U.S. Navy and the Army Engineers.

Returning to Northfield, he established a welding shop at his home, then located at 614 Water. A few months later, he bought the blacksmith shop of Jim Kofoed at 116 West Third, part of the West Side business district that was later destroyed with the re-routing of TH 3. He then put up a business building at 610 S. Water.

He'd had a life-long interest in iron as a material. After welding some wrought iron railings, he decided to try making railings and gradually worked into that field. He constantly sought new ideas in iron design and improvised methods for their development.

When he was 65, he sold his equipment at auction and rented out the building. He told the *News* that for years he could hardly wait in the morning to get out to his shop and get started, but that recently the work has seemed more like drudgery. He hoped to find something with which to keep busy on a part time basis, however.

Soon he did. He made grandfather, grandmother and granddaughter clocks with chimes. He was not interested in using clock kits, but designed his own cabinets. He said, "1 don't see any fun in buying a kit and just gluing it together." He much enjoyed learning to work with various kinds of wood.

He did not want to sell clocks, but made them for relatives. This work was done at his last home at 1118 S. Water where he and his wife moved in 1966.

His wife was the former Bernice Drentlaw, a native Northfielder. They wed on March 29, 1924. They had one daughter, Doloris (now Olson). After a very short illness, Bernice died from a heart condition on March 2, 1969.

Fremouw's public service began in 1937 when he was elected to the city council from the second ward. He served until 1942 when he moved to Duluth.

Seeking office again after his return from defense work, he was elected to the council in 1951. He was re-elected in 1954, but he resigned in 1956 in order to run for mayor. He was not elected to that office.

Much of his work on the council had to do with municipal finance. He helped the city come back from a tremendous overdraft to balancing the budget. He also at times chaired council committees on the poor, water, parks, ordinances and fire.

In 1957 he was severely injured in a motor vehicle accident and it was thought for a time that he would not regain full use of his body. He was able to do so, however, after walking with crutches for quite a time.

The cause of his death was not recorded in his obituary, but it stated that he had been in failing health for a year and had been seriously ill for six weeks.

His funeral was conducted in All Saints Episcopal Church and interment was in Oaklawn Cemetery.

16 July, 1999

1974: Frank Gallagher is 50-year member of Odd Fellows

After postal retirement, Gallagher served on City Council

Frank Gallagher received his 50-year pin for Odd Fellows Lodge membership in the spring of 1974, according to a story in the June 6, 1974, *News*. He had actually been a member since 1920 for a total of 54 years and was still a member when he died in 1981.

He had served in all of-  fices of the lodge and had also served in district office. He thoroughly enjoyed playing cards and for years helped line up whist games between the Odd Fellows and members of Masonic orders here.

Gallagher was born June 30, 1890, at Blooming Prairie. Soon his family moved to Faribault, then to Dundas. He lived the rest of his life in this area. He married Hazel Quinn, a native Northfielder. For many years they owned and lived in the house at 411 W. First.

As a very young man, Gallagher was employed as a cashier at the Milwaukee Railroad depot. Later he was an agent for the Minneapolis, Northfield and Southern Railway.

At that time the Gallaghers were renting their home from the Northfield postmaster, Charles Dougherty. Dougherty encouraged Gallagher to switch from railroad work to postal service. He urged him to take the examination when there was an opening for a substitute.

Gallagher's first postal job was on the parcel post route and he was appointed regular carrier after only a few months, on Dec. 1, 1919.

Gallagher was to recall that at that time parcels in the mail were limited to shoe box

size and a weight of 10 pounds. With a horse and wagon it took the whole forenoon to make the trip to each of the colleges and to the residences receiving packages. Two trips a day were made to the colleges. The horse and enclosed wagon were kept in a livery stable at night.

Very soon afterward, on Jan. 1, 1920, Gallagher won the contract to furnish the Northfield post office with its first parcel post truck. At that time the size and weight allowed for packages was increased and the volume of business also increased considerably. However the big increase came in the mid-1930s when postal regulations allowed the mailing of the laundry cases that were very popular with college students at that time. After that Gallagher also delivered cases of baby chicks, bees, what-have-you.

When he started his postal job, Northfield streets were muddy and rutted. By the time he changed assignments, the streets were mostly blacktopped.

It was in 1943 that Gallagher's doctor suggested he lose weight. He was able to change to a foot carrier's position, delivering mail to downtown stores and to households in 10 adjacent blocks. Interviewed at the time, he said, "The 11 stairways I climb every day takes care of any excess fat!"

The interview also stated, "Gallagher is known to one and all downtown for his hearty greeting and ready grin, his interest in what's going on in the town."

He retired from postal service in 1956. The following March, when city elections were held in the spring, he filed for office as alderman from the third ward. He was quoted in the *News*, "During the years I worked under civil service, I couldn't hold city office. Now that I am retired, I would like to have the opportunity. I feel it's my duty to serve my city in this capacity."

He won and was appointed chair of the park and building committees. He was also a member of the insurance and light committees.

When he was seeking re-election in 1960, a story in the *News* stated that he had given a great deal of time to the office, accompanying the mayor and other city officials on necessary trips to examine facilities and observe procedures. "He has also given considerable time to the Northfield park system, obtaining new equipment and making parks more useful to Northfielders." He was re-elected.

However in 1961 a city election was necessary in the fall because the adoption of an amended city charter made the city council smaller. Gallagher did not seek re-election.

His "retirement" was short, however, as a member of the council resigned in the fall of 1962 and Gallagher filed for councilman-at-large. He was the only candidate for the office and was appointed to serve the rest of 1962 as it was obvious he would subsequently be elected to the one-year term.

"We're glad to have you back," exclaimed Mayor W. T. Nelson as he appointed Gallagher once again chairman of the park committee.

In the fall of 1963 when he sought re-election, Gallagher was involved in a contest, but he won with a 124 margin.

He led in all but one precinct, the first precinct of the second ward.

In seeking re-election, Gallagher had said that he was especially interested in working with parks. Since the city was still acquiring land to be developed into parks, he was interested in continuing that work.

He was very active in city tree planting projects. He was also chairman of the council's fire and lights committees.

Gallagher served as an elder in the Northfield Moravian Church.

His wife died in July of 1978. Finally in ill health, Gallagher received care at the Odd Fellows Home. His death occurred there on

His obituary stated, "Gallagher may have known more Northfielders than any other one person and for years he knew all Northfield addresses."

The obituary also stated, "Through the years he faithfully called on fellow lodge and church members, as well as other friends, who were ill. With an infectious grin, he was able to spread good cheer."

Interment was in Northfield cemetery. The pallbearers were all former postal employees.

Gallagher was survived only by two nieces. Mr. and Mrs. Gallagher did not have children.

4 June, 1999

1975: George Machacek and other NEMCO people honored
Machacek was machinist, designer, teacher, manufacturer

George Machacek was president of Northfield Equipment and Manufacturing when NEMCO was named Industry of the Year in 1975.

In the issue of Sept. 4, 1975, the *News* saluted the company and traced its history

One of the illustrations showed Machacek with his son Jim, company vice president, with hammer and anvil that had been in the Machacek family for more than a century.

George was born in New Prague, a son of Mike and Anna Machacek. Mike, son of a blacksmith, farmed for a time in Wheatland Township, then started work in machine shops and foundries in Chaska and Carver. He was working in Superior, Wis., during the great iron boom in northern Minnesota in the 1880s and 1890s. Then during the 1890s he bought into the New Prague Foundry where George was to learn the family trade.

George graduated from New Prague High School in 1916.

During World War I he enlisted in the U.S. Army and because of his experience was assigned to the 368th Aero Squadron for research and development.

After graduating from the Willis Overland Aviation School, he was assigned to Langley Field, Va., as a chief technician in a research group. He assisted in the development of synchronized aviation machine guns, guns that could fire through the moving propeller of an American airplane; in the development of the forerunner to the Norden bombsight; in the development of radio controlled aircraft.

Because he wanted to gain manufacturing experience, when the war was over he took a position with the Townsend Tractor Co. in Janesville, Wis., where he designed, built and operated a crankshaft line. He also worked for Besleys, Fairbanks-Morse and Yates-American Machine Co. Then for a short time he operated a small machine shop

in Beloit, Wis., in partnership with Frank Melounek.

In 1920, his father Mike, his brother Oliver, Melounek and George established the Northfield Foundry and Machine Co. here.

Mike had wanted to locate in an area where the service of three major railroads would be available. He first thought of Farmington, but on the day that Mike and George set out to look around, heavy rain had reduced even main roads to quagmires. By the time they reached Northfield, they were too tired to drive on to Farmington and they stopped for a visit with an acquaintance, C. L. Brown who was president of the Northfield Iron Co., then a bustling industry. Brown highly recommended to them locating in Northfield. Although it was started in 1920, the company was not incorporated until 1926.

The foundry developed a line of woodworking machinery that soon become internationally known. George studied foundry melting practices and metallurgy and with his father, was often a consultant to the foundry industry in the Upper Midwest. They designed and held several patents on foundry and casting procedures.

In 1929 George married Antionette "Nettie" Proshek, a native of New Prague who had become a graduate nurse and had, in addition to working in hospitals, been an instructor at the University of Minnesota School of Medicine. She had also worked in Sacramento, Calif.

Having survived the Great Depression, with the advent of World War II, the foundry geared up for wartime production of machinery. The firm received the first Army ordnance award for excellence in production given in Minnesota.

After the war, George was issued a teaching certificate by the Veterans Administration and the Minnesota Board of Education to conduct an on-the job training program for GIs wishing to become machinists. He trained about 100 machinists and more than 250 welders.

In 1955, G. T. Schjeldahl, having used the Northfield Foundry to fabricate some earlier equipment, gave the local firm the job of producing his newly-developed side-weld poly bag machine. George persuaded Shelly to locate his new balloon and bag machine manufacturing operation in Northfield after he sold his Farmington plant.

In 1964, George and his sons, Charles and Jim, formed NEMCO as offshoot of the foundry. It began as a consulting and small sales firm, catering to area meatpackers. The company was joined by the late John Hager who developed an instantizing process used by the food industry. (The products so produced led to the formation of Ryt-Way Packaging by Glenn Haase.)

In 1967 NEMCO erected the first plant in the Northfield Industrial Park. That same year the firm developed the spiral freezer, a freezing conveyor belt system that gained wide use in the frozen food industry.

In 1969 Bill Cowles, former sales manager for NEMCO, formed Northfield Freezing Systems and took over the distribution and sales of the spiral freezers. Spiral freezers continued to be custom made to the needs of the user as to capacity, speed, dimensions and length.

NEMCO continued as well to make parts for Sheldahl and a number of engineering companies in Minnesota.

NEMCO was still operating under that name when George suffered a short illness and died at age 90 on July 4 , 1987. NEMCO was later purchased by York International as was Northfield Freezing Systems. Both were then purchased by Frigoscandia, a Swedish firm, and now that firm belongs to Food Machinery Corporation of America (FMC). The Frigoscandia division will soon move its main offices to Northfield from Seattle.

Beginning in 1956, George and Nettie spent winters in the Cayman Islands which, different from nearby islands, were colonized by British rather than Spanish. The Machaceks enjoyed both the weather and the people.

Eventually they operated a quarry that provided the island with building materials and a small machine shop, known as Mister George's Place, that repaired everything from small pumps to equipment for ocean-going liners.

George was an original member of the American Legion Post No. 45 of New Prague and for the rest of his life after moving to Northfield, was a member of Post No. 84, American Legion. In the early years of the latter post, he was a member of the American Legion State Championship Drum and Bugle Corps of Northfield.

For 68 years he was a member of King Hiram Lodge No. 31, AF&AM, at Jordan. He received his 50-year Masonic pin in 1969.

His wife survived him by two, years. They are buried in the Czech National Cemetery in New Prague.

2 September, 2000

1975: Robert Swanson took Boys' Chorus on tour 'up north'

Swanson taught in local schools, organized Boys' Chorus

Robert "Bob" Swanson, teacher of music in the Northfield public school system and organizer of the Northfield Boys' Chorus, managed to take his beloved group of boys on a tour almost every year the chorus existed. They were in northern Minnesota in the summer of 1975 and the June 26 *News* pictured a group of the boys stepping from stone to stone, crossing the Mississippi River near its source in Itasca State Park.

Swanson was born in Rush City on Aug. 28, 1929. When he was 6, he moved with his family to Minneapolis where he attended elementary and high schools. As an adult he credited his seventh grade music teacher and his senior high speech and drama teachers with giving him encouragement and guidance, helping him discover his talents. He also said that he had wanted to become a teacher from the time he was in third grade.

After attending the University of Minnesota for two years, he served in the U.S. Army field artillery in Korea. On his return, he graduated from the University in 1956. Several years later he received a master of education degree from the University's college of education.

In the fall of 1956 Swanson began nine years of teaching at Appleton. He taught music for grades 1–8 as well as an eighth grade English class.

That same fall he met Phyllis Vik, an English teacher. They were married in June of 1957 by the bride's father, pastor of Our Saviour's Lutheran Church in Waubay, S.D.

The Swansons and two of their children moved to Northfield in 1964 when he became a vocal music consultant in the elementary schools and vocal music teacher in the junior high school. Swanson had become acquainted with Yosh Murakami, NHS vocal music teacher, who was instrumental in getting Swanson here. Swanson said he was inspired by Murakami's example.

Swanson was to teach in the Northfield public schools for 26 years. He also taught private piano lessons for 35 years.

He was a very active member of St. Peter's Lutheran Church. There he directed choirs and musicals, taught Sunday school and played the piano.

Over the years he directed more than 25 operettas, from "The Wizard of Oz" to "Willie Wonka and the Chocolate Factory."

But he was without question best known for the Northfield Boys' Chorus that he organized in the summer of 1969. At that time all-boy choirs were not common in the Midwest. Nevertheless 65 boys, primarily from grades 4–7, responded to his invitation. Nearly 400 boys participated in the chorus over 15 years, many for two or more years. One youth sang with the chorus for five years and then served for seven years as tour accompanist and chaperone. The boys were members of 245 different families.

The first year the chorus sang only in the Northfield area, but from then on there was an annual tour. The chorus performed in 121 cities in the United States and Canada.

Two tours were to Washington, D.C., the first during 1976 when the chorus performed in the Kennedy Center, the National Cathedral and on the steps of the Capitol in the presence of Congressman Al Quie and Senators Hubert Humphrey and Walter Mondale. The chorus received a certificate of appreciation from President Gerald Ford.

The chorus sang twice in the amphitheater at Mount Rushmore in the Black Hills. The chorus once served as the Sunday morning church service choir in the Air Force Academy Chapel.

In 1971 the group performed at the Minnesota State Fair. They made many appearances in the Twin Cities and on Twin Cities television stations.

In the final year of the chorus, Myron Solid of the St. Olaf College Faculty, a "Boys' Chorus father" and former tour chaperone, wrote a tribute to Swanson which was published in the *News*. He said in part that the chorus had served as an unofficial ambassador of good will for Northfield.

"Everywhere the boys traveled they behaved and performed in a manner that positively reflected and represented our community," Solid said.

He continued, "But these aren't the real accomplishments of the Boys' Chorus and Bob Swanson. More valuable is the growth and experience of the boys under the guidance of their director. To be a member of the Northfield Boys' Chorus requires a large commitment, with many hours of practice, much individual effort in earning tour money, numerous concerts and mini-concerts throughout the year in addition to the main tour. This commitment is nourished by Robert Swanson who somehow develops within each boy self discipline, group discipline, poise, a good self image and pride in himself, the group and his community."

Solid further stated that "Bob has a talent for developing self-responsibility within the boys. He inculcates discipline, mixing love and affection with high expectations."

Solid also saluted Phyllis Swanson who, he said, "plays a major role in support and assistance, especially during concerts and tours."

During the final year of the chorus, the group entertained at the annual banquet of the Northfield Area Chamber of Commerce. The Chamber took the occasion to present Swanson with a plaque. Dan Freeman, in making the presentation, said, "It's only a plaque that must be dusted," but that it represented "all of the love in this room" as well as all the love that Swanson has given to and shared with Northfielders.

In responding, Swanson said that "people ask me where I find these wonderful boys. I tell them they are everywhere. Just give them a purpose."

In 1994, on the day before his 65th birthday, Swanson received the WCCO Good Neighbor Award. The award script stated in part, "Bob bought his first piano with money from his paper route and he's been enriching lives with music ever since. He taught hundreds of piano students, directed choir and produced musical productions for schools and churches. He spent thousands of hours — all without pay — as founder and director of the nationally recognized Northfield Boys' Chorus. Bob used music as the vehicle for life's greater lessons — perfection without judgment; commitment to self, group and community; discipline with love; caring; sharing; service; responsibility; poise and professionalism."

When Swanson decided to retire in 1988, a story in the *News* stated, "He is leaving the job with the philosophy toward children that has helped him along over the years. 'I've always said there isn't a bad child,' Swanson said. 'I've always felt if you believe in that, you can cope.' Those who have worked with Bob Swanson agree that his interaction with young people has done a lot to steer them toward a constructive life."

Swanson continued a busy life, giving piano lessons, gardening and more, until one Sunday evening in February of 1996. He had been driving, with his wife and was just blocks from his home when he suddenly became ill. He had suffered a stroke. With very prompt aid from a passerby, the rescue squad, the ambulance crew and Northfield Hospital personnel, he seemed to recover quickly. But then it was discovered that he had terminal pancreas and liver cancer.

Swanson had written an autobiography for his two sons, daughter and grandchildren, stating, "God has been good to me and I praise Him for His kindness and love! Whenever He decides to call me to His home, I shall be ready and have no fears of my departure. It would be nice to see the 21st century roll in."

But that was not to be. Swanson died the morning of June 22, 1996, at his home. The service was at St. Peter's and interment was in Oaklawn Cemetery.

Mrs. Swanson still lives in Northfield.

23 June, 2000

1978: Dacie Moses observes 95th birthday anniversary
Moses leaves home for cookie baking, cribbage, song

"Dacie Moses celebrates her 95th birthday today, probably amidst a crowd of adoring Carleton College students," a story in the Jan. 26, 1978, *News* began.

The story continued: "For years, Mrs. Moses has left her front door unlocked and her heart open to any Carls who choose to come by and chat, play cribbage or study. Nobody knows how many pounds of cookies or gallons of coffee have been consumed over the years at her house at 110 Union."

Moses was to live three more years, her death occurring on Jan. 3, 1981 — just days short of her 98th birthday anniversary.

Moses left her house, now known as the Dacie Moses House, to Carleton to be used by students as a home away from home, just as it had been used during her lifetime — for baking cookies, for rehearsals of music groups, for playing cribbage, for visiting, for just relaxing. Two students reside in the house, serving as caretakers. But everyone using the house participates in keeping it clean. Many more take part in major cleaning and repair efforts.

Continuing the rules of the house set by Dacie, there is no consumption of alcohol on the premises.

This coming Sunday, Jan. 26, the 120th anniversary of Dacie's birth, will be observed with a brunch at the house from 10AM to 1PM. Special guests will include singing groups including the Knights, the Knightengales, and the Sunday Morning Musicians. The committee planning the brunch stated, "Celebrate with us the legacy of Dacie's incredible gifts that continue to bless the Carleton and Northfield community."

Moses, whose real first name was Candace, was born Jan. 26, 1883, in Northfield, the daughter of Duren F. and Emma (Rounce) Kelley. During the following year she became a member of the Congregational Church and was, before her death, the church's earliest living member.

In Sept. 17, 1906, she married Royal H. "Roy" Moses who had lived in Northfield since 1896 and had graduated from Carleton College in 1904.

They spent the first three years of their marriage in Minneapolis, but in 1909 his ill health forced him to seek outdoor life and he joined his father in the latter's lumbering enterprise at Ladysmith, Wis. He regained his health and the couple planned to return to Minnesota. But two weeks before the planned departure, Roy was helping a neighbor raise a house. The equipment for the raising collapsed and Moses was struck on the head. He was completely paralyzed for a time and only gradually regained the use of his limbs and was able to resume activity. His obituary — many years later — stated, "He never fully recovered, but his spirit and that of his devoted life's companion were such that out of this tragic accident grew lives of outstanding service."

At various times he worked a milk route,

as city weighmaster, and as city recorder. He became Northern States Power Co. superintendent for Northfield, retiring in 1946. He was long active in various local organizations.

The couple had one son. Rounce, who graduated from Carleton in 1930, became a medical doctor, but died in 1963.

Dacie worked for several years at the Northfield Cooperative Laundry, located in the building now occupied by the Rueb-N-Stein. She became a Carleton employee in 1919 serving as assistant to the college treasurer, F. J. Fairbank, for 32 years. She combined homemaking with career in years when many labor saving devices had not been invented.

After her first retirement in 1951, she soon returned to Carleton as part-time reserve librarian. After her husband's death in 1960, she became a full-time employee at the library. She retired a second time in 1969, the 50th anniversary of her employment on the campus. She was then 86.

She was honored with an Alumni Association Exceptional Service Award in 1975. At the time of her retirement she was presented with an honorary master of arts degree.

Read at the ceremony was the following citation: "She isn't a graduate of any college but she has given her life to Carleton and its students. Now ending her 50th year as a Carleton employee, Dacie's philosophy of living is succinctly expressed with these words 'I'd just die without the students — what's to live for without them around?'

"She's been lauded, honored, written about and generally adored by Carleton students throughout those years. . . .

"The petite and always smiling Dacie is as historic a part of Northfield as she is of Carleton. Her grandfather in fact was Northfield's first resident minister — not only for the Congregational Church to which he belonged, but for the Methodist Lutheran and Episcopal churches as well.

"Carleton students take care of her and she takes care of them, and alumni send her on trips around the country, name their children in her honor, teach their grandchildren to say her name. This is having friends."

While Roy was alive, the Northfield Male Chorus of which he was a founder began rehearsing at the Moses home Other singing groups including the Carleton Knights, a campus singing group, also began to rehearse there. In 1967 the Knights honored Dacie by dedicating a record album to her. With a play on her nickname, the album was named "Dace and Knights."

Dacie, whose father was a Civil War veteran, helped a Carleton graduate write a book about the Civil War, furnishing letters written by her father to her mother during the war.

She joined the Josiah Edson Chapter of Daughters of the American Revolution in 1912. For many years she entertained the February meeting of the chapter at her home and had planned to be doing that just a month after her death. She had planned to serve cherry pie.

She was the first president of the Northfield Business and Professional Women's Club when it was founded in 1921, and was a member of the Order of the Eastern Star.

She was named grand marshal of the parade during Defeat of Jesse James Days in 1980. She hesitated. Heywood, the acting bank cashier who was killed during the bank raid in 1876, had been a close friend of her father. She did not believe in celebrating an outlaw. But she decided to join her fellow citizens in celebrating the brave pioneers who defeated the would-be robbers. A *News* story at the time reported that "typically, she had a wonderful time."

On Dec. 20, 1980, she entered Northfield Hospital in severe pain. She seemed to rally, however, and thoroughly enjoyed the letters and calls from all over the United States and overseas that she traditionally received at Christmastime. But her condition worsened by Jan. 1 and she slept most of the time. Her obituary reported, however, that "a student who visited her the night before her death recalled that she opened her eyes wide with pleasure and gave him a big smile."

Her obituary reported, "Over the years Mrs. Moses became a Carleton College legend. Her home at 110 Union, a half block from the college campus, was a haven for tired students and night owls looking for a cup of coffee, a bit of advice or a game of cribbage before going to bed.

"On Sunday mornings as many as 50 would gather there for coffee, orange juice and muffins before heading off for church or back to their studies. Most of them were students, but some were townspeople."

"It was for the warmth of her hospitality that she was best known. There was a time when relatives worried because Carleton kids thoughtlessly consumed pounds of coffee at her house every week and used her in-gredients to bake up dozens of cookies. But somewhere along the line, the realization came that they ought to be helping. They replaced an ailing refrigerator and later other equipment. They painted her house, shopped for her groceries, baked her Thanksgiving turkey, took her where she needed to go."

Former Carleton president John Nason was quoted, "Sometimes I think you provide more and better education than the rest of us." President Robert Edwards was quoted, "The warmth, generosity and love of this singular woman have touched the entire Carleton and Northfield community."

The *News* reported that when Dacie was once asked why she didn't have any friends her own age, her reply was, "What would I do with them?"

25 January, 2003

1979: Rand to be named next ambassador to Norway

Sidney Rand served as St. Olaf College president 1963–80

"Rand to be next ambassador to Norway" was a headline in the Nov. 1, 1979, *Northfield News.*

The story stated, "Dr. Sidney Rand, president of St. Olaf College, will be nominated soon by the Carter administration to become the next United States ambassador to Norway. That announcement was made Friday in Washington, D.C., by Vice President Walter F. Mondale before a group of Minnesota broadcasters."

The story explained that the nomination must be formally conveyed to the Senate's foreign relations committee which then would schedule a confirmation hearing. If the Senate then approved Rand's nomination, he would replace the retiring ambassador sometime after Feb. 1.

The story added that earlier that year, Rand, 63, had announced plans to step down from the college presidency following that academic year, after 17 years in the post. Personal retirement plans would now have to be postponed.

The story reported, "Rand told the *News* in a telephone interview (from Washington, D.C.) that he had not actively pursued the diplomatic appointment. He said he was approached six weeks ago by Mondale and became more interested as the idea took hold. Rand has traveled six times to Norway and has had extensive contact with the country and its people through his work at St. Olaf."

He was further quoted, "The United States and Norway have had a long-standing cordial relationship. One of the challenges is to see that it continues."

He also indicated that the appointment would not be a political plum. He had probably voted for more Republicans than Democrats.

When Rand appeared before the foreign relations committee, it was reported in a subsequent issue of the *News*, he was asked whether he could speak Norwegian. His re-

ply was, "Not as well as I should, and not as well as I expect to."

That story explained that although the appointment was officially made by President Jimmy Carter, it was actually Vice President Mondale who selected Rand. Mondale had told the president that he would like to have the opportunity of selecting the ambassador to Norway because of Minnesota's strong Norwegian ties and his own connections here

Rand and his wife, Lois, spent the last two weeks of January, 1980, receiving a briefing in Washington. They were not to leave for Norway until mid-February as the house in Oslo was being remodeled.

That house, purchased by the U.S. government in 1923, contains 24,000 square feet, includes several large reception rooms, and has 20-foot ceilings! It is located near Frogner Park.

It was on Feb. 14 that Rand affirmed the oath of office as U.S. Ambassador to Norway in Boe Memorial Chapel on the St. Olaf campus. Mondale administered the oath.

During the weeks before the couple's departure for Oslo, they were honored at several events. One was a community-wide dinner held on the Carleton College campus, sponsored by the Rotary Club of which Rand was an honorary member.

One of the speakers, Orval Perman, was a St. Olaf graduate and regent and owner of a Northfield clothing store. He recalled that when Rand arrived in Northfield to be president of St. Olaf, "he came around and introduced himself. We want him to know we appreciated it." He joked that he'd had other plans for Rand's retirement. He had learned that Rand had worked in a clothing store when he was in college. He concluded that "after Sid is done with hobnobbing with kings, he hoped the Rands would have a strong desire to move back to the serenity of Northfield and I want you to know that a job at Perman's is always open!"

Sidney Anders Rand was born May 9, 1916, at Eldred. He received his bachelor of arts degree in 1938 from Concordia College in Moorhead and his bachelor of theology degree from Lutheran Theological Seminary, St. Paul, in 1942. He did graduate work at the University of Chicago and Union Theological Seminary, New York. He received an honorary doctor of divinity degree from Concordia.

He was ordained as a Lutheran minister in 1943. After serving as parish minister at Nashwauk for three years, he became professor of religion at Concordia, serving there for six years, 1945 to 1951.

He was then for five years president of Waldorf College in Forest City, Iowa. Luther Seminary awarded him an honorary doctor of divinity degree in 1956.

He then became executive director of the board of Christian education of the Evangelical Lutheran Church. In 1961, at the time the American Lutheran Church was formed by the merger of three Lutheran synods, he became executive director of the board of

college education of the ALC.

It was in 1963 that he was installed as president of St. Olaf College. When he came to Northfield, he was married to the former Dorothy Holm who had been a college classmate. The couple had two children, Peter, a student at St. Olaf, and Mary who had just graduated from high school. The family had been living in Minneapolis.

When he had been here nearly a year, Rand was named by Gov. Karl F. Rolvaag to be chairman of a five-member commission that would distribute 25 million dollars in federal aid to Minnesota colleges and universities during the next five years. Also in 1964 he was named to the board of trustees of Fairview Hospital, Minneapolis. Fairview had served as the training hospital for the St. Olaf College nursing department for a dozen years. In 1965 Rand was elected a director of Northfield National Bank.

Dr. and Mrs. Rand made a five-week tour of Europe in the summer of 1965. On the Fourth of July, he delivered a sermon in Bergen Cathedral in Bergen, Norway.

In January of 1972 the couple left on a trip around the world under the auspices of a Danforth Foundation grant for college presidents who needed or deserved a break from routine. They visited New Zealand, Australia, the Philippines, Japan, Taiwan, Hong Kong, Thailand, India, Kenya, Ethiopia, Israel, Greece, Yugoslavia, Germany, Austria, Russia, Finland, Norway, France and Spain.

Also in 1972, Rand was elected to the board of North American Life and Casualty Co.

In February of 1973, Rand attended a meeting of the governing committee on scholarships and the exchange program of the Lutheran World Federation held in Beirut, Lebanon. On the way he visited Oslo, Norway, where, at an audience with King Olav V, he invited the royal family to visit St. Olaf during the college's centennial observance in 1974.

Later in the spring he was elected president of the Minnesota Private College Council. It was in 1974 that he was elected chairman of the National Council of Independent Colleges and Universities.

In January of 1974 Dorothy Rand suffered a massive cerebral hemorrhage and died.

During the St. Olaf centennial observance that year, Rand was made a knight first class of the Order of St. Olav, the title conferred by order of Norway's King Olav V and presented by the Norwegian ambassador to the United States. Later from King Olav V came the Commander's Cross, Royal Norwegian Order of Merit.

On Nov. 23, 1974, Rand was married to Lois Ekeren who was vice-president of Minda Public Relations in Minneapolis and was serving on the board of the Greater Minneapolis Chamber of Commerce. Friends had brought the couple together. Her husband had died unexpectedly. She had two grown children.

Rand received an honorary degree of doctor of laws when he delivered the commencement address at Colorado College in 1976.

He was one of 13 persons who represented the American Lutheran Church at the assembly of the Lutheran World Federation in Dar-es-Salaam, Tanzania, in 1977.

While he was ambassador to Norway, Rand returned to the St. Olaf campus in May of 1980 to deliver the commencement address. He was presented with an honorary doctor of laws degree during the ceremony.

While he was in Minnesota, he was presented with a doctorate of theology from St. John's University in Collegeville and here in Northfield a doctor of laws degree from Carleton College.

Rand was not to serve as ambassador for very long. Following the election of Ronald Reagan as president, after Rand had been in Oslo for not quite a year, he received a four-paragraph cablegram from the U.S. state department giving him two weeks to leave Norway. Several influential Minnesota Republicans tried to muster support for Rand's reappointment. One of them, Senator David Durenberger, called the episode a "lousy way to do business."

The Rands quickly relocated in a condominium that Mrs. Rand owned in Minneapolis.

Soon after his return to Minnesota, Rand was named to Minnesota Governor Perpich's 16-member tax advisory panel. A few months later when the commission's findings caused much controversy, Rand's remark was widely publicized, "Being on this commission I've learned one thing: A fair tax is one you pay and I don't."

In 1986, Rand was called out of retirement to serve as acting president of Augustana College, Sioux Falls, S.D. He served there again in 1992–93. In 1990–91, he served as interim president of Suomi College (now Finlandia University) in Hancock, Mich. He also taught homiletics (the art of writing and delivering sermons) at Luther Seminary, St. Paul, in 1984–85. While at Suomi, he served on the National Architectural Accrediting Board which accredits schools of architecture.

The spring of 1993 found the Rands in Oslo again. They were with the St. Olaf Choir when it flew from the United States to Europe, attending concerts in Copenhagen, Denmark, and the Norwegian cities of Trondheim, Lillehammer and Oslo.

In 1995 Sid and Lois Rand chaired the committee planning the Midwest portion of the United States tour of Norway's royalty, King Harald V and Queen Sonja.

Sid and Lois Rand, along with photographers Robert and Loren Paulson, prepared a coffee table book, "Norway," in 1988. In 1996 his autobiography, "In Pleasant Places," came out. He started the latter book as a family affair, but was encouraged by friends and colleagues to have the book published.

Rand died at age 87 in Northfield Hospital on Dec. 16, 2003. His obituary said that his wife, other family members and friends were with him.

The couple had moved back to Northfield and Lois still lives here.

The obituary quoted Walter Mondale,

"Sidney Rand was one of Minnesota's truly remarkable men. He was a great president of St. Olaf College, highly respected educator throughout the state and nation and a wonderful human being." Rand had worked with Mondale for many years on the Nobel Peace Prize Forum conference which Rand had helped establish.

The obituary also stated that during Rand's presidency, St Olaf's enrollment had increases from 2,094 to just over 3,000. Six major buildings were constructed and two fund-raising campaigns, which together raised about $25 million were carried out under his direction An additional campaign was well on its way to bringing it more than $21.5 million when Rand left for the embassy in Norway.

Other honorary degrees not noted above were from the College of St. Scholastica and Augustana. He also received from King Harald V of Norway the Commander's Cross with Star of the Royal Norwegian Order of Merit. He received the Brotherhood-Sisterhood Award of the National Conference of Christians and Jews and Luther Institute's Wittenberg Award.

Rand was well known for his quick, keen wit. Once when he was presented with an unexpected personal plaque for outstanding leadership by the Northfield Area Chamber of Commerce when St. Olaf was named Industry of the Year, with a straight face Rand threatened to speak twice as long as he had planned.

30 October, 2004

1982: Bunday remembers 19th century life
Area hardware operated for 26 years

The first in a series of stories about the late Thomas J. Bunday appeared in the Oct. 14, 1982, *Northfield News*. The stories were taken from a written transcription of a taped interview with Bunday, loaned by the Northfield Historical Society. His memories give a glimpse of what life was like in this area in the years just after the Civil War and at the turn of the century.

The story began, "My folks drove up from Wisconsin in the fall of 1865 (Tom was 14 months old). They drove a team, and had a covered wagon. We landed here in Northfield and our first stay was with Uncle Daniel Bunday who at that time lived about a mile south of Northfield (on what is now TH 246) and kept a tavern."

Bunday continued, "The farmers south of here, as far south as Waseca, used to haul their wheat through here on their way to Hastings and they'd either stay there (at the tavern) at night or for mealtime and then go on. He had a big barn and kept the horses all in there. . . .

"In the spring of 1866 we moved out to the Prairie Creek Valley. We lived there during that summer while we built our own little home over on the 80 acres that my father had bought east of that place, and then that fall we moved into our own little house. It was about 24 by 26, just a three-room house. We lived there until 1877 when we bought the farm that Uncle Chauncey Bunday had lived on adjoining us on the west. He went out to Redwood Falls. . . .

"I went to the old stone schoolhouse on what was later the Ralph Goodhue farm

— it was the only school that I ever did attend."

At the conclusion of this portion of his story, Bunday was quoted, "In the wintertime the neighbors used to get together and everybody would bring something good to eat and we would have the best meal and the best time that you ever saw in your life. They crowded into those little homes as thick as bees, you know, but everybody had a good time."

The second chapter in the series began, "A special day for the whole Bunday family was Nov. 9, the birthday of the three oldest children in my grandfather's family. They were born just exactly two years apart and that was why we had this celebration every 9th of November.

"At one of these birthday parties we met at Uncle Sidney Dickinson's and there weren't chairs enough to go around so that everybody could not be seated at the table and some of us kids had to stand up. I was one that objected to that. My mother took me into the other room and when she got through, I was willing to stand up. . . .

"In those earlier days we only got to Northfield about once a week and whoever came by brought the mail for the rest of the neighbors that were close by. . . .

"Before the stone schoolhouse was built that stands there now, the first school was held in what was later on Uncle Sylvanus Bunday's house. But at that time I think a fellow by the name of Field owned the home. They used to move the benches in the morning and have school — they didn't have desks, they just had wooden benches. They'd move them back at night, you know and then next morning they'd move them out in the room, in the kitchen, and that's where they held their school.

"The first seeder to sow grain that I ever saw, this Mr Field had up there at his place. It had one wheel with about an 8 or 10-inch face on it, and they drew it with one horse, and the box went crossways, you know, and they broadcast that grain. This seeder that was up there on that place didn't have any cultivators attached to it. It was a seeder just to sow the grain. My father used to sow by hand and he had a box in front of him that would hold a sack of grain. He was a pretty good hand at it because he could sow with both hands. A lot of fellows could sow with only one hand, you know, but he sowed with two."

In another chapter, Bunday recalled, "When I was about 7 or 8 years old, they had a fair on what is now the Carleton College campus. And they had about a quarter of a mile race track so they had horse racing there. There was quite a crowd there. I got away from my folks and got lost, and I was pretty well frightened. I didn't know whether I'd ever find my folks again."

Later (when he was in his early 20s), Bunday told about talking John Ferguson (who was teaching school south of Nerstrand) into opening a hardware store with him. (In another interview, Bunday said that his "first hankering for the hardware business came during visits he and his father made to the Joe Hyde Hardware on the West Side of Northfield.")

"That (plans to open the store) was arranged," Bunday continued. "And of course John had a sister Mary that looked pretty good to me at that time and always did afterward.

"John and I started our store out there (Dennison) in 1887 and were there for 26 years. In 1890 Mary and I were married on Thanksgiving Day in the old Ferguson home. . . .

"The first years of our business life in Dennison were pretty slow pickings because people had been accustomed to going to Northfield and Cannon Falls and Kenyon and we had to wean them away from those places to get them to come to our place to trade."

Talking more about his courtship and marriage, Bunday said that he would occasionally go over to the neighborhoods where Miss Ferguson taught in country schools to see her "but the first time I ever asked her to go any place was up at the Thorpe schoolhouse and that was the worst storm I believe we ever had and I couldn't get anywhere."

He remembered then, "Once I went up to Farrankops to a barn dance and danced all night until 4 o'clock in the morning, went home and changed my clothes and did the chores and sheared sheep all the next day and I made up my mind that was a little too much. So I quit dancing right there and then."

Interviewed in 1951 during a Diamond Club series celebrating the 75th year of the *Northfield News*, Bunday recalled more about the business in Dennison. "We (Bunday and Ferguson) were a couple of green kids, neither of us had ever worked in a store. We put in $500 a piece at the beginning. That wasn't enough capital then, but we got a lot further with it than we could today. At that time 75 cents a day was a good average wage.

"I didn't have $500 and my father had to sign a note with me at the First National Bank in Northfield. It wasn't until I renewed that note about the third time that G. M. Phillips, the cashier, would accept just my signature. He said, 'I've been watching you boys out there and I know you'll do all right.'" Bunday revealed that he only got $480; the bank deducted the interest in advance.

Bunday said, "We always tried to stock good merchandise. A farmer will remember the quality of his purchase long after he has forgotten the price.

"And we always discounted our wholesale bills, taking the customary two percent for cash paid before the 10th of the month, although we sometimes had to borrow at the bank to do it. This practice established a good credit rating and we made money. Even when we had to borrow the money we were able to do so at a saving."

Bunday recalled the hardware stock. "We had a complete line of cooking utensils, tools, fixtures, binding twine, barbed wire. We even had plows, plow shares, gas engines, windmills, buggies, wagons, oil, etc. One thing — we had a double line of wood-burning kitchen ranges right down the center of the store. I guess not many use them any more."

The firm also dealt in lumber and at times bought grain and cattle, sold farm machinery, engaged in pump and windmill work.

After the business was sold in 1913, the Bundays moved into Northfield. Mrs. Bunday had long admired the house at 808 Nevada (current home of Christine Hager). Bunday said, "She used to go by this when she came into town and always thought she'd like to live here. When we found it was for sale, I came over to see about it and when I got home I told her I guessed we were too late and she commenced to cry. Then I said, 'Never mind, put your duds on and we'll go in and close the deal,' and we did, we bought it that night."

The house, which the Bundays remodeled, was then surrounded with nine acres of land. At first the Bundays had two cows, a team of horses, chickens and raised prize-winning onions. But Bunday said, "We got tired of being tied down to home. We don't even have a cat now."

For several years after his retirement from the store, Bunday wrote insurance. He said he enjoyed the driving involved and the couple liked driving around the community and the state.

Bunday was born in 1864 at Raymond, Wis. His father, Jeremiah Bunday, was a native of New York state. His mother, Harriette Bunday, was born in London, England, and had come to America on a sailing vessel. Bunday said the voyage took six weeks and "some mornings they were further away from the United States than they had been the night before."

Bunday's wife had the misfortune of breaking first one hip and then the other in her old age. A week after the second break, she died in September of 1948. In addition to her husband, she was survived by a son Donald. A daughter had died in infancy.

Bunday and his son, who was handicapped, continued to live in the large and comfortable house with the help of a housekeeper.

The day after his 90th birthday anniversary, June 30, 1954, Bunday was pictured in the *News* with this paragraph: "There's nothing slow about Tom Bunday who celebrated his 90th birthday anniversary yesterday. Despite recent serious illness, Tom was feeling pretty chipper when he arose in time to see the total eclipse of the sun in the wee hours of the morning. During the forenoon, he drove his three-hole (engine hood trim) Buick downtown to greet his friends. Though he's lost a lot of weight, Tom looks like he's settled down to gun for the 100-mark."

But such was not to be. He died at Northfield Hospital the following Oct. 24.

The funeral was held at the Congregational-Baptist Church (now First United Church of Christ) where both Mr. and Mrs. Bunday had been very active. Both are buried at Oaklawn Cemetery.

16 October, 1992

1985: Museum's memorial room begun
Ted Scott — generous citizen

Although Ted Scott's death occurred just 14 years ago, Northfield's population changes so quickly that quite a number who enter the Northfield Historical Society's museum and see his name in stained glass over the entrance to the changing exhibit room, wonder aloud, "Who is Ted Scott?"

It was in the Oct. 10, 1985, *News* that plans were revealed for the exhibit room. A headline stated, "Historical Society Begins Scott Room Development."

The story began, "The first stage of the development of the Ted Scott Memorial Room in the Northfield Historical Society's museum is slated to be complete in October Other stages of construction will follow as the society can afford them.

"Since the space for the room will come off the back of the store space occupied by the Yarn Bin, the board has promised Chris Lee, proprietor of the store, that the new wall will be completed by Nov. 1 when the Christmas shopping season will be under way. (The adjacent store space is now occupied by Centerfield Music.) A new stairway to the basement and spaces for washrooms will also be built.

"There will be doors to the new room from both the society's office (now the introductory portion of the bank raid exhibit) and the director's area of the reproduced bank.

"Chip DeMann, member of the board, is shepherding the project.

"The room is being named for the man who helped organize the Northfield Historical Society, who served as treasurer from its inception in 1976 until his unexpected death in November of 1981, who watched carefully over the Scriver Building.

"Funds being used to cover the development of the room are those given in his memory by scores of Northfielders following Scott's death. . . .

"Later stages of construction, after the press of completing the wall is over, will include

electrical work and plumbing.

"The room, to be used for hanging exhibits, will assist the society in presenting other important historical aspects of Northfield besides the bank raid."

Development of the room was completed in the spring, the dedication taking place on May 3, 1986. A program and reception were staged with the late Lee Fossum as principal speaker. The first display in the room was that of paintings by Northfield painter, the late John J. Sletten.

The story regarding the dedication of the room stated that "the entrance (to the Scott room) has been built with arched top, following the prominent architectural feature of the Scriver Building exterior. At the top of the arch has been placed a stained glass window, work of well-known local stained glass artist, David Kjerland. Kjerland's share of the work was a gift to the society."

This story further stated, "Scott, for whom the room is named, died very unexpectedly on Nov. 14, 1981. A community leader, he had been very active in the founding of the Historical Society and the purchase of the Scriver Building in 1976. During the early years of the society, until his death, he devoted much energy to the nitty gritty function of the building as well as serving as society treasurer.

"His widow, Mary Zoe Scott, has recently become a member of the board, carrying on Ted Scott's interest in the society, and she is now serving as treasurer. Scott's daughters, Nanette, Heather and Dawn, have followed the development of the memorial room with interest.

"At the time of Scott's death and the establishment of the memorial fund for the room, Christine Hager, then president of the Historical Society, was quoted in the *News:* 'We looked upon this man as "Mr. Northfield." He gave his time and talents selflessly with no thought of recognition or reward. It would be impossible to enumerate the responsibilities Ted had undertaken for our organization. We shall all miss him as a friend and will never forget his kindness, generosity, thoughtfulness and patience.'"

At the time of Scott's death, the *News* ran an editorial headed, "Ted Scott will be missed." With all the important people who die in Northfield, this was unusual. But Scott had given so much to so many, it seemed necessary.

The editorial read, "There are a number of things that may not work as smoothly in Northfield these coming weeks, for a person who quietly assumed responsibilities in many activities has died unexpectedly and left broad gaps.

"Most people connected with banks serve often in such jobs as treasurer and financial officer for drives and organizations, but it seems that Ted Scott had an unusual number of such tasks.

"It was partially because as a long-time resident he truly loved Northfield and wanted to see its endeavors succeed. But Scott was also an exceedingly kind person who did

many things beyond what was required of him for individuals and groups.

"Though he was loved, respected and admired by many, he was surely never given adequate public recognition. Time was shorter than we thought. It's tragic that the recognition due can be given only after his death.

"In addition to his other fine characteristics, Ted Scott was an exceedingly modest person, and we're certain he didn't expect public recognition even though he greatly deserved it. Without doubt, he obtained great satisfaction in the love of his family, the warmth of friendships and the success of projects held dear."

Edward I. "Ted" Scott was 61 when he died of a heart attack. He was born June 2, 1920, at Rochester, the son of Irwin E. and Ruth (Whiting) Scott. He had Northfield roots as his maternal grandfather, Dr. D. J. Whiting, had his dental office on the second floor of the Scriver Building. Whiting came out onto the landing of the Division Street stairway to see what was going on during the Northfield Bank Raid, a detail that is now recognized during Bank Raid reenactments.

As a little boy, Ted lived with his family in the Elgin-Stewartville area. He was 7 when the family moved to Northfield.

He was a graduate of Northfield High School and attended Carleton College. His education was interrupted by World War II. A conscientious objector, he served with a soil conservation project in Ohio, as firefighter in Oregon and as a psychiatric attendant in Wiliamsburg, Va. After the war, he continued his education, earning a bachelor of arts degree in sociology.

He began working at the First National Bank of Northfield in 1949. He was made an assistant cashier at the bank in 1956; a cashier in 1968; and a vice president in 1970.

His marriage to Mary Zoe Fox was on May 17, 1952.

Besides his work with the Historical Society, Scott was a member of the Veblen Preservation group which made initial efforts at preserving the farmstead near Nerstrand where Thorstein Veblen, famed economist, lived as a youth and young adult.

Scott served on the ABC (A Better Chance) board which brought young people of other cultures to attend Northfield High School. He was active on the refugee settlement committee of Northfield. He was a member of the Lions Club. He served on the Northfield Retirement Center Board. He was a Scoutmaster for many years. He was an active member of the United Methodist Church of Northfield. He was active in the Organic Garden Group which had a community garden in Carleton's upper arb.

In the years when it was appropriate, he served in offices in the Northfield Elementary Parent-Teacher Association. He was one of the original parent founders and the first treasurer of the Minnesota Youth Symphony, Inc. His three daughters are among a large number of Northfielders who have been members of the symphony.

Besides all this, Scott helped many an elderly person reconcile a checking account. And when it is said that he watched over the Scriver building, that meant almost daily winter visits to the building to check out the temperamental furnace, year-round visits to check on leaks and the like before the society could arrange for a general repair of the building. When the society could not afford seating for its meeting room, he found a group of folding chairs slated for the dump and single-handedly repaired them and upholstered the seats.

When the Organic Garden Group planted some spring flower bulbs in his memory, they said of Scott, "His gentle, cheerful nature, common sense and uncommon ability to relate well to people of all ages were — and remain — an example to all."

13 October, 1995

1986: Les Drentlaw speaks his mind about city politics

Les 'willing to do more than his share' to effect change

People new to Northfield often ask, "Who is Les Drentlaw?" He's a man who frequently writes letters to the editor of the *News*, more often than not critical of Northfield city government. His letters appear less frequently in the winter because he's spending the cold months in Arizona — but he writes letters to the editor there also!

In the Dec. 18, 1986, *Northfield News*, Les was interviewed by Ross Daly, then a member of the *News* staff. The story was headed, "Drentlaw dislikes city policies."

The story started, "Les Drentlaw really doesn't have anything personal against the people at city hall, he said. It's their policies that bother him. . . . I don't dislike the people on the city council, I dislike the way they perform," he continued.

He further explained that it was really only certain city departments that he minded — the engineering, planning and administrative offices.

As to his letters, he said, "I see things that should be improved and I try to stir up enough people so they get up in arms and do something about it."

He was quoted, "I've always been a perfectionist." He said he always wants things done exactly right and so will criticize when he feels criticism is in order.

Les said that his criticisms have won favorable feedback over the years. "I've only had two people call up and complain," he said.

The story continued, "When people do call him to express their agreement, he turns those compliments into a challenge to others to try to effect change, Drentlaw said. 'I don't think one person can do it,' he said."

But he told Daly "I am willing to do more than my share" to accomplish the changes he wants. The changes often relate as much to background causes as to particular policies, he said. For example, he said that vandalism in Northfield is caused by a national attitude that allows for lax penalties.

He said that the people then serving on the city council were not qualified and that people who would be qualified wouldn't run because "they think politics are too rotten."

He charged, "The good man can't get elected. You've got to tell the people what they want to hear to get elected." He also said people don't get involved because it's easier to watch from the sidelines.

He expressed the opinion that only people who pay taxes and assessments ought to be serving on the council. "The people who should be on the council are the ones who are writing the checks."

He also charged that the council was merely rubberstamping policy that had been set by city officials. And he was highly critical of the foot bridge, then new, located between the Second and Fourth street bridges, calling it a "stinking, rotten bridge."

Les warned, "Northfield is well known as a nice city, but high cost from city projects could threaten that reputation. If we keep this group employed that we got in city hall, it'll soon be a nice little town that no one can afford to live in."

Les will soon have a birthday. He will be 92 on Feb. 16. And he still loves golf. When he was 90, the accompanying picture was taken in relation to the fourth annual Les Drentlaw Camp Courage Golf Tournament held at Northfield Golf Club. The fees, which benefited disabled campers at Camp Courage, included dinner, a riding cart and door prizes along with the round of golf.

Les was born here and grew up on a local farm. Interviewed some years ago for a story about the Great Depression, he revealed that he was at his parental farm during the Depression and remembered those days clearly. He expressed the belief that because so much work was done by hand in those days and because farmers helped each other, they were able to get through the Depression as well as they did.

"The amount of machinery we would have had on a 160-acre farm cost what you'd pay for a corn planter today," he said. "I can remember real smart people saying that the combine was a fad that wouldn't last."

He recalled that milking was done by hand and the milk was separated — cream from skim milk — in a DeLaval separator that was cranked by hand.

Les said that the home farm did have a home electric plant that provided a yard light and lights in the house and barn. He said that the family grew enough potatoes to last them all winter and to provide seed potatoes in the spring. They raised a lot of other kinds of vegetables and so many strawberries that they always had a lot to give away. They had apple trees as well that provided plenty of fruit.

Les also recalled that it was his job to churn the butter for the family. "You churned away, listening for it to thump instead of splash."

He said that beef was canned and hams smoked. Side pork was salted down in jars that were kept in the basement. Some meat was frozen despite the lack of home freezers. Les recalled that when the weather was very cold, the meat would be frozen outdoors. Then it would be well wrapped and buried under two or three feet of oats in the granary, this insulation keeping the meat frozen solid. "We knew how to cope," Les said.

He also remembered that the family did not have an icebox, but kept the cream cans in cold running water in a tank. The water was piped from a pump to this tank and thence to the stock tank where the cattle drank.

He said, "The secret of getting along in those days was not to want too much and to do it by hand. We didn't have or expect to have motorcycles, snowmobiles, etc. But we were satisfied and contented."

His share of the story closed, "Drentlaw recalled that neighbors used to get together and play cards and similarly amuse themselves. 'You really enjoyed your neighbors in those days. Now you don't know them.'"

Not long after the Depression waned, Les established a grocery store at the corner of Woodley and Division. After about five years there, he moved his store to the present location of VIP Travel Center, 309 Division. During many of those years, his wife Gertrude worked with him. They also raised a son, David. And during some of those years Les actively operated a farm south of Northfield.

After selling Drentlaw Food Market in 1951, Les soon became associated with the late W.T. Nelson in Nelson & Drentlaw Real Estate. Les took over the ownership and management of the agency in 1963.

There is nothing in Les's biographical file at the *News* to indicate when he retired from the real estate business. But through the 1960s and 70s, Les and Gertrude did considerable traveling, some of the major trips in the company of Sid and Lydia Freeman. They visited many areas of the United States including Hawaii, traveled in Mexico and made two trips around the world.

Gertrude died in the fall of 1984 and a month later, Les underwent a quadruple bypass. He's had periods of ill health in recent years, but he's wiry and always seems to rally. "I don't smoke or drink strong booze," he was quoted in a 1990 story.

27 December, 1996

1988: Carl 'Cully' Swanson, athletic legend, dies at home

Swanson fills several roles in his years at St. Olaf

Carl 'Cully' Swanson, 87, an athletic legend at St. Olaf College who later served the college as coach, dean of students, assistant professor of English and director of admissions, died Friday morning, May 6, 1988, at his home in Northfield." So read the opening paragraph of the story of Swanson's death in the May 19, 1988, *News*.

The story traced his young years, "Swanson was born in Minneapolis and graduated from South High School in 1920. He enrolled at St. Olaf where he was captain of the football and basketball teams his senior year and was an all-conference quarterback for two years.

"His skill in passing the football earned him a place in 'Ripley's Believe It or Not' (a popular syndicated newspaper feature of yester-years). Running the football was the prime method of advancing down the field in those days, but Swanson liked to fling the ball to receivers. He averaged more than 200 yards per game in 1924, a very high number of yards, especially in that era."

The story continued, "Those were the days of 'Cully to Cleve.' Frank Cleve was a speedy halfback in high school, but Coach Endre Anderson moved him to end when he enrolled at St. Olaf. Cleve became Swanson's main target, and the combination thrilled crowds with long completions.

"But Swanson was more than a 'passing fancy.' Some say baseball is his favorite sport."

When Swanson was among the 10 initial inductees into the St. Olaf Athletic Hall of Fame in 1971, it was noted that he won four letters each in football and baseball as well as one in basketball. It was also stated that he won national recognition for his 200-yards-per-game passing average in 1924.

Swanson played semi-pro baseball in summers for teams in Minnesota and South Dakota. He was once quoted, "Sometimes I think the baseball played back in those days was even better than it is today. That's all the kids did then. There was no golf, or autos, boats or TV sets for distraction." After his graduation from St. Olaf in 1925, Swanson coached at Kasson's high school for two years. He was later quoted, "I say coached advisedly because I taught four courses in English; coached football, basketball and baseball; coached and played with the town baseball team; even coached the girls' basketball team. I was young then and I could take it!"

Swanson returned to St. Olaf to coach baseball and to help coach the football team for the next years. He was there for the first unbeaten Ole football team, the squad of 1930 which included such star plays as Harry Newby, Norman Nordstrand and Mark Almli.

Swanson left St. Olaf to became a teacher, athletic director, coach and assistant principal of Marshall High School of Minneapolis. From 1935 to 1943, he coached basketball and baseball at Augsburg College. In 1940 he received a master's degree in education from the University of Minnesota.

In 1943, during World War II, he entered the Navy. He served as lieutenant commander and coached in the Navy's pre-flight physical education program alongside famous football coaches Bear Bryant and Red Sanders. He served both at Iowa Pre-Flight School and the Naval Air Base at Pensacola, Fla.

After the war, Swanson returned to St. Olaf to become dean of men.

"It was a hectic time," he once recalled. "We wanted to take care of as many men as we could. We put them in the attic of Ytterboe, the drama studio, Springbrook Farm, the fieldhouse and the Odd Fellows Hall. They were hanging on hooks all over the place."

He was also quoted, "Those were trying days, but we had a wonderful bunch of guys. I think the faculty will testify that this is the greatest experience they ever had in teaching."

In Swanson's biographical file at the *News* office is a clipping, a few paragraphs from the column of Publisher Herman Roe in February of 1947. Roe opined that Swanson should perhaps have opted for journalism instead of teaching and coaching, basing his remarks on a clever piece of writing that he quoted from the *Manitou Messenger*, St. Olaf student newspaper.

The notice written by Swanson read, "To all faculty members, this is a call to arms. The seniors, having chosen a team consisting of men whose shoulders measure 42 inches or more, have challenged the faculty to play a game of basketball on Winter Sports Day.

"I have accepted the challenge on your behalf, knowing, as did Napoleon, that superior forces endowed with intellect, will always triumph over minor uprisings of the proletariat.

"The uniform of the day will be sword and shield plus the clothing you think appropriate for the occasion. (We intend to have fun.) Do not forget first aid supplies such as gauze, bandages, iodine, liniment and a sun lamp. Dr. Cooke and two nurses, fully equipped, have promised to be in attendance. They have assured me that no faculty player, male or female, will be required to continue playing if he has stopped breathing.

"Special equipment such as shoulder pads, helmets, catcher's masks and hockey sticks, will be available for those who gave four-hour final exams.

"Our motto, like that of Bunker Hill, will be — 'Shoot while you still have whites in your eyes; tomorrow you will have only pupils.'"

Swanson's obituary said that his sayings and stories when he was dean of men had become St. Olaf fables. It quoted as an example,

"A freshman student once complained to the dean that he was becoming depressed because he kept falling out of his upper bunk. Swanson's advice, 'You ought to lie low for a while.'"

In March of 1950, Swanson was elected to Northfield's city council from the third ward. That spring he gave the address at the Northfield High School commencement ceremony. Following the tradition that the speaker is a parent of a graduate, Swanson was the parent of Stephen "Steve" Swanson.

After serving as assistant professor of English at St. Olaf in 1951–52, Swanson was appointed director of admissions for St. Olaf in the spring of 1952. He noted that the admissions process at the college had become more complex. Recruiting was becoming intense and standards were constantly being raised. "The admissions procedure changed drastically in those days," he later recalled. "I don't even remember bringing a transcript when I came from high school," he said.

When Swanson retired from St. Olaf in 1968, the St. Olaf Alumni Letterman's Association honored him with a luncheon on campus. They presented him with a color television set. More than 150 attended the luncheon including seven of Swanson's teammates.

Among those attending the luncheon was Swanson's son, Stephen "Steve." He was on leave from teaching at Texas Lutheran College while completing work on his PhD degree in English at the University of Oregon. Friends of the Swansons had purchased an airplane ticket to bring him to campus.

Swanson was also given a portfolio containing greetings and signatures of nearly 600 friends and acquaintances.

In the fall of 1981, Swanson required bypass surgery.

When he died in 1988, he was survived by his wife Dorothy, son Steve and daughter, Marilyn Haugen, also eight grandchildren.

Memorials were made to the St. Olaf Athletic Department scholarship fund and to St. John's Lutheran Church.

15 May, 1998

1990: Robert Shumway, longtime bank president, dies
'Bob' Shumway participates in many community activities

"Robert Shumway, 83, long-time president and chairperson of First National Bank died Tuesday at Metropolitan Medical Center in Minneapolis," said a page one story in the Feb. 15, 1990, *News*.

The story continued, "Shumway, who was semi-retired after a life of extensive community involvement, continued to make stops at the bank up until a week before he died."

The story said that at "First National, Shumway was known for his 'old-style' work ethic and extensive knowledge of banking. 'He always tried to get the best results,' Dave Shumway said. (Dave Shumway, current president of the bank, is a son of Robert.) 'He was meticulous, did his job well, and expected other employees to do the same. He was also loyal and modest, often diverting attention from himself. It was never below him to shovel the walk next to the bank if it was needed.'"

His son was further quoted in the story, "He was a character lender. An interview for a loan was often a simple conversation with a few business questions at the end."

The story stated, "At home he instilled in his children a tremendous appreciation for education. 'I always marveled over his thirst for knowledge,' Dave Shumway said. 'Shumway was a great fan of the classics in literature, and sometimes quoted Shakespeare.'"

Robert "Bob" Shumway was born Nov. 29, 1906, to Roy and Mabel (Ferguson) Shumway on the family farm in Greenvale Town-

ship. Because the parents wanted their six children to attend Northfield city schools, they made arrangements for the children to ride the Dan Patch train from the milk station, which was located on their farm, to town in the morning and make the return trip by train at night. This meant that the Shumway children's schedule was slightly different from those of other students but the school officials were tolerant of the variation, Shumway recalled many years later. The father also had to pay tuition for the children to attend a school outside of their rural district, but he accepted that as part of providing a good education for them.

On the farm, young Shumway was involved in chores including milking cows.

He graduated from Northfield High School and, in 1926, from Carleton College.

In 1927, the First National Bank, looking for a new employee, approached Shumway's older brother, having respect for the Shumway family and having learned something of the brother's abilities. The brother, however, was primarily interested in science and did not want to work in a bank. But Robert did and applied for the job the next day. He was hired.

His first job at the bank involved sitting at the table that is now being used as the director's table in the Bank Museum of the Northfield Historical Society. He was recording information about out-of-town checks, a painstaking job with a columnar sheet.

Years later when he was in partial retirement, he said, "I've done all of the jobs there are in the bank."

Through the years he also did many "jobs" for the community. One of the early ones was president of the Community Chest, forerunner of the United Fund, then 12 years old. In 1946 he was chosen as vice president of the Four County Clearing House Association, a banking group, and the following year he was elevated to president.

He was active in local Masonic orders and was elected illustrious grand steward of the Grand Council of Minnesota, R&SM, in 1954. In 1961 he became Grand Master of the Grand Council, the sixth member of the Northfield Council to serve in that capacity.

In 1960, Shumway — by then cashier of the bank — was appointed associate councilman for the Minnesota Bankers Association. The associate councilman was the representative of the state group in the county and his responsibility was to assist the banks in the county in improving operations and methods. A couple of months later, Shumway was elected Rice County director of the Minnesota Bankers Association. During the next year he was named a member of the MBA colleges and universities committee. That group studied banking material used for banking courses in colleges and universities and also worked with college placement bureaus to attract qualified graduates to banking.

In 1963, Shumway was elected a director of the Northfield Area Chamber of Commerce. In 1965 he was elevated to president of the Chamber.

In 1965, while he was still bank cashier, he was named Outstanding Boss, an annual designation given by the Junior Chamber of Commerce (now Jaycees). His citation noted that he had been a Jaycee.

The following year, Shumway became involved in CoDeP, Northfield's very successful community development program. He was named chairman of the committee on city government.

In January of 1967, Shumway was elevated to president of the bank, succeeding John D. Nutting who was made chairman of the board. Nutting had been president since 1926 when he succeeded his father.

It was during Shumway's presidency, in 1977, that the bank made its first major expansion of space into the adjacent building that had been Freeman's The Hub.

While he was president, Shumway made at least two trips to Washington, D.C., to attend the Washington Legislative Conference of the Minnesota Bankers Association. Both times he was accompanied by his wife, Dorothy, and they combined the experience with visits to relatives and friends in the East.

In 1979, Shumway was inducted into the Pioneer Club of the Minnesota Bankers Association. Members of the club had served at least 50 years in the banking field.

The following year, he was succeeded in the presidency by his son and became chairman of the board of directors. He later commented that he was very pleased David chose to follow in his footsteps. But he said that he had never tried to influence any of his children about their careers.

In 1982, Robert and Dorothy Shumway were chosen as representative citizens to be honored during the city's July 4th Heritage Days celebration.

By that time the couple had lived in Northfield through 48 years of marriage (they were wed in 1934). Mrs. Shumway, reared in Zumbro Falls, had attended nursing school and had been a teacher. She came to Northfield to work in a dental office and then met her future husband. In addition to bringing up the couple's three sons, she had been active in volunteer work and had served on the Rice County welfare board and the county public health nursing committee for many years.

Both Robert and Dorothy were active in All Saints Episcopal Church. He had served as junior and senior warden and presiding officer in the vestry.

In 1984, Shumway was chosen as the second recipient of the Joseph Lee Heywood Award given annually by the Defeat of Jesse James committee to a person who has served Northfield well. The award is named for the acting cashier of the First National Bank who gave his life in the 1876 bank raid rather than lose the uninsured savings of his fellow community members.

Shumway modestly suggested that the award should instead go to Chip DeMann who was in his second year as chairman of the celebration. "He's got us straightened out so we are emphasizing the aspects that should be emphasized," he explained.

When the bank celebrated its 115 years of service in 1988, Shumway was recognized for his 60 years of service to the bank. He was honored by bank employees with a wall clock and a golden shovel, calling attention to the numerous times he had cleared the bank's sidewalks of snow.

Shumway had then been a widower for a year. Dorothy Shumway died in May of 1987 at the age of 78.

When Shumway died three years later, his obituary mentioned that he had been a member of the Northfield Historical Society and had been a Boy Scout leader. It also reported that his hobbies included gardening, especially growing roses.

The Shumways are interred in Oaklawn Cemetery.

11 February, 2000

1992: Dallas Haas begins elevator addition to Archer House
With many projects under way, Haas dies at age 56

"Work has begun on an addition to the Archer House," a story began in the April 15, 1992, *News*.

The story explained that the addition to the west side of the building would mainly include corridors and an elevator. Owner Dallas Haas said that he was also planning expanded facilities for the Tavern, Treats and the Archer House banquet rooms.

Although as a younger man Haas never dreamed of becoming an "innkeeper," ownership of the Archer House provided him with great pleasure — and without doubt, some headaches.

His death was very unexpected — at age 56 — just before noon on Sunday, Aug. 13, 1995. He suffered a heart attack while doing some work in a lavatory in the Archer House.

He was born Nov. 28, 1938, at Farmington. He attended elementary school at Farmington and graduated from Bloomington High School.

He was a building contractor for most of his life. While he was still in high school, he convinced his father, also a carpenter, to co-sign on a purchase of four acres of land in what was then an unknown township south of Bloomington called Burnsville. He wanted to buy more, but his father drew the line, not sure that it would be a good investment!

After working primarily in Scott and Dakota counties, Haas first came into Northfield in 1959. He built Mt. Vernon Apartments which opened in 1964. More apartments were built in 1965 and Haas began building houses in the community in 1966.

He turned his attention to the business area of the city in 1980, purchasing the Nutting Block at 220 Division. The 1893 building had been well built and was still completely in plumb. But it had become shabby and needed a change in uses. Haas converted it into a business mall with offices upstairs instead of apartments. Care was taken to retain the historic front of the building. An elevator was installed.

One of the shops in the mall was the Golden Unicorn, opened by Haas's wife Sandy (current location of D. Butterfield's). The Cocoa Bean was born in the building. The Schmitz & Ophaug legal office was an original tenant on the main floor.

It was noted that J. C. Nutting had erected the building during a period of economic depression and had built it well as an expression of faith in the future of Northfield. Haas's restoration efforts were done during a period when his construction crew might not have been busy otherwise.

While work on the Nutting Mall had barely been started, Haas was honored as Northfield's Employer of the Year by Northfield High School's Vocational Industrial Clubs of America (VICA).

In 1981, The Haases were presented with a bronze plaque for their restoration effort by the City Council and the Heritage Preservation Commission.

After receiving much encouragement by Northfield business people (and he also credited Maggie Lee), Haas purchased the building next door — the 19th century Hotel Stuart (now the Archer House) which had become quite run down.

Also in 1981, Haas and Gene Jasnoch formed a new corporation and purchased Pheasantwood Town Homes from a Farmington company. The development had languished for a year under the previous ownership although streets and utilities were in place. (In 1989 this project was to be taken over by a new construction company consisting of Haas and Bob Carel.)

In 1982, the portico across the front of the hotel was built. While Haas had originally known very little about historic restoration, he had by this time become very interested in matching woods, preserving old tin ceilings and the like. In much of the hotel, the interior had to be removed down to the brick.

In 1983, Dallas and Sandy Haas of Dallas Haas Construction were honored as Industry of the Year by the Northfield Area Chamber of Commerce and the Northfield Industrial Corporation.

A story in the *News* concerning the award stated, "If Dallas Haas seems to be everywhere at once, that's because he is. He builds apartments and town houses, remodels office buildings, restores significant downtown buildings, manages a car wash, is part owner of a realty business, and still you can find him on a Sunday afternoon carrying freight out to the Jefferson Lines bus that stops at the Stuart Hotel lobby. . . .

"He flies around town in his small yellow pickup, working from sunup to sundown, supervising any number of projects in which his seven-man crew is involved at the moment. Up until a few years ago, the 44-year-old Haas worked right along beside his crew. Now, working with a hammer in his hands is a luxury his time rarely permits.

"His work restoring the Nutting Block building and the Stuart Hotel have become rallying points for those who champion efforts to revitalize Northfield's historic downtown."

Haas was quoted, "I've worked hard, but it still takes a lot of people's confidence and trust."

At the awards luncheon Haas was described as "both solid gold and gilt edged." But he was kidded about his personal un-filing system, his unopened mail, and his habit of always having left where you're looking for him about 15 minutes before.

At the luncheon, Haas was given a gag gift, a "Stuart bellhop" shirt. It was noted that he took a lot of kidding for helping hotel guests and bus passengers with their luggage.

"Sometimes I offer and they turn me down," Haas remarked. "I think they are afraid they will have to tip me."

"Have you ever gotten a tip?" someone called from the audience "Yes, a couple of times." "You kept it too, didn't you," suggested another. "Yes, I did," Haas agreed as the program dissolved into applause and laughter.

In September of 1983, Haas purchased the Medical Arts Building adjacent to the hotel.

In 1984, Haas received the Regional Development Award given by the Southern Minnesota Tourism Association during the Minnesota State Tourism Conference at Rochester. By that time he had changed the name of the Stuart Hotel back to its original name, the Archer House, named for the 1877 founders, Mr. and Mrs. James Archer.

After much work had been completed on the unusual furnishing of the Archer House rooms, a public open house was conducted in August of 1984. Very impressed, one of the guests suggested that the proprietor ought to be called "the wizard of Haas."

Renovation of the third floor of the Archer House followed. As in the rest of the hotel, each room was furnished individually; nothing was uniform. Fifteen tons of debris was hauled out of that third level when remodeling began.

In 1987 the banquet facility in a north addition to the Archer House was completed.

During Defeat of Jesse James Days of 1987, Haas was given the Charlie Pitts Award for his contribution to the celebration over the years.

Haas expressed pride that what he had accomplished had been done with his own resources, that he had not depended on public subsidy. He encouraged other downtown business people to restore their historic properties and he constantly encouraged tourism here.

In the spring of 1995 when the Pheasantwood Townhomes were complete, Haas and his partner, Bob Carel, began building 15 more townhomes in a development called Presidents' Way on Humphrey Court. Haas died before the end of the summer and Carel purchased the Haas share.

It was also Carel who saw to completion of the hotel addition and the installation of the elevator that had been started in 1992.

Inside the new elevator a plaque was placed, dedicating it to Haas' memory.

One of the last things that Haas completed before his death was the gazebo behind the Archer House. He thought it would be a neat structure for receptions and weddings. He was extremely pleased when he learned that early in the summer someone had proposed marriage in the gazebo.

At his untimely death, Haas was survived by his wife, Sandra "Sandy"; children from his first marriage which had ended in divorce; grandchildren and great-grandchildren.

The funeral was conducted in St. Peter's Lutheran Church where he was a member. Interment was in Oaklawn Cemetery.

Horsemen portraying the James Gang were part of the funeral procession. With them was a riderless horse. According to tradition, that horse had a pair of boots in its stirrups, facing backward, allowing the deceased to look back on his life.

A few weeks later, the Charlie Pitts award was not given during Defeat of Jesse James Day. Instead a special tribute was paid to Haas.

"Dallas was always helping us out," said Chip DeMann, leader of the James Gang. Among other things, Haas had let the gang camp behind the Archer House ever since he bought the property.

So after one of the bank raid re-enactments, the gang lined up, gave a 21-gun salute and heard the reading of a eulogy.

13 April, 2002

Index

This index lists individuals, organizations, businesses and locations related to Northfield and its history. Individuals profiled are in **bold type**.

Adam, Rev. Lorenz 168
Adams, Elizabeth Steele 28
Adams Lumber Co. 128
Albers, Clarence 168
Alexander, J.W. 108
Alex Marshall Co. 68
Allen, Laura Kay 37
Allen, Mary 118
All Saints Episcopal Church 9, 146, 174, 199
American House 50
American Legion 104, 115, 117, 137, 147, 152, 178
Ames Mill 16
Anderson, Endre B. 105
Anderson, Kathryn 91
Anderson Farm Hatchery 105
Archer House 120, 201
Armstrong, A. E. 158
Arneson, Fred B. 132
Arneson, Gust 104
Arneson, Rev. Frederick 133
Ause, O. H. 141
A Better Chance 193

Babcock, F. M. 61
Baker, Laura 37
Baldwin, Horace 58
Barrett, R. D. 20
Bates, Fred 16
Bennett, Elizabeth 54
Berg's Shoes 104
Beytien, L. F. 73, 77
Bickel, George Herman 73
Bierman, A.W. 61, 107
Bill, C. E. 61
Bill's Art Floral Shop 130, 136, 147
Bill's Kodakery 136
Blodgett, A. B. 61
Board of Education 47, 85, 112, 122, 128, 163
Boe, Henry A. 55

Boston Shoe Store 104
Branes-Johnson Garage 77
Brown, C. L. "Chan" 77, 177
Bryan, W. L. 66
Brynstad, Robert 64
Budd, Mabel Bierman 24
Bue, Hagbarth 46
Bunday, Thomas J. 107, **188**

C. M. Grastvedt Plumbing & Heating Co. 102
C. R. Griebie & Co. 51
Campbell, George 110
Campbell Dairy Products 110
Carleton Academy 80, 87, 107, 134, 145
Carleton College 29, 46, 66, 80, 120, 121, 137, 138, 147, 153, 181, 192
Carlson, Victor E. 103
Carlson's Shoes 104
Carter, Henry 11
Central Block 49, 145
Charlie Pitts Award 202
Christian, George 126
Christofferson, Anna Marie 63
Church of St. Dominic 19, 45, 51, 142, 147, 154
Citizens State Bank 120
City Council 75, 125, 143, 160, 176
Clark, Merril M. 25
Commercial Club 19, 44, 55, 142
Community Building 102, 141
Community Chest 64, 70, 121, 142
Community Club 55, 70
Community Development Program (CoDeP) 91, 164, 199
Community National Bank 112
Congregational-Baptist Church 109, 125, 190
Congregational Church 22, 30, 59, 75, 79, 81, 88, 96, 114, 120, 129, 140, 157, 163, 181
Corinthian Chapter No. 33 24, 30, 33, 70, 102
Cowgill, Rev. F. B. 134
Cowles, Bill 178
Curren, Frank 52

Dacie Moses House 181
Dahl, Fred 171
Dahl, Lee 171
Dahl House 68, 171
Dale, Borghild 131

Dampier House 50
Dan Patch Line 34
Dean, Edwin B. 170
Dean, Sophronia 11
Deckelnick, J. 43
Defeat of Jesse James Days 91, 98, 154, 162, 164,
  182
DeGross, Frank 49
DeLancy, J. L. 134
DeMann, Chip 191, 203
DeMann, Frank 124
DeMann Motors 124
Dilley, Everett L. 166
Dilley, Harry O. 75
Donaldson, Oscar 55
Drake, Frank 32
Drake, Stella Amoret 36
Drake's Variety Store 32
Drentlaw, Bernice 174
Drentlaw, Les 194
Drentlaw Food Market 195

Ebel, William 88
Enfield, Russell 124
Everett L. Dilley 166

Fairbank, F. J. 61, 182
Farmers Telephone Co. 87
Farrankop, Ervin G. 107
Federated Store 156
Felland, Elsa 159
Felland, Valborg 159
Fey, Lincoln 15
Fink, Jacob 63
Fink, Sam H. 153
Finkelson's Drug Store 21
First National Bank 7, 28, 50, 75, 85, 192, 198
Fishback, Mary 19
Fjelstad, Ralph S. 121
Fletcher, Harriet 11
Follansbee, Rev. Mark 140
Fox, Mary Zoe 192
Fox Foundry Co. 16, 77
Freeman, Henry 153
Freeman, Sid 153
Fremouw, Edward John 173
Fremouw, Frank C. 173

Fremouw, John Edward 66, 73, **173**
Friest, Al 66

Gallagher, Frank 133, 175
Garden Club 142
Gates Cafe 84
Gill, William R. 160
Goodhue, Horace 80
Goodhue, James M. 80
Goodhue, Ralph B. 80
Grand Theater 11, 54, 84, 166
Grastvedt, Christian M. 151
Grundy's Corner Bar 6
Gulbrandson, Carl 111

Haas, Dallas 201
Haase, Glenn 178
Hager, Leonard 126
Hall, William F. 55
Halvorson, Dr. David 97
Hauer, A. C. 61
Haugen, Sanford L. "Sam" 89
Headley, Leal Aubrey 138
Hegland, Edroy 64
Heibel, Carl 43, 132
Heywood, Joseph Lee 25
Heywood Award 85, 89, 200
Hill, F. B. 87
Hinds, P. B. 128
Hometown Spirit Award 96, 162
Houston, Alvin 92
The Hub 153, 199
Huestis, L. W. 54
Hunt, Dr. W. A. 20

Jackson, O. S. 23, 61, **66**, 116
Jackson Electric Co. 66
Jacobsen, Ralph A. 156
Jacobsen, Robert "Bob" 157, 158
Jacobsen's V-Store 156
Jacobson, N. M. 116
James-Younger Raid 56
Jarchow, M. E. 139
Jenkin's Tavern 6
Johnson, C. J. 61
Johnson, David E. 63
Johnson, Helen 104

Johnson, Stanley 'Tiny' 98
Johnson, Walter E. 63, 116
Junior Chamber of Commerce 85, 113, 131,
    143, 148, 199
Kaus, Mathilda 51
KDHL 131
Kelsey, Elizabeth 118
King, Henry 167
Kjerland, David 191
Klinefelter, Paul 84
Knights of Columbus 45, 117
Knights Templar 75, 104
Koester, Agnes 73
Kofoed, Jim 174
Kump, Henry B. "Hank" 63, 113, 116

Lajord, Mary 56
Larkin, George B. 19
Larson, John 101
Lashbrook, Alfred J. 46
Lashbrook Holstein Farm 46
Lee, A. O. 61
Lee, Esther 137
Lee Fossum 191
Leivestad, R. 151
Lillemoe, Annie 127
Lions Club 29, 45, 70, 79, 96, 112, 113, 125,
    129, 136, 155, 157, 167, 193
Lippert, Jim 44
Livingston, C. M. 60
Louis Tschann & Co. 49
Lyceum Building 8, 26

Machacek, George 177
MacKay, Alexander J. 52, 61, 68
MacKay, Alex Sr. 68
MacKay, Jessie 69
MacKay, Steve 99
MacKay & Company 68
MacKenzie, Donald 142
MacKenzie, Marian 142
Mader, Harvey H. 128
Mader Tire Shop 77, 128
Maitland, Rev. David 28, 140
Malchert, Norval 64
Manhart, Samuel L. 18
Manhart, W. F. 19
Manhart Coal Co. 19

Manning, A. R. 9, 55
Mansion House 118
Marshall, Alex 68
Mayer, Blanche 43
McConnell, Rev. J.E. 7
McGuire, Talford 167
McKenzie, Dr. K. J. 23, 61
McKenzie, L. M. 73
Medical Arts Building 97, 202
Meierbachtol, Rev. F. E. 25
Meldahl, Andrew 116
Mergen Building 68
Methodist Church 14, 17, 24, 33, 134, 193
Mikkelsen, Anna 54
Minneapolis, Nfld & Southern Railway Co. 34
Morton, John 55
Moses, Dacie 181
Moses, Dr. Joseph 95
Moses, Royal H. "Roy" 52, 61, 136, 181
Murphy, John E. 52

Nelson, Willard 'Red' 113, 176, 195
Nelson & Drentlaw Real Estate 195
Neuhaus, Marjorie 143
Nichols, Charlie 134
Northern States Power 182
Northfield (Area) Chamber of Commerce 69,
    85, 98, 115, 130, 141, 156, 158, 164, 199
Northfield Arts Guild 85, 96
Northfield Association 44, 64, 112, 142, 155
Northfield Baseball Association 163
Northfield Businessmen 117
Northfield Cemetery Association 26
Northfield Charter Commission 121
Northfield Choral Union 57
Northfield Cooperative Laundry 182
Northfield Council No. 12 24, 30, 33, 70, 102
Northfield DFL Club 163
Northfield Equipment and Manufacturing 177
Northfield Farmers Coop Elevator 47, 87, 108
Northfield Farm Bureau 157
Northfield Foundry and Machine Co. 177
Northfield Freezing Systems 178
Northfield Furnace Co. 8
Nfld Golf Club 45, 70, 131, 137, 146, 154, 161
Northfield Hatchery 105
Northfield Historical Society 96, 191, 200
Northfield Holstein Club 47, 86

Northfield Hospital 64
Northfield Hospital Auxiliary 143
Northfield Improvement Association 30, 70,
    139, 145, 148, 151
Northfield Industrial Corp 85, 157, 158, 164
Northfield Iron Co. 29, 77, 125, 173, 177
Northfield Light, Heat and Power Co. 11
Northfield Lodge No. 50 17, 66
Northfield Milk Products 29, 101, 126, 148
Northfield Moravian Church 168, 176
Northfield National Bank 19, 91, 125, 155
Northfield News 71
Northfield Physicians and Surgeons 97
Northfield Press, Inc. 72
Northfield Retail Merchants Assoc. 44, 136
Northfield Retirement Center 164, 193
Northfield Safety Council 148
Northfield Seed Co. 134
Northfield Social Lodge No. 48 75
Northfield Volunteer Fire Department 163
Nutting, Elizabeth 28
Nutting, John Claudius 29, 50
Nutting, John D. 28, 199
Nutting Block 201

O. A. Lysne's West Side Hardware 55
Oaklawn Cemetery Association 19, 160
Odd Fellows Lodge 10, 115, 170, 175
Olesen, Anna Dickie 44
Ole Store 63, 116, 126, 159
Olin, Clara E. 7
Olsen, Norman "Norm" 130
Onstad building 105
Orr, C. D. 13
Osman Temple Shrine 21, 24, 30, 66

Paper Shop 70
Park, Bertha 59
Parson, Nels 86
Perman, Martin 84
Perman, Orval 83
Perman's Store 83, 171
Perman Building 124
Peterson, A. T. 77
Peterson, Casper "Cap" 149
Phillips, G. M. 50, 75
Phillips, Nellie W. 10
Phillips, Ross 8

Piesinger, Marie 141
Pioneer Club 59, 199
Pioneer Farmers Club 134
Plaisance, A. J. 128
Pye, W. W. 54, 61, **144**
Quinn, Hazel 175

The Racket 32
Rainbow Saddle Club 157
Rand, Sidney 184
Rasche, Dr. Robert 75
Reese, Hilbert 158
Remes, Dr. David 74
Revier, Nellie 19
Revier, W. H. 136
Revier, William E. 136, 147, 167
Reynard, P. G. 104
Rice, Edwin R. 41
Rice, F. O. 41
Riddell, Dr. E. G. 50
Roe, Herman 24
Rotary Club 33, 64, 66, 85, 104, 106, 117, 139,
    158, 162, 164
Ryt-Way Packaging 178

Santino, Gustaf A. 26
Schilling, W. F. 35, 44, 46, 87
Schjeldahl, G. T. 178
Schmidt, Dr. A. J. 95
Schrader, Delmer 160
Schrader Hardware Store 160
Scott, Ted 191
Scriver, Hiram 6
Scriver Building 56, 99, 130, 191
Sheba Chapter No. 73 14, 33, 79
Shirley, O. H. 110
Shisler, May Fremouw 40
Shorrocks, Dick 167
Shumway, Dave 198
Shumway, Robert 198
Simpson, Lillian 13
Skeffington, Jack 153
Skogerson, Mary Louise 79
Sletten, John J. 191
Smoke Shop 98
Social Lodge No. 48 14, 24, 30, 33, 59, 66, 70,
    81, 102, 104, 113, 129
Spear, Everett 20

Spears, Lambert E. 16
Spink, Mary E. 134
Springsted, D. D. 63, 116
St. John's Lutheran Church 56, 64, 85, 104, 106,
    112, 121, 131, 133, 159, 172
St. Olaf College 63, 84, 89, 106, 159, 163, 184,
    196
St. Peter's Lutheran Church 179, 203
Stacy, Elias 9
Stake, Edna 46
Starks, Margaret 8, 40
State Bank of Northfield 51, 146
Stavig, Rev. Lawrence M. 56
Stewart, Solomon P. 118
Stranahan, Effie M. 25
Street, Dr. Bernard 95
Sumner Building 104
Swanson, Carl 'Cully' 196
Swanson, Robert 'Bob' 179

Tholstrup, Martin 16
Thompson, W. E. 160
Thye, Edward J. 71, 121, 132, 137
Tri-County Cooperative Oil Co. 149, 170
Tschann, Louis 49
Turner, D. D. 51
Tuttle, Emily 118

United Way 85

Vanderbelt, Delia M. 7
Veterans of Foreign Wars 137, 147
Voss, Burnett 158, 163

W.T. Nelson Realty 114
Ware, A. K. 11
Ware Auditorium 11, 54, 166
Warn, Robert 169
Way, John 20
Weicht, Carl L. 70, 76
Wells, Guy 'Barney' 60
Wescott, Allie 32
West Side building 105
Whitford, Ellen E. 9
Whittier, H. A. 34
Williams, Rev. J.K. 28
Wilson, Dr. Warren E. 95

Women's Christian Temperance Union 88
Wyant, Andy 166

Zanmiller, George J. 66, 116, 147
Zanmiller, Elizabeth 116

Maggie Lee has for 61 years been a member of the *Northfield News* staff.

A native of Northfield who prepared for a career in accounting, she came to realize that serving as news editor of her high school newspaper had been the most pleasurable experience in her life.

She used the accounting experience to gain employment at the *News*, suspecting that if she were "on location," she would get an opportunity to write.

Through the years she served as reporter, news editor, managing editor and for 19 years, editor. Since age 65 she has been a staff writer.

She is a founding member of the Northfield Historical Society, keenly interested in her community's history. She has served for several years on Northfield's heritage preservation commission.

Printed in the United States
31162LVS00005B/70-255